FINDING THE WAYFARER

Also by Emma Rose Barber

111 Churches in London That You Shouldn't Miss

FINDING THE WAYFARER

PHYSICAL, SPIRITUAL AND POETIC SURVIVAL

EMMA ROSE BARBER

TANDEM PUBLISHING

First published in Great Britain in 2025 by Tandem Publishing Ltd.

Copyright © Emma Rose Barber 2025.

Emma Rose Barber has asserted her right under the Copyright, Designs and Patents Act 1988 to be identified as the author of this work.

ISBN: 978-1-0687613-7-9

10 9 8 7 6 5 4 3 2 1

Image on title page and ornaments: detail from *The Macclesfield Psalter*, fol. 98r.

A CIP catalogue record for this book is available from the British Library.

Printed and bound in Great Britain by CPI Group (UK) Ltd, Croydon CR0 4YY.

My shoots are tipped with buds as dusty-grey
As ancient pilgrims toiling on their way.
Like Thursday's child with far to go, I stand,
All ready for the road to Fairyland;
With hood, and bag, and shoes, my name to suit,
And in my hand my gorgeous-tinted fruit.

Cicely Mary Barker
'The Song of the Wayfaring Tree Fairy'

CONTENTS

LIST OF ILLUSTRATIONS

Integrated illustrations

Figure 1: *The Macclesfield Psalter*, Cambridge, Fitzwilliam Museum, MS 1-2005, fol. 98r, c.1330–40, 170 x 108 mm.

Figure 2: *The Seven Works of Mercy*, Norfolk, St Andrew, Wickhampton, 14th century.

Figure 3: *Figure of a man*, Yorkshire, Pocklington, All Saints, north arcade, 12th century.

Figure 4: *Psalter-Hours*, Baltimore, Walters Ms. W.82, fol. 193v, c.1315–25, 111 x 162 mm c.1315–25.

Figure 5: *The Macclesfield Psalter*, Cambridge, Fitzwilliam Museum, MS 1-2005, fol. 168r, c.1330–40, 170 x 108 mm.

Figure 6: *The Ideal City*, Fra Carnevale, Baltimore, Walters Art Gallery, c.1480–84, 77.4 x 220 cm.

Figure 7: *The Seven Works of Mercy*, West Sussex, St George's Church, Trotton, 14th century.

Figure 8: *The Gorleston Psalter*, London, British Library, Add. MS. 49622, fol. 48v, c.1310–24, 374 x 235 mm.

Figure 9: *The Ghent Psalter*, Oxford, Bodleian Library, MS Douce 5, fol. 74r, c.1320–30, 86 x 63 mm.

Figure 10: *The Ghent Psalter*, Oxford, Bodleian Library, MS Douce 6, fol. 136v, c.1320–30, 87 x 62 mm.

Figure 11: *Bestiary*, Oxford, Bodleian Library, MS Bodley 764, fol. 16v, 13th century, 298 x 195 mm.

Plate section

Plate 1: *The Macclesfield Psalter*, Cambridge, Fitzwilliam Museum, MS 1-2005, fol. 98r, c.1330–40, 170 x 108 mm.

Plate 2: *The Macclesfield Psalter*, Cambridge, Fitzwilliam Museum, MS 1-2005, fol. 85r, c.1320–30, 170 x 108 mm.

Plate 3: *The Taymouth Hours*, London, British Library, MS Yates Thompson 13, fol. 95v, c.1325–30, 170 x 115 mm.

Plate 4: *The Rutland Psalter*, London, British Library, Add. MS 62925, fol. 47r, c.1250–60, 285 x 205 mm.

Plate 5: *The Ghent Book of Hours*, Cambridge, Trinity College Library, MS B 11 22, fol. 23v, 14th century.

Plate 6: *The Gorleston Psalter*, London, British Library, Add. MS. 49622, fol. 132v c.1310–24, 374 x 235 mm.

Plate 7: The Wayfaring Tree (*Viburnum lantana*), coloured engraving after J. Sowerby, 1796, Wellcome Collection.

Plate 8: *The Wayfarer*, Hieronymus Bosch, Rotterdam, Museum Boijmans Van Beuningen, 1516, 71 x 70.6 cm.

Plate 9: *Our Mother*, Grayson Perry, Victoria Miro Gallery, 2009, 84.5 x 65 cm.

Plate 10: *La Legenda Aurea*, London, British Library, MS Stowe 49, fol. 220r, last quarter of 13th or early 14th century, 270 x 180 mm.

Figure 1: *The Macclesfield Psalter*, Cambridge, Fitzwilliam Museum, MS 1-2005, fol. 98r, c.1330–40, 170 x 108 mm.

INTRODUCTION

Throughout the cities the blind were given sight. He
fed five thousand men; the companies sat down, sad
at heart; weary after wayfaring, they enjoyed the rest;
they received food, the men on the ground, as was
most pleasant for them.
'The Fates of Men', *The Exeter Book*, 10th century

A man gestures towards a seated, red-cloaked fox
holding up a jar who is sitting on a decorative mound
(see Figure 1, opposite, and Plate 1). The figure looks as
though he is walking. Nobody knows who he is. Painted
on parchment and shown in a short white tunic with
crutches, he is part of a very expensive medieval illuminated manuscript. Depicted only in profile, he is barefoot, his
calves are accentuated. Indeed, he looks quite fit.

One might think him a lucky man, since he is surrounded by a treasure trove of gold leaf, clusters of foliage and
ornament, decoration, bands of geometry, delicately drawn
flowers and sprays, as well as religious text to guide him on
his way. For this is a *bas-de-page* image in a fourteenth-century luxury Psalter, which contains the *Psalms*, accompanied by illustrations. In a sense the decoration he stands

on protects him, while the glorious illumination lightens his way. But in truth, he is more likely a needy, impoverished wayfarer at the limits of life. Soon, though, he will disappear from view as the page is turned, and he becomes invisible. If he were an actual person, he would likely have been gripped with fear about dying from hunger. This sort of figure was the inspiration for this book about wayfarers through time. Loosely chronological but also meandering. And which also weaves in personal reflection and observations on the natural world as I record some walks I made following in the spirit of the wayfarer.

The book was written with the view that wayfaring as a form of walking, quite often associated with the poor, going from place to place to survive, has not yet been comprehensively written about. Not that this is an easy task, as wayfaring is imperceptible, transient and incidental. Historically, people's movements were rarely recorded while walking. But the word has always been there. Wayfaring is permanent, despite the shifting nature of what it might mean. And in all of us, walking is a constant if we are fortunate enough to be able to. And like so many ordinary things humans do every day, it can be taken for granted.

I wrote this book as somebody who yearns to walk a lot, even though I am nervous about walking alone, whether in town or in the countryside. For me, to sit still is to invite atrophy, boredom and sleepiness. Going outside gives me a sense that I am doing something. If I am in the country, I prefer a walk that is circular, with that sense of completeness, coming back to meet the start of the circle – which I have made myself, sometimes with the OS map's assistance. If I am in a town, I like to walk on streets unfamiliar to me, even though I can never remember which ones I have already walked, which becomes then a never-ending, frustrating quest. There is no empty space in the *A-to-Z* index to tick off the 'streets that I have walked' and that is a good thing, as it would cause such a boulder of ambition that I would not sleep. I do not remember walks done, places seen, buildings viewed, the 'been there' of touring and ticking off.

I have been restless since I was a child. I wrestled with schooling and said goodbye to friends at school gates and beside cars before I moved to another school at the start of a new term. And another school after that. While I lived in the same house for my childhood, I became accustomed to moving places, changing dormitories, cubicles, desks and classrooms, companions and ways of teaching. As an adult, I tend to move house more than I need to. I have always been a magpie – as a child, picking up the numerous leaflets at the South Bank arts venue; now, looking at websites, sifting through all the mailings from museums, galleries, publishers, libraries and cultural organisations. Lists of lectures, authors to follow, books to read, beauty products to read about. It all takes time, and it is a ceaseless activity. No sooner have I removed such information from my inbox, more emails arrive. And so, the wheel's turn is over-loaded. It is all a way to exist, a sort of frenzied being, rather than a being still, which I say I will learn about when I am old. And so, I wonder if this restlessness is a metaphor for transience.

Romantic writers knew that walking, like life, could be

brief, even unsatisfactory. In Wordsworth's verse tragedy *The Borderers* (1796–97), the character Oswald speaks:

> Action is transitory – a step, a blow,
> The motion of a muscle – this way or that –
> 'Tis done, and in the after-vacancy
> We wonder at ourselves like men betrayed:
> Suffering is permanent, obscure and dark,
> And shares the nature of infinity.

Studying the landscape in minute detail, pausing to stop at a branch or a bough, a pocket of woodland or the corner of a grove, a gully or a running stream were the elemental joyous particulars of nature that caused walking poets such as Wordsworth to stop. As he said of the poet, 'he considers man and the objects that surround him as acting and reacting upon each other, so as to produce an infinite complexity of pain and pleasure…' The specifics of nature fostered the poet's imagination. Walking, then, can be motivated by a driving, curious poetic spirit.

It is not just the province of the poet, though. Walking can be inspired as much by safety and survival, or a flight from pain and hunger. This is where the word wayfaring comes in. And the image in the medieval manuscript.

The hallmarks of a wayfarer in the Middle Ages were to be somebody who walked barefoot, somebody with little clothing; as well, homeless and rootless. The depiction of wayfaring in holy books such as Psalters (Figure 1), which to this day are in pristine condition, takes place incongruously in these richly painted artefacts which only the rich could afford to commission or buy. But on the road, a wayfarer's destiny was to find themselves where they might have hoped to rely on at least one of 'the Seven Works of Mercy', acts of charity expected of you by the Catholic Church. These were: feeding the hungry, giving water to the thirsty, clothing the naked, sheltering the homeless, tending the sick, visiting the prisoner and burying the dead. These 'Seven Works' frame the chapters of this book. After all, to be a good Christian, you would, in theory, be judged if you did not perform these good deeds to alleviate the bodily distress of others. But could you get away with having an indigent wayfarer painted into your personal book of *Psalms* (the Psalter) instead? We can never know. In the image, the wayfarer gets noticed, even at the bottom of the page, as your eye is drawn to him. The figure must have been painted for some reason.

Other than in this book form, the medieval wayfaring figure is intangible. Like a bear, whose feet leave only faint traces, unless walking through mud or snow, the medieval wayfarer can really be glimpsed only by those who observed them, and who probably did not have or want to have much to do with such people. Unless they were thought of as a nuisance. For, just as today with people we routinely or carelessly call migrants tramping from country to country, or place to place for safety, the historical wayfarer was often viewed with suspicion and associated with anti-social behaviour. So, the evidence that exists about them comes largely from labels made by people carrying the word with them over time. But there is no consistent definition.

There must be some accuracy in the painted wayfarer as historical reality. The figures are presented as if they are on a path or at a threshold hoping somehow to be let in to a society to care for them. They are shown walking and are engaged in some form of physical effort. They might be disabled, moving with trestles. Their clothing can look ragged and worn out, they can be accompanied by a dog or hold a sack or basket; they are sometimes begging. They might be shown with exposed legs, slightly turned calves and clumsily drawn bare feet, one foot leading away from the other. They might face out to the beholder as if to arouse compassion; they look needy. But it is unlikely hugs from strangers would have been on offer.

I am not writing a comprehensive study about wayfarers. The exploration features manuscript images of them, medieval images of Joseph – the legal father of Christ, who was also for a time a peripatetic – as he guided his wife and child to safety in the narrative of the Flight into Egypt. The book explores medieval variations on a theme such as apes: yes, it was, of all the creatures, apes, who parodied wayfarers. For the early modern period, the book looks at Hieronymus Bosch's *Wayfarer*. Later, from the eighteenth century, there are the artists and writers, as if they, themselves are abiding wayfarers, who see a distant figure walking, who might appear as an outcast or a misfit, which is then construed through careful crafting to become something romantic. At this time, a peripatetic embodied a figure who wandered, and writers found these figures walking along in the landscape a source of wonder. There was the poet of the path, such as John Clare or

Robert Bloomfield, who were themselves the wandering, wondering wayfarers. Writers such as the eighteenth-century poet Charlotte Smith and the legendary nineteenth-century writer Thomas Hardy wrote both rhapsodically and realistically about life on the road. So, while the wayfaring poor continued to exist, walking to survive was not the only form of wayfaring. In the nineteenth century, poor wayfarers would become objects of social misery and justice in literature – you only need to think of Charles Dickens here. For the twentieth and twenty-first centuries, the book looks at Samuel Beckett's *Waiting for Godot*, the wayfaring stranger who belongs to the world of folk and rock singers, wayfaring in Sufism, and even Grayson Perry's *Old Mother*. And then, the quintessential contemporary Will Parsons, who left *his* mother one day to go walking. You can see what he does on his website – Pilgrimage and Wayfaring in Britain.

Yet for all time, wayfarers hover between being the wayfaring poor and the anonymous. But walking in general is a recurring theme of interest for artists and writers.

Through a selection of images and portrayals in literature, drama, music and poetry, we can at least look at how wayfarers have been represented through time. And we can do it in slow time. There is no other means to follow them as largely anonymous figures in history otherwise. By unplanned means, the words, like people who walk, are eternally out of reach, but in thinking about what wayfaring is, we might see how the word is fused with ideas and memories to do with something always beguiling – if at times in danger of being just a little quaint. The word's use, though, has changed over the course of its history, showing us a language that ambles to reflect the passing, even improvident, figures, but consequential for us who have always been dependent on our legs and feet. Like an adapting law or a growing tree where branches appear as if overnight, the word is shaped over time. A bit here and a bit there. The word has its own undefined logic and path. While the word cannot be neatly drawn from one epoch to another, from the beginning the word 'wayfarer' has undergone a kind of dalliance with different artists and writers and has withstood fluctuating linguistic travels over the course of its history. But within 'wayfarer', there is a core idea and a person, as somebody who walks.

What also seems true is that the word was more commonly used when we walked more than we might have to today and when people had to think more carefully about the ground upon which they trod, since they were leading harsh lives in harshly regulated societies. Walking now, even in some supposedly rural areas, is quite a municipal experience. More than ever, urban pavements, boardwalks by the sea, country footpaths and trails in the nature reserve are clean and bordered with fences and barriers, manufactured and organised to show us the way. This is the walking of the post-enclosure movement (the 1809 Parliamentary Act and others – to enclose land and parish land to maximise its use), where common land diminished. Here, you are guided by a host of policies, signs, information boards and authoritarian attitudes to displace what had been before. Such changes are imperceptible day to day, particularly when we are encouraged to go out and take exercise, but they have changed in my lifetime.

There is another way. We might also apprehend wayfaring as being about just getting through life on that turbulent and bumpy road. Wayfaring can be a bodily disposition, but may also invoke something of a spiritual, restless or vagrant mental state where the heart is vulnerable. For others, it might be a way to track one's walking, wandering self, while redefining a word that can seem so useful and flexible. Or wayfaring might just conjure up a collective state of being that is unsettled, shifting, melancholy. It can be synonymous with life as a journey, which, incidentally, I have only touched on in this book (for fear of overkill), as this has already been written about extensively. The word 'wayfaring' is also used as a title for poems to do with the spiritual journey.

Encountering wayfarers in art and literature is often a silent business. We might see them from afar, or beyond us in the distance; and in life, if they look wretched, we might not even want to get too close. They are not often imagined as figures you might strike up a conversation with. For they pass, and they go, peripheral, fragmentary, where their road or path stretches out before them. They are often alone, which was the case when I walked to write the book. Traipsing, plodding, heaving, footsore. From that, the predicament of capturing them follows, as we do not always hear about their homecoming where they could be traced in a concrete way.

I think it is fair to say that I have never encountered

anyone I know who has used the word wayfarer or wayfaring in their conversation. I would like to think that this book could change that. I sense, too, that this particular way of walking is an 'untold' one.

As well as the cultural explorations, my own geographical searches were done through walks in Sussex and Norfolk, partly to follow in the footsteps of the ambitious and acquisitive de Warenne family, who it is likely commissioned the manuscripts where the wayfarers feature. The family were originally seafarers, coming over as they did from northern France at the time of the Norman Conquest, and who became, we hear, great knights for the Norman Conquerors. From the shores of Sussex, they made homes and acquired land in Lewes and then in other counties in England, including Norfolk – Castle Acre, Thetford and north of Gorleston. Their manuscript illuminators may have come over from the Low Countries. So, these are the places where I went – on path, road, in summer drench and sun. I had shoes though and I was well-clad and tummy-full.

This is not a definitive study, but I hope it might bring to the reader a sense that to be a wayfarer is something migratory, moving, changing, reflecting and with all that, something sustaining over centuries. Or it might merely remind you that you are blessed to be able to walk.

ONE

WAYFARING WORKS 1:
FEEDING THE HUNGRY

… and savoury steams of hot dinners salute the
nostrils of the hungry wayfarer, as he plods wearily
by the area railings.
Charles Dickens, *Sketches by Boz*, The Streets –
Night (1836)

Medieval Wayfaring

I clock up a record number of steps in the city at the year's
end. The bellied shadows hang low in the narrow, dark
streets of Madrid, while New Year revellers walk past the
man without any legs in a wheelchair. This is his ill-abode.
He is bound to his fate. The dark makes it hard to tell if
people look at him as they pass on by. Scantily dressed,
he shakes a white plastic cup from his mouth. This is his
only glint of light. He is waiting. Waiting for the coins
to drop in, one by one; or better, two by two. Gathering
them in to save him. But the people are the twos, or even

the threes; he is the one – and anyway, they do not have many coins on them. They will not throw him a plastic cash-card. Even before pandemic pleas for help. They do not need to be saved. But at this moment, nobody knows yet that soon we will not be travelling and walking in the streets, but that we will all want to be saved.

Everything above the wheelchair-bound man is bright, light and right. All around him people walk along the clutch of festive streets, holding colourful New Year celebratory sparkles on sticks. These are like the bright fragments scattered from a dropped kaleidoscope, as if they are the answer to a new decade of hope. We are in the European south, where late afternoon winter sun lingers long. Soon, though, that butter-pat light becomes the artificial and brittle glow of a waiting world, a modern fairy world of portable neon lights and the streetlamps we take for granted. Soon, the midnight hour will strike.

Would people in the Middle Ages have ignored the man? They knew all too well then that to give food or money to others would be a way to save themselves from the indefinite pains of Hell. And one of the ways in which repentance could be found. After all, they would have known the liturgical instructions on how to be a good Christian from 'the Seven Works of Mercy' (*The Gospel of St Matthew*, 25: 35–46), often found in wall paintings in churches, such as at St Andrew, Wickhampton, Norfolk (Figure 2).

Figure 2: *The Seven Works of Mercy*, Norfolk, St Andrew, Wickhampton, 14th century.

In 1215, a decree at *The Fourth Lateran Council* stated that '… parish priests must make provision both for the reception of pilgrims and wayfarers and for the relief of the local poor.' From the beginning, to be a good Christian was to prepare for a good death through a good life. And that good life was determined by your goodness to others. Doing by others was one way to safeguard your passage to Heaven. That walk through the heavenly gates was an either–or situation. The wall paintings of 'the Seven Works of Mercy' were a form of instruction to the seven things you could do to help the poor and needy – offering and extending yourself. You were not a good Christian if you insisted on social distancing then. There were no exemptions for whether you could perform the 'Works' or not.

Through number-rich to-do lists your moral integrity was exposed, exercised and stretched. You were responsible for your own salvation in accordance with the Church's instructions. The fourteenth-century lay folks' *Catechism* also reminded you of your duty to the poor: 'Furst men schuld wilfully fede pore hungry men and þrusty / Forin þat þey fede Ieus Crist he hym self sayþ in þe gospel.'

Words and images consistently reminded those who could read and see that concern for the poor and vulnerable was a Christian imperative. To be a good Christian was to remember those who were not far from your door. Being charitable was, too, a way to bind rich and poor. The problem is that seeing and reading about doing good by the poor was one thing. Doing was another.

The man in Madrid sits in a big square, a place where he knows there will be people. This is close to the narrow *Calle Pelegrin* (meaning pilgrim). It is a street lateral to two main roads, which at night is a shadowy channel to get from one urban hum and hub to the other. It is not obvious today it is a pilgrim's route. Groups are walking in both directions, as we do in every street, everywhere, all hours, all the time. To the eye, figures are blurred and dark-coated in the quickening black of the evening, like the buildings that surround them. The pavements hold a dim hue from the odd shaft of streetlight on either side. People walk right in the middle of the pavement, rather than near the steps and entrance ways where gloom hangs and lingers. Around that thick dark, our sight is impeded; we could fall into the glass, brick or stone of a building, the gutter of the street, or an unprotected hole. As I go, I am barriered and I respect the lines and logical movement dictated by the buildings' margins. As if a spin of the dice has determined an equal flow of people, some going in one direction, some in another. This is an understated exercise in the act of the anonymous body, moving along an ordinary street. Even so, at a less than ordinary time.

I walk on. In that excited city, there is a group of people queuing to get near the firework display. Part of me is drawn to them, imagining I could try and speak Spanish. I am pulled away by the motivation to keep moving. The queue gives me disquiet. The bodies are there now, they were not there before, soon they will not be there at all. All that coming and going makes me uncomfortable. I do not know why but walking and moving away removes that discomfort. I hear little as my wandering eyes are too preoccupied with the paradisical New Year's Eve. But I wonder about the walking. Some participate in the revels of the new decade. But for some, walking in solitary fashion away from the excitement is preferable. There is a man ahead, walking in the other direction from the illusionary colourful heat and heart. There is a sense of sadness too, as this excitement is temporary and for each step we take, something is lost. And the people are only transitory walkers – as soon they will return home, where their possessions are taken for granted. I wonder where the man in the wheelchair might go.

In 'A Ten O'Clock Lecture' (1885), James Abbott McNeill Whistler, the painter of mood, water and mist with murky, inky, iridescent colours and tones, alludes to the pleasure of returning home for those who can:

…and when the evening mist clothes the riverside with poetry, as with a veil – and the poor buildings lose themselves in the dim sky – and the tall chimneys become campanile – and the warehouses are palaces in the night – and the whole city hangs in the heavens, and fairyland [*sic*] is before us – then the wayfarer hastens home – the working man and the cultured one – the wise man and the one of pleasure – cease to understand – as they have ceased to see, and Nature, who, for once, has sung in tune, sings her exquisite song to the Artist alone, her son and her master – her son in that he loves her, her master in that he knows her –[1]

To be a wayfarer in the Middle Ages is often to be endlessly on foot, which is to have your own form of transport, but to be a wayfarer out of need or hunger knows no boundaries between night and day. Rather, there are impediments to destination, place and fortune. Following light to dark and shadow to illumination shows up itinerancy in a somewhere setting; not home. This is merely a string of passing habitats which you might not return to. After all, after the dark, light is what we crave. There have always been home goers and home leavers as well as all those in between.

In the wide street neighbourhoods of outer Madrid where the land is higher, the roads wider, pigeons perch on overhead cables. There are one, or two to three together, occasionally hopping onto another branch, or darting to the side. They are aware of one another, but they do not appear to care what is going on down below. There is no doubt about their precarious position, but they balance, touch, jump and land with perfect precision. Whether it is day or night. And somehow, they find their food. Pigeon power high up there. All together, all at ease with life on a cable.

As in all cities, the traffic lights go from red to green. And the driver waits impatiently for amber. For the pedestrian in Madrid though, a bell that sounds like an alarm indicates that it is time to move and cross the street and a sign is illuminated of two people walking together hand in hand. Street life and the passing through it can be communal. It offers solidarity but can also be solitary. Something of these passing perambulating scenes makes me think of the medieval walking destitute, for whom life on the roads was a perilous norm, and where the shadows of a city gate, wayside shrine or church provided actual or illusionary shelter. To be received without scorn. And hope.

The ninth-century monastic Alcuin of York wrote, 'What is speech? The betrayer of the soul. What is a man? The slave of a death, the guest of an inn, a wayfarer passing.' The means by which this 'universal' man travelled is not discernible. But Anglo-Saxon poetry also uses the theme of travel in the sense that it could be expansive. The Old English poem 'Widsith' (meaning Far Journey) known as well as the Traveller's Song (from *The Exeter Book*, tenth century) is a list of the battles for lands fought by the Goths and Huns, encompassing Scandinavian and Baltic territories. We do not know who Widsith is, except that *he* is, he does, *he* is Widsith, *he* is the third person, and *he* could be the poem's voice. He. Widsith. *He*, a personification?

Never mind his identity. Widsith is a man journeying far:

> Widsith spake,
> He unlocked his treasure of words.
> He who among men
> Had travelled most in the world,
> Through people and nations.

Definitions of Wayfarer

Documents from the medieval and early modern periods contain many words to describe the needy indigent, including 'wayfarer', usually characterised as those who walk, often out of need and not in any way rooted. More recently though, 'wayfarer' has not fared very well as a word. Yet it has cast its spell on me. But what a diffusion of words and related words. In *The Oxford English Dictionary*, wayfarer is a 'traveller by road, especially one who journeys on foot.' In the word way-fare, way refers to a road or path; while fare, is a going or a journeying, a course, or passage. It seems that people go wayfaring, write wayfaring poems and songs, and think about what it means.

What a busy time the wordsmith had though. Just this one word brings variations and distortions, which have played into its imprecision and ambiguity over time. In Latin, the word *viator* (*viatrix*) had two meanings: traveller and then summoner (one summoning people to a magistrate), and Cicero, Horace, Virgil and Juvenal all used the word. In Anglo-Saxon terminology, the noun is *weg-férend* translated as a wayfarer or traveller. The Anglo-Norman word for wayfarer is *wagarer*, defined as vagrant and vagabond.

In *The Consolation of Boethius, Se nacoda wegférend vacuus viator* means 'the naked empty wayfarer', using both Latin and Anglo-Saxon here. Also, *wei-f ring(e)* is one who is engaged in travel, an itinerant, a traveller, a transient, or vagrant. And in the Low Countries, the word was *trekker* and the movement *trekkend*, which look as though they have become anglicised, but not to the same word. In the Middle Ages, a pilgrim was a *peligrin* to describe a traveller and wayfarer, but also, a wanderer, wandering beggar. And peregrination, or *per-agros*, was to go through fields as stranger or outsider. And as time passed, all these words inhabited overlapping ideas and worlds. What remains constant is that this type of figure is going somewhere. Their place is the road or path, pasture, field, heathland, shore and wood, but until recently, rarely on a marked trail. While language might seem to be the most comfortable context in which to understand a wayfarer, their voyaging is often defined before it is begun, and then disrupted whether by law, decree or by an evocative written or artistic weaving.

And despite the medieval Church's words about the need to give, the poor were often forced onto the streets hoping for a little bit of hospitality and kindness. They walked to find food, lodging or help. And if they were bare-foot-ed, they might have had a deep physical attachment to the know-how of mud, ruts, troughs, roots, stones and all the detritus that make up a path's surface. With eyes downwards, they might have seen a discarded sole of an old shoe and wondered if they could make something out of it for protection. The ground was their habitat, while looking upwards to Heaven, where in *The Gospel of Matthew*, Christ had said that the poor would enter the Kingdom of Heaven (5:3). Those in need, driven to the roads, were not forced to the land like the peasant, a victim of the ferocious feudal system, who had to serve and till a strip of land with crops, and then give a large sum of the harvest as tithe to the lord whose land they were farming. In a sense, then, the medieval indigents had more freedom to roam. They were free of servitude but chained by survival and fearful of the law. And, despite what the Church said about kindness, the medieval wayfarers, vagrants and beggars were subject to all sorts of laws and statutes, which must have been hard to police. In this punitive and insistent language use, we see the antithesis of the religious exhortation to be kind to the indigent, where attention was placed on the rich who were encouraged to think of the poor, in part to assuage their own spiritual conscience about gaining salvation. But the law could act against those wayfarers.

Statutes Against the Wayfarer
As early as 1168, there was unease as to who was worthy of charity. The law book *Summa Elegantius in iure Divino, Seu Coloniensis*, stated:

In almsgiving there should be distinction between people. You had better give to your own than to strangers, to the sick rather than to the healthy, to ashamed rather than aggressive beggars, to the have-not rather than to him who has, and amongst the needy, first to the just and then to the unjust.

That is ordered charity.

Able-bodied beggars in medieval law were singled out as undeserving of support. But it was less clear how 'able-bodied' was defined. One summer, I walked past a London church in a quiet residential square in Notting Hill and on the porch of the church was a notice saying, 'No rough sleepers here.' It was shocking to see such a command at the entrance to the very place that historically is meant to provide when the law so often works against the needy. As it was then, as it is now. And so, Amen.

During the reign of Edward I, *The Statute of Winchester* (1285), a proclamation targeting vagrants in the city, was made. It was ordered that the city gates were to be closed. If strangers entered the city, they would be detained under suspicion until morning. And this suspicion extended beyond the city barriers:

> That highways leading from one market town to another shall be enlarged, whereas bushes, woods, or dykes be, so that there be neither dyke nor bush whereby a man may lurk to do hurt, within 200 feet of the one side, and 200 feet on the other side of the way.

One act led to the next. The alienating force of language carved out pejorative words and expressions marking out those that society objected to, such as 'able-bodied beggars'. *The Statute of Labourers* (1350), during post-plague time, was intended to restrain desultory wandering and mendicancy and indiscriminate almsgiving, the implication being that such charity was misdirected. Adding to the waste of the resources of those who could work:

> And because many sound beggars do refuse to labour so
> long as they can live from begging alms, giving them-
> selves up to idleness and sins, and, at times, to robbery
> and other crimes – let no one, under the aforesaid pain
> of imprisonment presume, under colour of piety or alms
> to give anything to such as can very well labour, or to
> cherish them in their sloth, so that thus they may be
> compelled to labour for the necessities of life.

Church and state could not have differed more in their attitudes towards itinerancy. In a later Statute of 1376, lepers were ordered not to beg in the streets as they risked spreading disease. An office for the seclusion of the leper with a familiar ring to us in the nervy post-pandemic world, commanded that:

> When you are on a journey not to return an answer to
> anyone who questions you, till you have gone off the road
> to leeward (against the wind), so that he may take no
> harm from you: and that you never go through a narrow
> lane lest you should meet someone. Also, I charge you if
> need, require you to pass over some toll way over rough
> ground or elsewhere, that you touch no posts or things
> whereby you cross, till you have first put on your gloves.

Bridges were threshold points. The wayfarers' toll was a sum extracted from those crossing them. Even though it might seem they were places to accost the unwanted. In the 1377 *The Commons' Petition against Vagrants*, another word with a pejorative reputation, complaints increased about these figures and what they were about. In some cases, they came to be seen as idle and mendacious beggars. Records labelled a person without a fixed home or occupation, a wanderer, a vagabond, and an idle or shiftless person, a good-for-nothing, even a criminal. The classification of people sticks in the mind. There was, for example, the 'Removal order and examination of Sarah Hayward, apprehended as a rogue and vagabond, from Brighton; married at Cowfold to Thomas Hayward of Brighton, "waggoner", (5 August 1812).' Poor woman. What had she done?

The Suspicious Wayfarer

People are wont to put suspicion before understanding and we see this in evidence during the medieval period. Walking and wayfaring, even just existing could not be taken for granted. *The Statute of Westminster* (1383) ordered an enquiry concerning vagabonds, who were allegedly, 'Wandering from place to place, running in the country more abundantly than they were wont in times past.' Other statutes declared that travelling beggars and servants had to carry testimonials describing reasons for being on the road. Likewise, lepers were not allowed to 'wander' anywhere. Those on foot were chased down by edict after edict. Even the innocuous travelling cloak aroused distrust. Bishops had to refrain from granting a tonsure and habit unless they were very sure they would be used appropriately, as, so often, it was said, it was a cloak for wandering. After all, suspicion sometimes had good reason. At *The Council of Salzburg* (1274), it was reported that: 'Three beggars stole three children at Lynn. They put the eyes out of one, broke the back of a second, and cut off the hands and feet of the third, in the hope that these infirmities would draw forth abundant alms from all who beheld them'. It might well have been feigned, but the strength of narrative can hold anyone in suspenseful belief.

Laws were drawn up, executed, made again, modified, and made again. This was the word, the state, the deed and the law trying to deal with people collectively, even though not everyone saw people on the move in the same way. The language of statute-making was precise when dealing with something so imprecise. Wayfarers and vagrants were chased, caught by classification even when walking to search for food. And that form of movement when in dire need would have been, for some, a slow process. Some were often ridden with unimaginable disability or disease: accumulating pockmarks, buboes, rashes, scabs and scabies. Like the Common Eider, the poor were out in the cold, but without the bird's protective covering. Yet they were encouraged to take comfort in God's watchful gaze to watch over them. By our standards, this was a hard call.

Writings about the wayfarer in the Middle Ages could also be contradictory. The word was often associated with trepidation. For any sort of traveller, whether on horseback or on foot, the ways of the road could be dangerous. People were often the victims of robbery, such that the Emperor Charlemagne (reigned 768–814 CE) issued legislation to try and protect them. In Italy, the 'killing of wayfarers and *peregrini* who hasten to Rome or to other bodies of the saints in the service of God' was an act punished by huge fines. 'Wayfarer' was at times a catch-all term. It is recorded that 'wayfarers were robbed on the King's Highway in 1388–89, somewhere between Dartford and Swanscombe and two men admitted to robbing a man of Canterbury of twenty shillings in gold and silver money and of a black horse'. There was one place of protection: the pie powder courts which received those with 'dusty feet' and disputations to make (in French, the *Pied Poudreux*). Like those they saw coming and going, these courts were temporary, held at fairs and markets to administer justice over those 'selling' itinerants such as pedlars and 'wayfaring folk.'

Wayfaring is also used in connection with the recording of deaths. John Bare, who died on 21 January 1574 in North Mundham in Norfolk, was listed as a 'wayfaring man.'[2] A euphemism, I suppose, for a man without an occupation. Similarly, another record declares someone as being 'born of a wayfaring woman', as was the case with somebody who died on 19 April 1584, but who was 'of no name buried' in Linchmere.[3] And later records show the use of the word 'vagrant' conferred on those who had died. One 'William, vagrant, 50, congestion of the brain at Rye Workhouse, Rye' is listed for 6 Nov 1848.[4]

In the Middle Ages, even the walking of monks was governed. Some were organised by an order called the *Ordo Vagorum*. So holy was their wandering, it brought itinerants into the all-seeing realm of a haloed world. And like wayfarers, monks and the mendicant friars would wander here and there, seeking shelter along the way. How could you tell one from the other? On 12ᵗʰ September 1224, a group of friars including Agnello of Pisa arrived at Dover. 'Nine wayfarers of all ages, clothed in rough and patched tunics, without visible means of support, who had crossed the Channel by charity and sought lodging as beggars; seemed to those unfamiliar with the friars to be mere vagabonds.' And according to one account they were actually treated as such soon after landing.[5] Acting as models of need gave the wayfaring mendicants some kudos, even though they, too, were subject to the law's reproving eye. The Dominicans (Black Friars) and Franciscans (Grey Friars) were more likely to have been in the front-line when it came to caring for others. What a good thing they had those hoods. They looked after the poor and often died of plague. The friars way-fared and begged, with scrip (a small bag used to carry food) and staff. Like the poor, they were there to urge the rich to remember to give; all of this in a 'faithful' religion that walked from the start to spread its word and power. Christ urged his apostles to 'take nothing for the way, but a staff only: no scrip, no bread, nor money in their purse…' (*The Gospel of St Mark* 6:8). They were to go west preaching to people as they went, practising the command.

Just a few weeks into 2020, walking ceased to be thought of in the same way as it had been. In the UK, emergency legislation brought 'movement restrictions', such that leaving home without a reasonable excuse was prohibited. Similar laws were passed all over Europe. The criss-cross of city streets and alleys would no longer contain people, save for key workers. Nobody knew on New Year's Eve 2019 that soon they would crave a walk or anything to step outside again. The pandemic brought forbiddance. Commands followed. Only walk when you must – for shop, errand, necessity or work. Walking would suddenly become a precious thing to do in locked up continual doom days of never-ending uncertainty, drawing mass media attention on a minuscule scale to this 'unprecedented' time. This word became a new meme. In Britain, a daily walk was allowed, but no more; lest the neighbours reported you. Yet suddenly, on the lane where I live, people were popping up like meerkats from nowhere to do their daily walk (luckily, not in the nude), for that is what they had been told to do. We were walking more than we had done before. No longer though could you walk with a friend, embrace them or hold their hand. Rarely before had your feet, your body, your footprint become a traceable thing. Rarely before did you see your home's threshold as a portal to danger. Rarely before had I seen such palpable concern. While the statistics tracking, tracing, monitoring, checking, reviewing and reviving were 'more or less' every day, there was the daily report of the death rate and the 'more or less' of statistics as susceptible things for interpretation. To go walking more than ever somewhat ironically was a healthy sign. Where you walked and how and what you did or didn't touch became the subject of daily governmental updates that we lived through in 2020–21.

Like the hunter-gatherers who once walked out, to run,

to catch, or hunt; or the questing spiritual pilgrim, or the hungry vagrant, walking came out into the open. One of humanity's greatest gifts – walking and its mores – became carefully considered things. The act of moving about is a reminder of our ancient roots and humanity. Religions and ideologies spread through walking, as those who wanted to change the way we think would stop – to speak and preach. The pandemic of 2020, the year of nature's most beautiful spring, caused walking to be a precious thing, when for many previous centuries it had been the only way for many to move about.

I first learnt to walk on the routinely cut grass of the garden lawn at home in suburban London. It felt cool, fresh, safe and comfortable on my smooth-soled feet, which had not yet learnt to jump or climb trees. I would lie on the grass, staring up at the flat plain of a summer's sky listening to birdsong, invisible in the high trees around the garden. To this day, that image provides an instant jolt back to my childhood. I remember the manicured flower beds of annuals in the local park, around which paved paths had been laid. I had safety and certainty within those boundaries and margins.

A patch of grass, or lawn made new from mowing brings aching painful memories of what was. As do children. The baby's foot yet to form, with arch, curve, knots and bumps, long before the arrival of bunions and blisters, is like a perfectly shaped block of wood. You can almost stack it up like sheaves of paper to be bound for a book. I wanted to squash or squidge my babies' feet out of pure delight in their smooth tactility. I also remember my children first learning to walk, at about the age of one. It was a hesitant, slightly jerky footstep, encouraged to make another when they heard the soon-to-be-learnt cue of 'ooh, you clever darling'; 'take another one for Mummy'; or any other cooing sign that to the baby was nothing but encouragement and pure unconditional delight. Here a step, the foot could do no wrong. Here a fall and a little cry to elicit further, never irritable, attention. There was the standing on tiptoe to see a tempting jar of something on the kitchen work surface, like a court tumbler who performs on feet upturned; the brain working fast with anticipation, or the curiosity when looking out of the window for delivery people. After the age of about five, the parent ceases to watch the foot and the walk, as the child has learnt to own what their feet can do. Later though, with each passing year, the foot's flesh would gradually be shielded from me, as big black shoes or boots for street-life, tube, airport and escalator journeying showed that the children were inching further away from my maternal protection. Their feet were gathering with their sense of adventure to assert rightful independence. How I remember the butterfly flutter movement within me at about twelve weeks' gestation, when the toes, floating in liquid, but forming bulk and delineation started to ripple against my tummy wall. As toddlers, out on the other side, they jumped on it joyfully. My belly was a trampoline, or a play-cushion as they lolled on my tired physical frame when all I wanted to do was lie down from exhaustion.

Footwear and balancing are something taken for granted, unless you do not have any shoes, or, for that matter, legs – like the man in the wheelchair. Or, if you need a type of shoe to help with a severe balancing disorder. My brother used to wear special grippy shoes to help him stay upright; something quite heart-breaking when for over fifty years I saw him walking effortlessly, even and straight. He had to obtain grip rails and the support of other people's arms. He used a frame for walking when before it was just a carefree business. Then his feet and legs became totally unreliable; he had to surrender to the unsteadiness of the most terrible condition. As he himself, said, his legs would not do as he wanted them to, even though his cognition was as sharp as ever. And though a crucial part of the fundamental mechanics of his brain ceased to be, he remained smiley, quick and witty until the very end.

The King of Covid fund-raisers, Captain Tom (1920–2021), once a motor cyclist, then broken-hipped, but determined, used his feet with a walking frame. He walked a constant, steady up and down, slow-moving pace, where the country was watching him journey around his garden, every step counting towards a huge sum of money for the National Health Service. This was a man who had also been the recipient of care by an institution that in a sense grew out of the longstanding Christian tradition of giving and hospitality, where people were urged to look after the crippled, the sick and the poor. Captain Tom was not going to allow his slow gait and age tether him at a time of great need. Then, when he died, an honoured man, there were outpourings of grief and messages of condolence that he would never have expected. Plaudits and obituaries, and the anticipated sense that the memory of him would live long. But while his warm heart and mien connected with others, in the fast-changing screen world of clicks and likes and dislikes, where one insouciant caress of the filmy filter of the phone changes both image and then memory, how will he really be remembered? Will we reminisce about that moment of need and longing harbouring the idea of heroism he created in his garden, his slow walking on a garden path, bordered with grass and brick? Or will we remember how his kindness was turned into blatant greed by his family, misleading us with conclusive misuse of money saved by his generous venture? He warned us of the consequences of too much fear. But not of all too easy temptation in his wake.

The Literary and Artistic Medieval Wayfarer
In Geoffrey Chaucer's translation of *The Consolation of the Philosophy of Boethius* (523), a wayfarer is also seen as a traveller with the advantage of money, but vulnerable to another:

> Yif thou haddest entered in the path of this lyf a voide wayfaring man, thou woldest thou singe beforn the theef; as who seith, a pore man, which berth no richesse on him by the weye, may boldly singe beforn theves, for he hath not whereof to ben robbed.[6]

The medieval wayfaring poor, often unwelcome at thresholds when they were most tired and hungry, tugged at the conscience of those who encountered them. The resistance to give was often derived from the concern of the other. In *On the Deception of Certain Signs* (9th century), Agobard of

Lyons warned against attacks on demoniacs. He advised that the best people could do to overcome fears was to distribute gifts to the poor and wayfarers.[7] The fact of saying 'give' could be a theoretical balm, even if that meant that the true deserving poor did not get what was due to them. If we don't give, we put up justified objections for why we can't.

Language was also voyaging with variations on a theme to do with feet. An Anglo-Saxon poem speaks of misery: 'One shall perforce go on foot on far paths and bear his needs with him, and on a dewy track tread the perilous land of alien people. He has few of living men to entertain him; the friendless man is everywhere hated because of his miseries.' In *Le Livre de Seyntz Medicines* – a devotional treatise, in the form of many a confession – Henry of Lancaster (who died of the plague in 1361), objected to the smell of the poor, and in his most intimate confessions sought a way to restore his spiritual health as he remembers turning away from paupers. Confessing on paper was a way to nourish your integrity.

Even better, as owner of a sumptuous religious book, you could touch a carefully painted wayfarer. And consider conscience done. The page – border, edge, margin. This is a place for those who do not want restrictions. Be like the illuminator of religious manuscripts such as the book of prayers (a Book of Hours) or a Psalter. The artists would doodle or draw little figures; they had fun with pushing the boundaries of how to be in a pictorial sense. The page in an illuminated manuscript is characterised by strictly bordered blocks of text with, at times, illustration or floral decoration running amok beside it. For the illuminated borders do not always respect the text's place, as the decorations expand within the place strictly ruled out for the script, which can be below or beneath the main text or image or in some sort of place or empty space at the side. The life of a page has its own order, a structure and system. In bright, bold colours, though, wayfarers are painted to stand out. Although the beholder can leave that figure behind, never to look back, allowing the viewer the power to forget and discard what has been seen. That sense of arriving and departing is seen in medieval illuminated pictures. A female wayfarer with a baby attached to cloth, like a *papoose*, walks towards a seated female figure holding out what looks like an apple, framed within an arch. Other people come and go, they know that spot. They are not so easily noticed, as they are doing something purposeful such as delivering goods. The wayfarer is convincing as she is doing something that, throughout time, has always caught the eye. Another figure is bent double, leaning on the staff to help them move. Other figures are half naked, revealing bare bottoms, yet loosely draped in decorative red and blue capes – colours which stand out. They are framed by two beautiful page decorations, but they are also rooted to the page, the colour catching them. Toes and feet are shown using the horizontal bar to walk along. Another figure looks slightly upwards to ask and repeat, his left hand outstretched to echo what he asks. His right foot is forward, rather balletic, almost like a nobleman with a swinging sort of walk, but all exaggerated by the artist to get noticed. If he had clothes on, he would be called foppish. And another figure bent over and completely naked, slightly stretched out, holds a T-bar staff. His right foot stands on a decorated initial.

These figures needed healing, hand on the head or on the arm. A touch to sense they could be acknowledged. When the manuscripts themselves provide that curative element, to us now they are objects of tactile joy. The touch of a medieval manuscript is like the power of healing from the flesh – consider just the feel of the page's surface: the gold leaf all burnished smooth, the parchment, on a microscopic scale, is still a bit hairy from its raw, pre-treated state, the page's surface a bit worn over time, bubbly, crinkly, all touchy feely, like a paper bag. The attention to colour and gold surface and touch in the manuscripts is the equivalent to lamination making all smooth and shiny today.

The colour of the illuminated manuscripts is usually in top-notch condition. A colourful gloss covers the truth. If the painted figure had a voice, they would cry out, 'Give me a home, a hearth, a haven.' Hostile hounding was probably what they heard. All they could expect in return was a road where they could go and where they might feel safe. Yet who was really looking? There was more sympathy I suspect from the bumpy, weathered, crumpled whorls of tree bark with lines stamped, as if forming faces. If you see a face in the tree, your eyes could be tricked into seeing the sort of monster that the medieval artist carved into stone on corbel and gutter. A wayfarer on the ground was likely to be invisible despite the Church telling people to look after them, only becoming visible, uplifted from the ground, on a beautiful painted page.

On paper, these religious contexts provided a sense of hope. Whether or not they experienced Christian kindness or not, the wayfarers were at the edge of survival. In the manuscript books, they are also on the edge. And at a physical border express the very power structures that cannot ever break down. There is the possibility of penetrating a porous structure, finding a place where there is always a space, but the in-between rarely survives.

We see another painted wayfarer on a page from *The Macclesfield Psalter* (Plate 2), where a figure and dog walk on a gold border at the page's margin: he wears a short tunic, a red cape, and a black hat hangs from his back. He holds a T-bar staff, maybe a sign of poverty. The dog looks back at him, all jaunty, lithe and energetic, and as if to hurry him on. The small but prominent figure (that red stands out) could show the book's owner how to find God's Divine light. He might have tried to dwell on the words of the *Psalm* (58:15) written there: 'They shall return at evening and shall suffer hunger like dogs: and shall go round about the city.' Man and dog look as if they are walking towards a brightly coloured, embellished edge and onto the next page. Although the man cannot see it, or others like him on other pages. A gold path has been made for him, to guide him to Heaven. Distractingly beautiful for the beholder. Less good for his conscience. A book commission was something you could do to remember the souls of those who might die without having enacted the works of mercy. Athanasius, the bishop of Alexandria (d. 373) wrote that: 'he who recites the psalms … sings them as if they were written concerning him … he handles them as if he is speaking about himself.'

All this visual matter, so lovingly illuminated, may have been some sort of prompt to memorise the words of the *Psalms* as well as giving. Such images were made to give the book's proud possessor a spiritual stability to help them in the difficult journey to save their soul. They could remind a book's owner of the plight of homelessness, even from the confines of a most precious object, a spectacularly luxurious devotional book. Here, then, a glimpse of how to awaken your morality in a 'moving' figure. The illuminator tried to please their patron aesthetically, but with just hints of the wayfarer's impoverishment. Those casting a cursory eye over them had castles, watchtowers, fortifications, iron-gated oak doors, draw-gates and moats to return to. They had fires, warm dining halls, tapestries, prayer books, amber rosaries, leather accessories and pewter on their tables. They had animal flesh to gnaw and ale to drink. They had musicians and songs to soothe their ear. They could look out to the peasants, mulching and nourishing their soil, tending their sheep and fattening their pigs. Then the doors of their households were shut and bolted, with fist and might. And at night-time with dying candlelight, a flickering conscience, sleep could harden your attitude. Put simply, castles are symbolically less incorruptible than feet. They were all the wayfarers had.

Out in the open, though, a wayfarer was at least ac-knowledged.

We see the word used on an eleventh-century sundial above the south entrance at the parish church of St Michael and all Angels, Great Edstone in the Ryedale region of Yorkshire, on an old drovers' route. The inscription, though incomplete, is written in Old English, and Latin. You can see it above the horizontal equinoctial line: +ORLOGIVM VIATORVM, translating as Wayfarer's Clock or Wayfarer's Day Mark. In a place where they could find sanctuary, it assumes a role as guiding travellers on their journey.

Figure 3: *Figure of a man*, Yorkshire, Pocklington, All Saints, north arcade, 12th century.

Medieval carvings of wayfarers were sometimes formed out of stone. And shaped, carved, commemorated, to stay. At the church of Pocklington in East Riding, on the twelfth-century capital of an arcade (Figure 3), there is a carving of a man strung across the stone, with a travelling pack slung across his shoulders. Stone becomes him and is his survival. See how he looks down at us as we look up at him. He is surrounded by carved foliage. Grooves to make drapery folds in the legs give him the air of a hair-clothed desert figure of endurance, and maybe soon, he is to enter the Kingdom of Heaven, even if he has fallen getting there. He is precariously perched in-between.

If the status between having and not having was felt, then Shakespeare's *Richard II* provides a richly evoked commentary on this unwelcome sense of just surviving. Exchanging one thing for the other, not out of choice, makes us desire the thing we have lost. When he has been imprisoned, the king muses about changing his regal things for those of the beggar – with alms-gown, alms-dish and palmer's staff:

> The name of king? I' God's name, let it go.
> I'll give my jewels for a set of beads,
> My gorgeous palace for a hermitage,
> My gay apparel for an almsman's gown
> My figured goblets for a dish of wood,
> My sceptre for a palmer's walking-staff…
> (Act 3, scene 3)

And later he comments on the thought of trading places:

> Thus play I in one person many people,
> And none contented. Sometimes am I king.
> Then treasons make me wish myself a beggar.
> And so I am; so crushing penury
> Persuades me I was better when a king…
> (Act 5, scene 5)

The veil between the outside and the inside that marks who you are is porous and fragile; even a king could fall on hard times. The medieval wayfarer may have imagined themself as a king or queen in their dreams.

Perilous Times

By the fourteenth century, England's native forests had largely been cleared for farmland. Just as surplus harvest, in theory, would be good for feeding the poor, the woodland offered wayfarers shelter and other forms of sustenance, and a place free from the eagle-eye interference of the law. Between 1315–20, when many manuscripts illustrating wayfarers were made, a Great Famine struck northern Europe. A sequence of unusually wet winters caused a high grain price and a scarcity of food due to crop ruin. Chroniclers reported on deserted villages with the poor left to die on the streets. And it was reported: 'so bad were things that the poor ate dogs, cats and even their own children.' Was it Divine punishment that had occasioned these disasters? Was God wreaking wrath upon all?

Cattle and sheep were also dying. Alms were withheld. Many people who had been living above the subsistence level were forced to be vagrants. People went in processions barefoot, sometimes in the nude. The Archbishop of Canterbury ordered that every Friday the religious should go in bare feet to the church of the Holy Trinity.[8]

This terrible time was captured in the poem 'Simonie', or 'The Evil Times of Edward II' (c.1320):

And though that mortality was stopped of beasts
  that bear horns,
Then God sent on earth another dearth of corn,
That spread over all England both north and south,
And made simple poor men hungry in their mouth
Came there another sorrow that spread over all the
  land;
A winter that was stronger than a thousand that
  came before
To bind all the many men in mourning and in
  care,
The cattle died all forthwith, and made the land all
  bare,
So fast,
Came never a wretch into England that made men
  more aghast.
While some are blessed and rich, where they can
drink or sup solemnly and elegantly, those crushed
to poverty 'devour' in rapid, ravenous exultation:
Then beggars tho cowered before
Began to grow bold and to devour
And drink up everything they might get.[9]

As the land was ravaged by incessant rain, humanity in
northern Europe confronted profound misery. These
hardships fomented strife and social unrest. The poor,
the dispossessed and the lowly started to demand a better
living and fair wages.

Perilous Wayfaring

People in the Middle Ages had to travel from their localities just as they have always done. Their ancestor hunter-gatherers did and their earthen or grass tracks, paths of flint and soil, were still perceptible in some places. A medieval person walked for basic needs. They, too, had to gather. They, too, were hunter-wanderers. They, too, needed sustenance. They would stand out for their lack; not a girdle at their waist to mark the sharp cut of a dress, nor a bead about their breast to mark their praying hours. And when fairs and markets were established (by 1349 in Norfolk alone, there were 121 weekly) by lords of the manor, travel on foot and for those that could with horse, only increased.

To way-fare, from the earliest times, was borne out of a necessity to endure against the odds. A medieval wayfarer walked, but they would have struggled. And they trudged, exhaustedly, shuffled through mud and grit, hobbled, with staff or crutch, limped, pausing once or twice, watchful to see who might be lurking, or, to look at injury, wound, blood, blister, scratch. They saw the scuffed earth, marks made by others before them. We do not know if they recorded their walks or destinies, or the earth's beauty, unpredictability, or mutability. The medieval wayfarer may seem to be more like the vagrant we understand today as a beggar or homeless person.

Then there was pilgrimage. Pilgrimages brought together a ragtag mix of travellers: hawkers, beggars and those seeking redemption or profit, or on the make. Some were said to feign miraculous cures to gain charity. To be seen in this vein was to navigate a void of compassion, while perceived or genuine contempt added to their alienation. Although it is fair to say that pilgrimage often had an end destination, such as a holy shrine, whereas, with their enforced transiency, wayfarers were often on the move. Though the lines are blurry, as the axle of hardship pressed down on many caught up with pilgrims. By its very nature, to travel on foot caused derision. And that continued beyond the medieval period. In the *Vagabond Act of 1547*, (Edw. 6. c. 3), it stated that 'Divers wemen and men goeth on begging wayefaring.' The Act tried to implement the enslaving of vagabonds for two years; but it proved to be a very challenging thing to control.

Bartholomew the Englishman as he was called, said in *On the Properties of Things* (1220–40) that:

Strange men ofte erre and go out of the waye: and take uncerten waye, and the waye that is unknowe, tofore the waye that is knowen…Therfore ben ofte knottes made on trees and in bushes, in bowes and in braunches of trees: in token and marke of the highe waye, to showe the certen and sure waye to wayfaring men.[10]

Both the noun 'wayfarer' and the verb 'wayfaring' could invoke responses, feelings and emotions, beyond the neutrality of how they sound and how they gradually acquired different meanings and contradictions. Even though the Church had said that walking on foot was the noblest form of travel, Aelred of Rievaulx wrote in *La Vie de Recluse* (1158–60):

Many, either not knowing or not caring about the rules of this way of life, think it sufficient to contain their limbs within four walls, while not only is the mind unloosed in wandering and dissipated in cares and anxieties, but the tongue wanders all day through towns and villages, through fairs and markets, over the lives and customs and works of men, seeking out things which are not only useless but shameful.

During the wintry lockdown intended to curb the coronavirus pandemic of early 2020s, the travelling Hermes would visit many of our homes. The couriers were still delivering. In our intensified desire to shop from home, the shopping experience came to us. With commercial premises closed, at least we could rely on mobile buying. According to Alfred Watkins in *The Old Straight Track* (1925), 'Hermes guides wayfarers on unknown paths.' The patron of market traffic became the god of tradespeople. Hermes wears wings on his traveller's hat and his shoes. Having been a messenger of the gods, Hermes was to become traveller–messenger for all. The everybody of lockdown. Meanwhile, in the clutches of Covid, walking through its slow minutes and hours, holding onto rural gate post, stile, urban escalator rail or staircase, people wondered about 'viral load', and the chances of catching the infection. Yet worrying about touching surfaces did not stop us from ordering cardboard parcels and jiffy bags. And while those in homes had warmth and comfort from the road in the winter lockdown, some felt imperilled by the restrictions. Utterances of discontent, scepticism, anger and suffering were made publicly in the days that ended so quickly through the physical dark, as well as by the darkness in people's spirits. I recalled the sonnet 'A Dark Day' (1855) by Dante Gabriel Rossetti, remarking on the uncertain quality of travel:

> The gloom that breathes upon me with these airs
> Is like the drops which strike the traveller's brow
> Who knows not, darkling, if they bring him now
> Fresh storm, or be old rain the covert bears.

The twentieth-century playwright Samuel Beckett saw vagrants and tramps in Paris, and as a young man was moved and shocked by the pain and suffering of beggars and indigents. It is held that, like St Martin, he once took off his jacket and gave it to somebody with his wallet still in it. An act of kindness perhaps, but he was watching too. Acts on the street became the inspiration for his actors.

We know too that Beckett also adored art and studied paintings with intense scrutiny in galleries in Paris. He was drawn to seventeenth-century Dutch genre paintings with their tiny images of ordinary scenes and people: beggars, pedlars, the disabled. Medieval marginal images could have been the prototype for this later form of art. Beckett said that 'the walking up and down is the central image […] The text, the words, were only built up around this picture.'[11]

The sense of nothingness in art has a power. Day, night,

moment, the prick of hardship. The quite simple things about survival are evoked to draw us in, while the portrayal of figures moving are pointers for that tough existence. Beckett's novel *Mercier and Camier* (1970), concerns two figures walking – and wondering and waiting. Accessories are scant: a bicycle, an umbrella, a raincoat, the contents of a pocket. They drink at bars from time to time. In what seem like futile conversations, they talk about where to go next. And when they are not on the move, they talk about the next stage. And like all travelling companions, they bicker, they speak rudely to one another – and they part. Then … they get back together again. But where they are or why they are together is unclear; when, how or why are things that do not matter to Beckett. The novel's protagonists, themselves, are not even sure. We are transported into the being and existence of two shadily viewed men. In one of their many conversations, when they reflect on their needless lot, Camier and Mercier talk about how they should find their way. They note too that they are not on the road because they love it. In one of the more unusual features of the novel, a description of a scene with valleys, moorland, ruins, the sea beyond, tarns and paths, Beckett writes of how a wayfarer might not suddenly expect to see tall crags when they were surrounded by land that was flat. All is strange to the characters, and all is unyielding to the reader.

Such a wayfarer. To way-fare as an itinerant in the Middle Ages was a compulsion to continue through the manner of walking. It was with a balance of foreboding and longing that drew subsequent writers and artists to dwell on these figures without getting to know them in a biographical sense.

Going on your feet is one thing, covered and protected in a shoe. Going on your feet with nothing on them is another thing altogether. And yet as itinerants, they would have had an uncomfortable lordship of the path. The world of the Middle Ages was reinvented from closeted, book-led worlds, where little incidents and vignettes inspired a sort of voyeurism.

And so, in the new year after Madrid, I walk down a country lane in the south of England. The winter sun's radiant reaches do not make it here. It is bird-time, the time of early morning when birds sing carelessly, without hesitation. This is loud, clear calling. As if they relish that humans have not yet brought their various audible eruptions to the day to compete with them. As John Clare wrote in 1848, they are: 'incessantly louder than the busy hum of men'. As I walked, before me a dirty tyre, the odd scattered tree, further off a scrubby field and the isolated house. Then I hear from afar the cockerel's morning call. I am reminded of the man in Madrid. Is he being led away against his will?

The mud runnels on the tracks by the lane were high. They were pristine, untrodden on after the high winds and rain. The gullies had become sunken watery stews as the weather had hit hard. One, though, rose, erupting everywhere and out back onto the lane. A little way down, opposite the white boarded house, the other side of a bordering fence, partly broken down, part concealed were puddles. Tawny, murky, like the corner of a Rembrandt picture. Watery mayhem. Channels breaking up the lane to the gully mingle pool and groove. All the features made more entrenched barriers than normal, as mid-winter's monotony alters the land. The next day perceptions shifted. The same area felt darker, even muddier. Another path and on either side a grass verge. But the path was divided up – one side, puddles, the other was relatively dry. This was no place for bare feet.

Humanity's interventionist laying down of the landscape has become something for us to go to, from this to that and back again. It gives us a structure, like the page or stage. Lanes and paths give us a sense of direction. Paths spill over into lanes fringed by weeds and sometimes rinsed by rain, where mud and detritus made by burrowing creatures and nosy worms take over. Rifts and trenches, marks made by nature from creatures and human contact over thousands of years. Has a fleck of dry mud moved much in its life cycle? How far along a road verge does a twig move once it is settled? Seeds are tossed and thrown, dispersed and destroyed without the naked eye seeing. The lane meets another road, or jolts into a main road, or pushes to an end. It is hard to record the minuscule goings-on in nature unless you wait patiently for hours, days, weeks – like a natural history filmmaker. But each imperceptible alteration makes all the difference.

The narrow lane bordered by a shaved-off hedge governs where and how I walk. I look up and beyond. I look behind and aside, forwards and backwards. The birds hop, and I watch. They go too fast for me to see if they are looking all over too. I imagine a vertical lane in the sky falling on the one I am walking on. This one too could be pushed up out of its foundations; it could become a slide and then a vertical. As it is, the bordered lane has precious boundaries to both bird and human. The horizon is another border: a fine, misty line of early morning sky that has not yet released all its collected vapour from the night. Then there is the transparent boundary at the side of the lane, where gaps are made by branches of small trees or shrubs that grow in isolated fashion away or separate from the edge. The birds use these holes to root and probe the foliage, they dive up and down while ducking the electricity wires or sit on them. Their boundary flows, mine is harder to break through, as I do not do anything but walk on the lane. I choose not to go through a hedge, though possibly I could. This is not my natural habitat, but I take from it what I can as I walk. At ground level, the plants in the lilt of the unsteady air veer a bit to right and left or grow upwards, invisible to my beady eye. All of nature seems to gravitate to vertical or horizontal, or a little to the right or a little to the left.

Wayfaring takes us somewhere we do not always know or understand. Feet and the steps they make take us to foreign lands and places and remind us of critical and current crises. As the anthropologist Tim Ingold says, 'Wayfaring is the fundamental mode by which living beings inhabit the earth.'[12]

Sometime later during the new decade year of 2020,

'bodies' began to re-emerge. Parents put summer shoes on their babies, they laced up the trainers for their children who were then let outside after two months in confined circumstances. The children walked and skipped once more, their parents not far behind. The dust-cart men, with their big, heavy boots were visible again, as they plodded from the cart to the bin and back, heaving the rubbish. Old ladies in Madrid who always relied on doing their daily shopping in the local market, put on the shoes they might have had for forty years with the solid sole and heel to take them steadily down the road. People and children no longer wriggled their toes inside; they walked again, at first by the hour, then the hours, then maybe for longer walks by the day, by river or on road and path. They even wondered when they might go to the shoe shop to buy a new season sandal. Once more, we moved. Repeat programmes on the radio talked to us of men on the moon. The astronauts' feet were the first body part that had contact with the moon's surface: excitedly, nervously, placing them down while knowing in theory that the surface was something they could touch, press and stand on. Feet first. Holding and standing. Taking the weight of years and years of research and preparation. So, like the men on the moon, people could bravely tread on surfaces they might have forgotten about. Spring's step held poignant movement and meaning in the later months of 2020. Once more, we became figures of expectation and optimism as we went. But as we were soon to discover, not for long.

Two

Wayfaring Works 2:
Giving Water to the Thirsty

As the hart panteth after the fountains of water; so
my soul panteth after thee, O God. My soul hath
thirsted after the strong living God…
The Book of Psalms, Psalm 41 (2–3)

Wayfarers walked far in shadow and light to ease their
thirst. In 1387, in *Polychronicon Ranulphi Higden
Monachi Cestrensis,* John Trevisa tells of the 'refresshynge
and socour of way farynge men.' Any travelling figure
could receive these rhetorical offerings. But did these
words ever apply to him or her or them 'over there' on
the road? Were these just words? It was all about sounding
hospitable to the bare-footed indigent. We can find places
where words account for the taking in of these figures. But
we do not know what 'sort of wayfarer' St Peter's College
(now called Peterhouse), Cambridge had in mind, when
in the 1388–89 *Compotus* or Bursar's Roll it stated that
wayfarers should receive 16d, one at a time.

Despite laws, statutes and doubts about the 'other' wayfarer, those with means in the Middle Ages were encouraged to give to houses for the sick or leprous, often known as hospitals, but where travellers and wayfarers might drink and rest as well. At St Giles's Hospital in Norwich, thirteen poor men (what of women?) could sit by the fire; there was a poor box for 'passing people' to receive alms and free charitable assistance, beds and a distribution of bread every Saturday between the feast of the Annunciation and the Assumption (25 March–15 August). Donating here, it seems, was only a passing summer act. Moreover, a door can always close, a door can always shut out those not wanted. But sometimes verbal encouragement might be all that was needed. We might imagine wayfarers at the Hospital of St Cross in Winchester, at the bottom of St Catherine's Hill, where the ancient practice of hospitality continues. Here is an old, sturdy medieval building founded in 1132 by Henry of Blois, grandson of William the Conqueror. It was run by monks whose primary purpose was to give shelter and succour to those travelling, precisely to one hundred poor 'men' at the gates. The tradition of giving a piece of bread and the 'Horn' cup of ale is alive and well today. As a tourist attraction. Ale would once have been the healthier option over water. It was this drink that provided the sustenance so needed.

Hospitals had a variety of functions in the medieval period. If you ill, a bed was found, but in the knowledge that only your soul could be saved; little was on offer medically. It was assumed a hospital was the final call, with the priest for last rites, the swinging incense-full censer, a Bible reading, the hope of seeing an angel to whisk you away; above all, the time to banish all those demons and seek forgiveness through the last rites. While the medieval wayfaring poor had little of material value, religious acts and liturgy enabled some form of charity towards them. Think of an open door, stool, ledge, even a cupboard door and a water vessel, as templates for how to look after the poor coming by. These objects tell the story of giving and receiving, echoing the origin of the expression 'dole', the casual word to describe unemployment benefit, from the Middle English *dol*, a kind of dividing of something. While it might have pejorative connotations, those in need could benefit from charity. But a medieval hospital was also a place to feed and give drink and lodging to the better-off traveller or pilgrim, and at times, maybe even the itinerant artist.

While it might not have been safe to drink, water was associated with spiritual healing. And for those anticipating a long journey over the water, being without a drink was something to withstand. The North Sea separates the broad bulky hump of East Anglia on one side from the Low Countries, now Belgium and the Netherlands, on the other. Two frail lands. One cold, northerly sea connecting them. I am standing on the shore in Belgium, not far from the border with the Netherlands. Above me is a sky that cloaks the land, prone to a sepulchral grey. The North Sea connects, but also now divides the two regions. The cut to drift was made some six thousand years ago. Here, a landscape sharing similar geographical features with its East Anglian counterparts: that is mainly flat and marshy, some land banked up with sea barriers and flood plains, while some of it is reclaimed from the sea. Lands that share the same open skies and atmosphere. The writer, essayist and publisher E. V. (Edward Verrall) Lucas wrote in *A Wanderer in Holland* (1905), that North Holland is really the Norfolk Broads. A geography from long ago knew no borders. Land looped around embracing waters. A gull glares and swoops down – indifferent to the boundary between sea and air, as it flirts with both, darting down, and then back up again. Birds cross continents and seas; for them, these expanses have no meaning.

This mass of cold sea with its forbidding horizon, meeting shores of sand and mudflats, may also have been the place imagined in the Anglo-Saxon poem, 'The Wanderer' (late tenth century) which tracks the perils of journeying abroad:

> … though much he endured
> On wintry seas, with woe in his heart,
> Dragging his oar through drenching-cold brine,
> Homeless and houseless and hunted by Wyrd.
> These are the words of a way-faring wanderer,
> This is his song of the sorrow of life…

The Illuminator Seeks Work
Immigrant medieval illuminators went across the sea to

East Anglia to engage in the laborious, exacting, minuscule, candle-lit work, that was their skill and talent. There, painters were casting their talents abroad, fulfilling desires to obtain profoundly beautiful books for the beautiful holy words. Unlike a poor wayfarer, they probably wore shoes, but they too found themselves cast adrift between the two edges of sea and land. God had told them to go forth to paint the Christian way. Find a road that is less dark than what was before.

Their task was to fill up parchment pages with images of religious figures and scenes from the lives of Christ or other saints; and calendars and roundels illustrating the Labours of the Months. Maybe they were seeking other forms of work too. Illuminating may have been only a part-time job. We will never know for certain. Only the painted pages left behind tell us something: that there were those who coveted a book full of colour and figures and decoration designed to aid access to the Divine mysteries – with their specific needs in mind. The artists from the Low Countries may have had skills favoured by those in England who could afford to buy such works as *The Macclesfield Psalter* which I wrote about in Chapter One.

Danger, fear, weakness and what was to become of them must have been in the illuminators' minds, as the boat was swept away by a cursed wind. Yet they had a talent that painstakingly learnt to lighten the page. Following the paths of outcasts into the unknown, leaving what they knew, hanging on tight to their brushes. I wanted to imagine them leaving their homeland for new painting opportunities, with the tools of their trade packed into a saddlebag. The polish long faded, the leather worn white in places, marked by creases softened with age, from being wedged into boats and pockets on other journeys. The bag was less likely to hold overnight things. It would have been a container for pigments, gold leaf, brushes, and seashells for mixing the paints. The twelfth-century storyteller of fables, Odo from Cheriton (now a suburb of Folkestone in Kent), wove some of his tales from his own travels. He belonged to a family who had migrated to Britain with the Normans, and it is said that he took himself off to Paris in a small boat to get educated with a satchel for his books. His narratives are reminiscent of *Aesop's Fables*, with titles such as 'One Dog, Two Men' or 'The Wolf and the Fox.' If the artists travelled across seas as well, Odo was hardly unique. We will never know, but the artists may have disembarked at an old medieval port called Nieuwpoort in present-day Belgium.

Nieuwpoort is about an hour's drive from Calais. If there ever was a Paradise here, if the town ever hosted a carnival or a colourful travelling fair, or merely had been a town of colour, with dressed up boats bobbing up and down, I was late, as all of this and more left long ago. And the apple and pomegranate trees had gone, and the people scattered, and even the birds and angels had flown away. This 'new port' is today, something indistinct and murky, pulling itself inside out, trying to change, but still chugging towards what was. Nieuwpoort once had a ferry service to Norwich via Great Yarmouth. Trade, goods, exchange and lively debate, with a sea that saw the conquering headways of the Vikings and the Dutch later in the seventeenth century as they built and maintained their empire. Boats coming and going, goods, jobs and people too, all representing a new life and prospects; but for some, of course, the sea was also a barrier to going further afield. Unless you knew somebody with a boat that was going over the sea, unless you had a skill to offer, or unless you just got lucky. It is likely that at the highpoint of its maritime history, the sea at Nieuwpoort was closer in than it is now. Proper wave-tossed sea, sea that would seem dangerous feels a long way out from where I stood. The boats are in a large basin of water with no obvious link to the wider seascape, as the town has a huge marina and harbour, with a conurbation stretching far and wide. It was hard to find a centre, or, for that matter, any sign of life. Just the odd bicycle bell and the distant whir of something. The small box-like houses, painted red, provided the only passion of colour on this greying coast. There, too, a neat window on one side and a neat one on the other, replicated on the storey above; all is reassuringly organised and uniform.

On the outskirts are large intersections broken up by flatland areas of green, somewhat like Milton Keynes. Trees line these roads, looking like gnarled branches or dog bones, creating a barrier to the small dykes that edge the tarmac. Cyclists pass by insouciantly and their cycling is fast; the people here seem fit and healthy, propped up on their high bikes, serene and casual, yet pedalling with purpose. There are wide streets, but few cars. There are windmills too, looking like modernist structures of garden trellis. Dozens of solar panels sun worship on rebuilt barn buildings, all these projects for a land that may soon in a changing climate provide more warmth in the winter. More than ever before. A river feeds into the sea, and a massive approach road, hints of the bustling, enterprising international status that Nieuwpoort once had. It felt a bit like looking at one of those Dutch maritime or landscape paintings, with a mass of sky and cloud commanding much of the picture and then not much else besides. That took some artistic bravery, in a sense anticipating the great swathes of colour of abstract art; but when this sort of landscape was painted in the seventeenth century, the sea was everything to the emerging powerful Dutch republic, as it set about colonising far distant lands. The sea brought wealth and prosperity and fine goods to people's narrow, but tall and gabled homes, and allowed power and domination. I sensed there is less colour and obvious materiality at docks these days, as post-industrial ports are more like the minimalist modern of the white-walled art gallery, where goods are in massive containers and ships are so large that only a few are needed. And people even less.

Port Life
There was no real working port to see, and I was disappointed. The name – Lombardsjide – is still listed as the old port, but that way of life has been replaced by yachts rather than seafaring, trading ships. Where had the port gone? How had it declined so sharply? These were questions that might be answered by a local, but I found nobody to ask as

they were either cycling or getting in and out of cars while trying to avoid the wind. The area is vast, there are no crowds. Imagining or even knowing how to track medieval people stepping onto boats heading for East Anglia was proving difficult.

On that cloudy, intermittently windy, at times sunny, day, the boats and their masts, rudders, engines and sails were churning and blowing. Glinting in a grey, silvery, blue sort of way. But the chaos of colour and urban thrill I wanted was not there; I had been looking at too much glorious technicolour from the medieval manuscripts' palette. I had been looking at too many topographical images by the Dutch seventeenth-century masters of steeples, windmills, and towers from various types of buildings, all delicately painted in oil. Viewing yachts and cars parked in a huge watery basin with flat slabs of paving going down to the water's edge makes the distinction between land and sea where you can imagine journeys taken, remote. I might as well have been looking at a Lowry painting with the stick people he depicted seemingly so effortlessly, but all too far to see from the picture plane. There was nothing really to latch onto. I stood there wondering where to go and what to look at. I tried not to let the inevitable question take hold, 'What am I doing here?'

Why had I relied upon such a stereotypical view in my dream? Today, the port town is not for transporting immigrant craftspeople, paints, pots, spices, cloth, wool and other such sundry items from one harbour to the other. No amount of tourist hype, to replace what was, will bring people here.

As for over there, across the sea.

All I know is that there were scattered homesteads and hamlets in East Anglia in the Middle Ages, united by farming, which provided mobility and some sort of community from place to place. There were, too, monastic settlements. And those wayfaring were close to the land. They probably understood how it worked according to the seasons, the farming calendar and the altered moments of light and dark. And people moving between places provided a form of cohesion and connection, sometimes favourable, at times not. As well as illuminators, entertainers crossed the seas. A privy seal of Westminster, dated July 9th, 1372 (Edward III's reign), records that:

> Myttok, king of the minstrels of Brabant, Guynaud the Blind, Swankyn and Rolethere and other minstrels were to pass the port of Dover towards Calais with 6 horses to return home to Brabant in 1368, their grooms [garceons] Clynkes and Wauter, 20 marks by exchange, and each of the said minstrels with 20 shillings (soldz) for expenses.[13]

Protective measures for those who travelled to entertain the king and his retinue. Skills, like the waves, went back and forth and minstrels, too, were in peril on the sea, but once at court, they found a stable status as entertainers. They reminded people of how close they were to the animals, putting on animal-like masks, as part of their subverting, carousing entertainment and mimicry.

There were signs to the old town. I drove along the coastline looking for old wharves and warehouses, cobbles (that would take me back in time, joyful like a child), a small harbour, some sign, something to make my journey worthwhile. But the coastal road was situated by rows and rows of neat houses with lace curtains, with more red front doors and pots of flowers on the windowsills. It was hard to see beyond Nieuwpoort, hard to accept that I had merely built up a medieval port in my mind. And a medieval Paradise charting what had been was a fantasy of an overzealous imagination.

Soon, I was longing for coffee. But cafes with hot waffle aromas, so prevalent in other Belgian towns such as Ghent and Bruges, were in short supply. I became a romantic pretender of the nineteenth century, questing for the medieval Holy Grail, but not quite finding it. The cathedral was entered by an automatic door. Automatic entrance to your Judgement? I imagined a pulley taking me down to Hell as well, but with an abrupt stop in Purgatory first. A woman was tending flowers outside on the pavement where there were metal containers for window-box flowers. A kind of municipal garden city had been created by conscientious citizens: flowers and order, quiet and safety to accommodate the mercy and forgiveness of God, care for the sinner and weak and, above all, the birth and salvation of Christ.

Later, at lunch, I sat next to a woman in a wheelchair, who was unable to speak. But still she tried, and, as she did, painfully wrought sounds came from her mouth, new articulations of consonants and vowels, stretched out, like wringing out clothes. Sounds that strain hearing for those trying to communicate with her. To understand her, one would need to enter her unmoving head. It is possible that her cognition was as mighty as the horrible degenerative condition that had beset her. I sensed that a part of her brain had ceased telling her body what to do. I could not get her out of my mind. She had no escape from her plight whatsoever. I knew that she would not walk or talk clearly again. A while later, I came to see why I had not forgotten this woman. The same sort of affliction cruelly brought on, unexplained, unavoidable, arriving from nowhere like a stranger in the dark, had just started to affect my brother, who was only fifty-five when he realised something was wrong. This woman epitomised a prophecy without me knowing it at the time. It seems that I had come to Nieuw-poort for other reasons.

Illuminations

I became a bit distracted from my original purpose. But then I remembered the illuminations. The medieval illuminators working in the Low Countries, including those who may have travelled to East Anglia and other places in Britain, painted manuscript images of the weak, including the wayfaring disabled.

In a *Psalter-Hours* made in Ghent (Baltimore, Walters Ms. W.82, fol. 193v, c.1315–25, Figure 4), the holy book is shimmering with gold. Quotidian vignettes are mixed in with the dazzling and glittering decoration which almost levitates the page. No matter the size, a book for prayer, organised around the liturgical hours

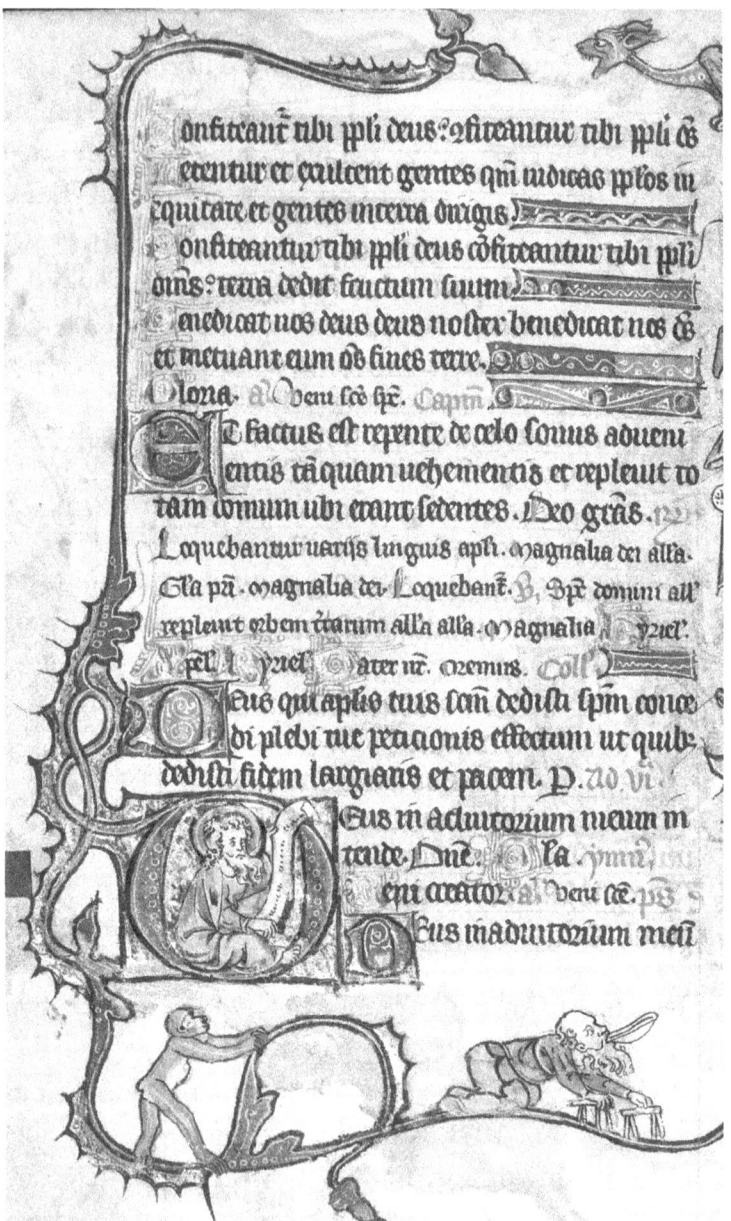

Figure 4: *Psalter-Hours*, Baltimore, Walters Ms. W.82, fol. 193v, c.1315–25, 111 x 162 mm.

of the day shows the plight of an incapacitated wayfarer trestling towards hope. With a bowl in his mouth, as his hands must move the trestles, he is painted as if moving towards the next page and maybe the light. Behind is an ape holding onto part of a painted, partially gilded tendril, doubling up as a tail, who also follows that line of hope. An ape can move on all fours, but here, he is showing his skills in imitation. He bears a naked similarity to a human, standing upright, against somebody who might never stand up again.

Collecting the Modern Word

As people walk through time, in county, city and country, words gather, change a little, alter their meaning a little, break a little. Words can be uprooted like people can. Words to do with vagrant walking and wandering become fixed for use in one period and are then adapted or changed in another. The word moves in time with what it represents. There is also a reason, often unclear, for a word used in a certain way. Similarly, a clarity of meaning around wayfaring and wayfarers has always been elusive, since people walk for a number of reasons. As different categories of walking emerged, language evolved. Society tried to organise itself around categories. We like to classify, but classification is a blunt tool, wherein lots of word groupings escape note and attention. That is also the case with walking words. Word use is convened by humanity, so of course it will be inconsistent and contradictory. This reminds me of my hoped-for epitaph – 'Mean what you say. Say what you mean.' Like the carry out fast-food, the quick to dispense with forms of communication. Language becomes an effective tool for us to contradict ourselves and shift our intentions.

Throughout history, a common thread in language around people who were itinerant has been one of fear. In 1572, *The English Act for the Restraining of Vagabonds* lumped together 'all fencers, bear-wards, common players in interludes and minstrels … all jugglers, pedlars, tinkers and petty chapmen and forbade them all to wander abroad without a licence from the justices of the peace'. By some accounts, even those who were selling goods on the roads had become nuisance figures who needed to be classified depending on how or whether they were considered undesirable or not. Fear, then, was declarative.

A brief 'hoarded' chart of words to do with wandering and wayfaring over time gives both positive and negative inferences.

Peregrine	Strangers
Homo Viator	Wayfaring man
Aliens	Alien
Baffa bone	Vagrant
Farrow	A wayfaring, a path
Gangrel	Vagabond
Viator, aviatrix	Traveller, summoner
Jeopardous	Dusty footed wayfarer
Vagrants	Wandering scholars
Hedge creeper	Vagabond, thief
Gadling	A vagabond

A stranger can be a wayfarer, but also a pilgrim. But a wayfarer can also be something else. In the way in which we assess, weigh and measure, we are subtly changing a word's intent and meaning, I suspect, quite inadvertently. Wayfaring as an idea, even if somewhat elusive, might have developed out of a recognition of those wearied with life. But it was accompanied with a distrust simply about a person seen walking on the road, over time, there were other expressive observations that caused wonder and intrigue about people seen walking from afar, where a virtue was made of those on the path or road. So, the use of the word has straddled both mythic musing and the sharp stab of reality.

The poet, William Browne of Tavistock (1591–1645) who wrote during the reign of James I was cloistered for a while in the Inner Temple, getting a 'portion' to survive in a marriage from a knight's daughter and wrote in 'A Devonshire Walk' of the perils of the path for a wayfarer:

> As when some wayfaring man passing a wood,
> Whose waving top hath long a sea-mark stood,
> Goes jogging on and in his mind nought hath,
> But how the primrose finely strew the path,
> Or sweetest violets lay down their heads
> At some tree's root on mossy feather-beds,
> Until his heel receives an adder's sting,
> Whereat he starts and back his head doth fling.

The lusciousness of the plants, the colours they offer – the primrose yellow, the purple violet, the mossy green, is contrasted with stinging danger as well and a rawness that continued to be explored with the word wayfaring. I have always been intrigued by the sight of others walking. The 'I wonder as I wander' is for me wondering about where somebody is going and where they have come from, which must in part be what Browne had been thinking about.

There have always been wayfarers in one form or another: begging and surviving but also being made anew poetically. By the eighteenth century, the act of wayfaring was still a physical thing, but was also described by the privilege of writing, by those who could, and the act was to walk and 'see' and to go within, to feel and experience. Wayfaring on paths in the Romantic period attracted poets to write about this form of journeying. With satchel, pen and paper, a writer or artist usually had the proper means to go wayfaring, with a coat, decent boots and no time limit, as usually they had homes to return to. Walking along a road or path which was wet or dry, muddy, rutted, bumpy; walking at night or day, accompanied by a wistful mind and an ineffable conjuring, 'moved' by visions and poetic yearnings. That was the spirit.

And then, through peripatetic self-fashioning, the restless mind, seen by a moving sensibility, became something to mull over. Poets and writers began to make something of the 'grey' in language and classification around figures such as wayfarers, vagabonds and travellers. There were poetic descriptions of wayfaring to rhapsodise the emotions and provide a commentary on roaming. Wayfaring was often used in writing about scenes, bound up with longing, wondering and feeling. We see this in Wordsworth's 'Old

Man Travelling' (1802):

> He travels on, and in his face, his step,
> His gait, is one expression; every limb,
> His look and bending figure, all bespeak
> A man who does not move with pain, but moves
> With thought…

And later,

> He hath no need. He is by nature led
> To peace so perfect, that the young behold
> With envy, what the Old Man hardly feels.

Those walking, looking, writing, and painting studied the gloaming light, the moon's changing shape, or through the light of its gaze, found a plant to probe. Accompanied by a magnifying glass, to look within or beyond the wondrous surfaces of nature's plenty, they sought suitable words to describe their wayfaring selves and the minute essence of beauty as they went. Their walks might have meandered with no particular point or fixed destination in mind. In this case, they were different to the medieval wayfarer who went in a linear fashion to somewhere where they might get help.

But not always.

Some writers assumed that wayfarers might have chosen or wanted to live as if they were struggling vagrants. In William Cowper's six-volume poem *The Task* (1785), in 'The Sofa', the poet recalls witnessing a vagabond family eating flesh of dog, or vermin, or stolen cock. 'Hard-faring race!' he comments. 'They pick their fuel out of ev'ry hedge.' He wonders later if they really must live like this, or whether they 'self-banish'd from society' out of choice, preferring 'sloth' to 'honourable toil.' And in another passage, the wandering illustrates the torment of love and loss:

There often wanders one, whom better days
Saw better clad, in cloak of sattin [*sic*] trimm'd
With lace, and hat with splendid ribband bound.
A serving maid was she, and fell in love
With one who left her, went to sea, and died.

She heard the doleful tidings of his death,
And never smil'd again. And now she roams
The dreary waste; there spends the livelong day,
And there, unless when charity forbids,
The livelong night. A tatter'd apron hides,
Worn as a cloak, and hardly hides a gown...

Poetic wandering is not all about dreams and hope. We learn that the maid begs for pins, hoarding them, but never asking for food, even though she must be hungry. 'She is craz'd', the poet says. Her name, he says, is Kate. She is, however, known as 'Crazy Kate' who once was sane and clothed but then became unstable and unwanted in her almost naked state. Like the composers of an edict or law, a poet could never really know what being on the road truly meant, unless they had experienced it. And it was easy to shrug and slur.

That sense of wayfaring misery is also seen in James Thomson's 'Seasons in Winter' (1726). With a fiery sky, reeling clouds that stagger, and a bleak circled moon, a storm starts. Rift and surge, angry, roll and billow, the scene is set to reduce a 'feeble man' still further, where the mountain growls while 'its sturdy sons' stoop so low:

> The dark wayfaring stranger breathless, toils,
> And, often falling, climbs against the blast –
> Low waves the rooted forest, vex'd, and sheds
> What of its tarnish'd honours yet remain;

In the nineteenth century, romantic and miserable ev-ocations persisted, but emerging prose anthologies about country life and lore depicted struggle, in ways that now we regard as romantic. In *The Rural Life of England* (1840), William Howitt assumes a wistful stance, designed no doubt to arouse sympathy: 'Well may the weary wayfarer / Lean on such humble gate and think the while'.

Only a few years before she died, the invalided Elizabeth Barrett Browning, writing from her *chaise longue*, wrote her epic poem, *Aurora Leigh* (1856). She uses the metaphor of being 'far from home' against embattling elements:

> 'You're poor, except in what you richly give;
> You labour for your own bread painfully
> Or ere you pour our wine. For art's sake, pause.'

I answered slow – as some wayfaring man,
Who feels himself at night too far from home,
Makes steadfast face against the bitter wind.

Indeed, for Browning, the word brings a sense of danger and fear:

Sublimest danger, over which none weeps,
When any young wayfaring soul goes forth
Alone, unconscious of the perilous road,
The day-sun dazzling in his limpid eyes,
To thrust his own way, he an alien, through
The world of books!

Nonetheless, Browning's wayfarer has a home.

Charles Dickens reflected on travelling hardship, but also the sense in which you can be a wayfarer, and all the while observe the wayfaring of others. In *The Old Curiosity Shop* (1840–41) he wrote: 'Gipsy camps they had passed in their wayfaring', making me wonder why he would not think the gypsies were the wayfarers. And in a delightful contradiction, in *The Mystery of Edwin Drood* (1870):

… time was when wayfarers, leading a gipsy life between haymaking time and harvest, and looking as if they were just made of the dust of the earth, so very dusty are they, lounge about on cool doorsteps, trying to mend their unmendable shoes.

All is wrought generically, even vaguely and unthinkingly,

to be descriptive. In *The Woodlanders* (1886–87), Thomas Hardy wrote: 'No wayfarer would have perceived that here the cottager did not sleep as elsewhere.' Hardy could strut or posture with the word as well. When he once visited the writer John Cowper Powys (1872–1963) at Montacute, Somerset, he was asked to add himself to their list of names in a play-den. He wrote, 'Thomas Hardy, a Wayfarer.'

In his *Tess of the d'Urbervilles* (1891), the act of walking to meet another is a romantic lynchpin, yet wretched wandering weighs heavily as well. Towards the end of the novel, when Angel Clare and Tess are together as tormented lovers, judged by Tess's past as sinner, they are only briefly reunited. Clare sees Tess walking between the edge of a valley, as he takes the road to the station. Hardy observes them as figures moving, writing: 'To avoid meeting any possible wayfarers he left the high road and took a footpath under some fir trees.' While wayfaring carries an enigmatic, romantic feel, here, it is invoked to carry love and its bearers towards a dramatic destiny. Earlier in the novel, Tess goes as far as the house of Clare's parents when he has abandoned her but stops just before as she overhears Clare's two brothers and Mercy Chant discussing a pair of old boots left by a tramp, or 'some imposter' who had come into town barefoot, to 'excite our sympathies.'

Using it as a label in *Wayfaring Men* (1897), Edna Lyall describes a man trying to get a lift from another in a cart: 'I am just a wayfaring man … grateful for the shelter of your hay-cart on a cold night.' Living with her sister Amy Agnes, from 1884 in Eastbourne, the novelist (her proper name was Ada Ellen Bayly), spent much of her time and money on charitable causes. She was also a supporter of women's suffrage and was a strong advocate of social reform. Her vivid childhood imagination allowed her to believe that a tramp had once entered her bedroom. For 'others' had told her that afternoon that, one day a beggar woman had followed them begging. Out of a sense of protection, the child's aunt told the beggar to leave them; she responded, 'I hope the Almighty will say so to you at the day of judgment'. This deeply upset the child, who thought it was a wicked thing to say. And that night, she convinced herself that the woman was in her cupboard, and she would not be comforted until the contents of the cupboard had been checked. Her mother's advice when you feel fear was robust: 'Take the bull by the horns.'[14] The account may, however, reveal more about religious sensibility and contradiction then, as she did not like the woman's reference to Christ's Judgement. The words you hear as a child often stay with you.

In the late nineteenth century, the law caught up with the ambiguity around wayfaring. In 1884, the following definitions were constructed by *The Central Committee of Poor Law Conferences*:

"Vagrant" means professional wanderer; "Tramp" means an honest traveller in search of work; "Wayfarer" means any destitute traveller without distinguishing the class to which he belongs; "Casual" means any wayfarer who receives relief in the casual wards of a workhouse.

Poetry, however, continued to be a refuge, for wayfarer

and vagrant *et al* were the objects of romantic musing. In 1894, the Canadian poet Bliss Carman and a fellow (American) poet, Richard Hovey, published the hugely popular *Songs from Vagabondia*, carefree poems celebrating community and freedom. In 'The Joys of the Road', rhyming couplets list unsurprisingly, we might think, the joys of the road: 'By marsh and tide, by meadow and stream, / A will-o'-the-wind, a light-o'-dream', accompanied by luscious references to 'an easy shoe, the crickets, a fairy fire, the forest loam, the cold new moon'. And all is image rich: the corn, the bubbling spring and other sights and sounds. And the vagrant even has wine and a maid to anticipate. There is no question then, that the subject is male and, on this occasion, speaks to being free.

The elegance of poetry barely conceals the fact that the road of the wayfarer was normally one of hunger and hardship. The abrasive grip of the law paved the way for the poetic flirtation of walking with words. The voice in John Masefield's 'Vagabond' (1899–1911), denies all the talk about knowledge, or life, or God, or being. Instead, he declares that his understanding is the dusty road, because, as he says in the fourth line of the first verse, 'Earth's jest [*sic*] a dusty road.' This is the place where he feels himself, with the last stanza concluding:

> An' why I live, an' why the old world spins,
> Are things I never knowed,
> My mark's the gipsy fires, the lonely inns,
> An' jest the dusty road.

The path. Contained, finite, marked and bordered, characterises the English country landscape. It links field with wood, wood with church, church with hamlet or village; all laid out before the walker as if they have always been there. American writers also observed the quaint attribute of the English path, which often provided the basis for a narrative or character walking along it. In 'Leamington Spa', one of the sketches in *Our Old Home* (1863), Nathaniel Hawthorne wrote that paths:

> … admit the wayfarer into the very heart of rural life, and yet do not burden him with a sense of intrusiveness. He has a right to go withersoever they lead him; for with all their shaded privacy they are as much a property of the public as the dusty high-road itself, and by an even older tenure…

The history of wayfaring has no singular course or direction. The word captures the irresistible quality of romance on the road but enduringly hints at disadvantage.

Documenting Wayfaring Life
Despite the reality of wayfaring, the nineteenth century also embodied a nostalgia for a past that was naively thought more worthy. Many writers, including William Morris, looked back to the Middle Ages as a time when all just might be well. They cherished walking in landscapes offering an escape from places that were smoking, steaming, misting, clouding and changing due to steam, vapour, velocity – the ineluctable power of industrialisation. Too

fast for some who continued to want to dream. And who wanted to rejoice in the pre-smoky furnaced world they felt was enveloping the land. The French cultural historian J. J. Jusserand (1855–1932) clearly thought the same. Not long after the establishment of the railways, his romp through different forms of travel in *English Wayfaring Life in the Middle Ages* (1898 and fourteen further editions by 1931), shows us all sorts of wayfarers from minstrels to pedlars, and preachers to pilgrims. In what can be seen as a form of ethnography, he also encapsulates a mood of warmth towards wayfarers. He lists a broad array: lay wayfarer, the ordinary traveller and casual passer-by, herbalists, charlatans, minstrels, jugglers and tumblers, messengers, itinerant merchants and pedlars, outlaws, wandering merchants and peasants out of bond. There are, too, the religious wayfarers: wandering preachers and friars, pardoners and pilgrims. In other words, anybody who walked.

You will see that his classification sounds absolute. As well as broad, if not overly capacious. The quest to order wayfarers according to category is also a way to structure his chapters. In gathering these types together, he was collecting in the manner of somebody sourcing Toby jugs or stamps from Romania. Included in his colourful pantheon cataloguing the wayfarer was the quack, drug purveyor, *triacleur*, tinker, *gleeman*, *jongleur*, scholar, wandering hermit, itinerant gospeller, preacher, messenger, chapman and beggar. His book is a charming, if rather wayward, circumnavigation round modes of wayfaring.

In an enthusiastic gesture, Jusserand created a kind

of wayfaring type. He may also have contributed to the romantic notion of the wayfarer, as he witnessed train replace foot and the newly established permanent shop favour the pedlar or chapman carrying linen cloth. All around Jusserand were slums, cholera, tuberculosis, dirt, mud at the skirts and trouser hems, death and poverty, pestilence and prostitution. No wonder there was a retreat to the past by reading ballads of the Middle Ages and wondering about the pedlar and his pack, and the colour of his ribbons, the glint of his mirrors, the shine on his combs, singing joyful rhyming songs of curiosity and jocularity. Although the reality of a travelling salesman was less romantic, a pedlar had always presented an odd mixture of appeal but also dread and disdain. Armed with travelling stick from home and back again at the end of the day, he enjoyed the hearth and a jar of ale. There is a medieval rhyme expressing how nobody would lay hands on a chapman or a pedlar, knowing they needed to sell their wares – 'Than might chapmen, pedlars, fare / And bladelike (boldly) beye [*sic*] and sellen' [*sic*].

Jusserand even goes as far as saying wayfaring was a passing practice. His opening sentence reads, 'At the present day there are but few wayfarers', selectively choosing to ignore the fact that while he includes beggars in his list, there would have been no shortage of them at the time he was writing. There is some concession to the plight of some out walking: 'Those who travelled on foot, were used to all sorts of misery.' He just spares us the detail, I suspect, in the interests of getting people to read his book, keeping the content dirt and filth-free. Much of Jusserand's inspiration came from Chaucer, who, he claimed, loved travelling narratives. But Chaucer does not mention wayfaring in *The Canterbury Tales*. No, Chaucer was clear he was writing of pilgrims on horseback, purposefully travelling to the shrine of Thomas Becket at Canterbury Cathedral.

Jusserand stretched the meaning of 'wayfarer' too, as he wrote of them wandering about like ramblers, ceaseless roaming, without direction. In his wistfulness, they are referred to at one point as a 'race'. His writing is partly theoretical, partly historical, boldly anecdotal and joyous. He left no walking diary, making it unclear as to know where, how or why he became so entranced by the notion of wayfaring. I have not read that he was a self-fashioned wayfarer. Though he writes of the odd time when he was out with the peasants in his later youth, on rocky outcrops and muddy tracks in Scotland – and with no real improvement in roads. That gave him the best practical way to imagine the life of the wayfarer. From a distance, a group of people he creates and affirms became interesting; but the bulk of the research was not done by going along with such people.

On a microscopic scale, there was not much difference between the notional wayfaring literary or literate collector like Jusserand and his / her medieval predecessor. Both relied on their feet to travel, both looked up and around, far out to the distance, behind and beneath, and both might have carried something, at times thirsty, weary or hungry. What is more, the shape of the steps might have been similar: some short, some long, some slow, or quickly striding. Their feet may even have been the same size, and yet they were not all on an equal societal footing. The former was at times pictured as the equivalent of a footnote on a page of manuscript with text; the latter were often their own main subject writing down their observations in notebooks.

But while writers and poets dreamt of walking freedom, the laws against wayfaring types continued. In 1906, in *The Report of The Departmental Committee on Vagrancy, with especial regard to Labour Colonies*, it stated that:

> the *bona fide* wayfarer who can satisfy the police either that he has worked at some employment (other than a casual job) within say three months, and that he has reasonable ground for expecting to get work at a certain place, and is likely to keep to it, or that he has some other good ground for desiring to go to some particular place, would obtain from the police a way-ticket, giving his personal description, his trade, his reason for wanting to travel, and his proposed destination, with his signature (if any) and possibly his finger-print.

The report refers to women separately. It adds that this ticket, including the wayfarer's signature and fingerprint, would last a month and would entitle the person to a night's lodging with supper and breakfast. Here is hospitality with a twist and with many demands placed on the wayfarer who is not really defined. Casual labour and wayfaring for work was common in the nineteenth century, tilted towards an underlying fear of people going from place to place. This miserable destiny is also commented on by Fabian and activist for the poor, Beatrice Webb. In a report she co-authored with her husband, *The English Poor Law Policy* (1910), she notes 'that the proportion of *bona fide* tramps among wayfarers is surprisingly large.' In *The Abolition of the Poor Law* (1918), she urged for the Poor Law's abolition, which stated people could only get help by going to the workhouse. She wrote: 'The honest wayfarer in temporary distress might, it was suggested, be given a certificate showing his circumstances, destination, object of journey etc., upon production of which he was to be readily admitted to the workhouses and provided with comfortable accommodation.' She rejected unfair treatment of those who were genuine. Yet linguistic contortions of classification continued. Conditions inside the workhouse could be so horrible that wayfaring on the road, even sleeping under a bush, was preferred. As late as 1918, people spoke of the degrading treatment of wayfarers where some would prefer to go to prison or even starve to death, rather than end up in the workhouse. Simultaneously, the romantic use of the word continued.

Wayfaring Back in Time
Alison Uttley (1884–1976), author of *The Little Grey Rabbit* books, loved paths and lanes and dividing walls and ditches, borders and hedges. In her books on country lore, she made extensive notes about the flowers and birds found there. She even comments on a 'trembling civilisation, with an earth on the point of extinction' in *A Year in the Country* (1976). Perhaps we have always known. Here, she writes of the ancient roads of England, the different types

of roads and how we can trace historical groups through tracking their journeys – often, she notes, in bare feet. In this book, she also writes of two glasses for the 'thirsty wayfarer' at an unnamed church somewhere in Buckinghamshire, but does not give the reader its name, taking pleasure in imagining ancient feet and spotting signposts to ancient ways. She writes of bordering trailing plants such as white bryony and guelder berries and traveller's joy. She observes gaps through hedges for views and distant hills, she finds places sinister or cruel, she imagines ghosts and fairies, haunting thoughts revealing her imagination. As a child, I read her children's novel about the imprisonment of Mary Queen of Scots called *A Traveller in Time*. I loved it and it became intertwined with a particular memory: a hot August in Portugal, where on a family holiday, I was holding the book, while walking along a hot and dusty path. Little stones caught in my sandals. The smell of exotic and dry mountain plants, such as wild thyme, lingered in the air. I can still picture this path today. Was it the book that helped etch this memory in my mind, or the intoxicating heat associated with my walk?

The Flight into Egypt

As I write, people will soon be thinking about going home for Christmas. It has also been a year of continuing crisis, with refugees making a perilous journey across the sea. After the birth at night in Bethlehem, Joseph and Mary and baby Jesus were in flight to Egypt for a while, having heard that King Herod was planning to massacre the innocents. Joseph becomes a wayfarer with his family.

Take the frequently painted medieval image of *The Flight into Egypt* (*The Taymouth Hours*, London, British Library, Yates Thompson, MS 13, fol. 95v, c.1325–30, Plate 3), in an illustration from *The Gospel of St Matthew* (2:13–15), and other apocryphal texts. Here, Joseph, from Nazareth, is protector as he leads Mary out of danger. In this image, the family walk across a border, but they are contained within it, protected and comforted by the decoration. In the account, an angel visits Joseph while he sleeps and advises their escape. In this depiction, Joseph, dressed in a long orange tunic, holds a staff across his back from his left hand, which has a garment slung across it. In his right hand he holds the rope that pulls the donkey that carries Mary and the baby. Joseph looks back on his wife and child who are wrapped within Mary's blue robe. They have just passed a tree. The donkey looks down, as they habitually do. As the family physically cross borders, they embody the might and indomitable merit of Christian devotion. And for a brief while, Joseph and his wife and child are like other vulnerable vagrants or refugees escaping and the page is part of that fugitive journey. It is easy to mistake this scene for a charming family image out travelling for a picnic. But Christians knew what had really gone on. Christ would have been killed along with thousands of others if Joseph had not taken his family and left. These swiftly recorded moments between one frontier land and another are captured before they walk into another page and another scene in the life of Christ, painted to persuade and affirm.

The family might also have been thirsty. One version of

the narrative – *The Pseudo-Matthew*, from the *Ante-Nicene Fathers* (eighth / ninth century), describes how, on the third day of their journey, the desert sun is especially hot. Mary sees a palm tree and asks if they can rest under it. She notices that the tree bears fruit and asks if they can have some. But Joseph thinks it is too high and instead, says he is thinking more of the lack of water, as their 'skins' are empty. Jesus, the baby, hears the conversation and asks the tree to bend to their wishes. Instantly, the branches bear down so that fruit can be gathered. Sensing perhaps that even the Divine can offer a two-for-one miracle, Jesus then asks the tree to open roots to bring water, and duly a spring comes forth.[15] There were other versions too. *The Arabic Infancy Gospel*, translated from Syriac, became known to the Muslims and some of the legends were adopted into the Koran. There was *The Armenian Infancy Gospel* and *The Protoevangelium of James*; this is a narrative that appealed to all religions and applies in a timeless way. Stories of survival and hardship overlap. Like the travellers, narratives migrate and pierce boundaries.

And like the shepherds who had been to see the recent birth, the family are poor. Like the medieval wayfarers, their poverty, according to Christ's later teachings, brings hope. To be poor is to be chosen for the Kingdom of Heaven. It is believed that the family stayed in Egypt for one year before returning to live in Nazareth in Galilee. It is good that, as the mortal father of Christ, Joseph gets some sort of recognition. Joseph, the carpenter, the quiet old man with his wood, who also knew how to trade in animals such as the ox. But not always, so the legends recount – sober, and often sleeping. In images at the Nativity, he looks tired, his head bowed, as he sits. The old man who had little part to play in Christ's birth, but still, he is sleepy. Joseph walks, but he also sleeps.

Christ is known as a miracle worker and preacher. Christ also conveys his storytelling abilities. In the *Ante-Nicene Fathers*, we hear about Joseph's life and death through the words of Christ as he speaks to his Apostles about his 'flesh' father and speaking of him with as complicated a family history as anyone's. As an older man, before he married Mary, Joseph had another wife, with whom he had four sons and two daughters. She died and soon after he met Mary, who they say was only about twelve. At his death, Jesus explains how Joseph cried out about the woes of his life: 'Woe to my feet, which have too often walked in ways displeasing to God. Woe to my body, and woe to my miserable soul.' It sounds like the call for forgiveness that Christ was later to implement. Jesus then says that he goes to see his father, who is comforted by his presence, while saying, 'You are my Lord.' Then Jesus says that at his death, Mary touches Joseph's body and his feet, which are already stiffening. Jesus recalls how he remembers the difficulty Joseph had when he had to take his family into safety. Of course, Mary Magdalen was later to touch Christ's feet, anointing them with oil. After his death, when he has been taken down from the Cross, she is depicted covering his feet with her head and hair. In these intimate moments, body parts connect and unite in trouble and grief.

Although Joseph is poor, he guides a figure who, himself, is destined to speak of the riches of Heaven and the truth of poverty. Feet are a not just a cypher to show that deficiency can bring you rewards. They say that Aristotle went barefoot on the road, with the dust on his feet and stick, and a few books of grammar in his knapsack. But he considers the legs as the seat of folly, more than the head. A bare foot did not always mean the same thing. For, to go on barefoot could be a punishment for those who had sinned through bestiality. Thomas of Cobham (d. 1327) said that an offender had to go barefoot for the rest of their life. And that they were never to enter a church again.[16] Where did somebody go then when they had to flee from the religious embrace as well as derision from society? If you moved, too, you were seen to be prone to folly, sin and decay of mind, even though, as the Flight into Egypt shows, going from one place to the other was not just necessary, but a transformative means of survival.

Samuel Beckett may even have thought of the Flight into Egypt. In a letter to Thomas MacGreevy, a poet and art historian, and eventually director of the National Gallery of Ireland, dated 14 February 1935, Beckett writes of *the two Rests on the Flight*, School of Patinir (National Gallery) as being lovely. He does not say why. But the 'Rest' depicts another moment in the narrative of the Flight when the family are, literally, resting. There is no obvious context for the comment.

In the seventeenth century, Dutch landscapes showed people walking on distant paths, walking away, along a road or beside it, walking past another or walking beside a church, a house with a smoking chimney, an inn, often shown as the den of iniquity. Over there may be a

windmill, or a field of bleaching cloth. All is episodic and
itinerant: one figure with sack and staff walking by a low
fence, another, with only their back visible, but showing
a staff and a pack on back which obscures the head, as the
figure walks past a seated woman holding out a bowl. Such
scenes were observed, happening all the time, everywhere,
without notice. Yet something draws us to the image of
moving figures, walking across, left to right, away from
our gaze. These are the anonymous pedestrians with their
daily existences. Painters and engravers took delight in
depicting them from afar. Figures who are on the go invite
speculation and attract because we do not need to get too
close. But they can also be important as they populate the
commonly painted localities, so often a feature of Dutch
landscape painting. The figures become the vertical forms
occupying little patches of space to contrast with the rest
of the landscape. Which is often icy. Cold. Wintry.

John Langhorne's (1735–79) poem 'The Poor' evokes the
image of the disenfranchised, wearied by life's long war,
insulted, laboured and hardened and invokes the Dutch
painter Teniers as a descriptive analogy:

> If, when from heav'n severer seasons fall,
> Fled from the frozen roof and mouldering wall,
> Each face the picture of a winter day
> More strong than Teniers' pencil could portray…

Wayfaring Reimagined
Reimagining the past is an accretive and creative act. And
a way to enable those who loved old engravings, scraps and

fragments to cut out papers from old books, including, rather shockingly to our eyes, pages from illuminated manuscripts. Only to then reconstitute all sorts of paraphernalia to make ephemeral anthologies of everyday figures from the past. And such figures were culled in the resourceful mind to inform the idea that the past is always better. The process was like a swagger through the ephemerality of the everyday. As if to try and record the time when people stopped drinking tea out of a cup and saucer in favour of the mug; now reminiscing on the day before and the day before that when the tea was drunk in a different way. When was the last sip taken by the person who then replaced the cup and saucer with a mug? This is the sort of imperceptible action on a minute scale that rarely gets recorded. The odd thing about these manuscript pages is that we know something about them because nineteenth-century antiquarian scholars reconstructed them in their 'Customs and Manners Books'. Such volumes romantically recreated past historical periods like the Middle Ages. The daily life of the time long ago was reproduced by men, like William Morris, even Jusserand, who sat in fine and ancient libraries, sharing a common belief that industrialisation had ruined society with its black soot and grimy faces. The scholars' mission was to show what life was like then. The lens was wide: the activities of different classes of people, their movements, crafts and daily living. Sometimes these pecking magpies would strip bare an illuminated manuscript in the manner of collage-making to compile anthologies of illustrations from original images. They would then re-compose them into an attractive display, like a dinner table – on pages, to make a sort of visual encyclopedia of life in the Middle Ages. Cutting and pasting to give a partial effect which in the act of rearranging could not be further from the truth. Antiquarians made it their business to 'find' the material to discover the medieval past through the extraction both physically and photographically (or in line drawings) of the small images of people and objects that populate the illuminated manuscripts / religious books once so preciously guarded. And they took keen delight in the little marginal decorations.

Joseph Strutt (1749–1802) 'cut' medieval manuscripts to reproduce them in his anthologised feasts, such as *The Sports and Pastimes of the People of England* (1801). In his indefatigable quest to reimagine medieval life as an encyclopedist, and led by anecdotal curiosity, he way-fared through paper, print, ink and colour, collecting little depicted figures such as pedlars and tinkers and arranged them artfully onto a page. With paper in abundance, scissors to rashly cut the manuscripts, access to publishers and printing presses, he razored his way through a time that he had little in common with. He had the training of a traditional artist: first as an engraver, and then he went to the Royal Academy schools where he drew from the antique. Yet he turned to the historic commonplace which he made all quaint and quirky to suit what must have been a taste for these compilations of history. Well, I wonder if he really did believe life was better before industrialisation. After all, had he not read about the plague, the famine, infant mortality, the poverty and destitution? His approach to history was presumptive and partial. But even if he did not truly think life was better in days long gone, he excelled at making it look so.

Thomas Wright (1810–77) also used medieval manuscripts as illustrative sources in *A History of Domestic Manners and Sentiments in England during the Middle Ages* (1862), introducing his study as 'plain facts in popular form.'[17] He was lavish with his imagination as well. The vernacular of medieval life appealed, at a time when industrialisation was seen as gross, grimy, grim and ugly. Women were cast as an exotic species in *Womankind in Western Europe, from the Earliest Times to the Seventeenth Century* (1869). But these antiquarian fogies, with pipes in their breast pockets and sherry at the ready, had good intentions, and Wright tried to show the similarities between what was called high and low culture. Cataloguing medieval life introduced the reader to the baronial hall, drunken brawls, gardens, money dealing, chairs, lanterns, pets, the stocks, conversations and bedchambers. Wright also featured medieval travellers in his book. For example, in the section on the Anglo-Saxons, he wrote, 'The pedestrian carried a spear or a staff. Pious ecclesiastics were more confident with the humility of their sacred character to journey on foot.'[18] He enumerated the pitfalls of moving around during the medieval period: 'Travelling in the Middle Ages, was assisted by few, if any, conveniences.' The act of cutting out quaint pictures from manuscripts originally designed to get people to pray, made the harsh realities of travel in the Middle Ages feel even more remote.

In *Scenes and Characters of the Middle Ages* (1872), the

Reverend Edward Cutts included a section in his anthology on itinerant traders using a florid style to describe the objects they carried with them to sell. All is evoked in loving and descriptive ways where, 'the paths are ploughed up every year and made afresh by the feet of the wayfarer.' Ah, so the wayfarer helps the worm too!

As a child, I owned books by the Quennells – Marjorie (1884–1972) and her husband, known as C.H.B., or Charles Henry Bourne (1872–1935), who, together, compiled books of text accompanied by quaint line drawings of different periods in history. The books became a hugely popular series called *A History of Everyday Things in England* (published from 1918–34). I grew up with this quaint conception of history. Marjorie was a historian and illustrator, who installed the period rooms of the Geffrye Museum (now the Museum of the Home) and one of her sons, Peter, a prolific writer, became founding editor of *History Today* (1951–79), whose autobiography *The Marble Foot* (1977) offers an insight into the family. Yet in this memoir, at times raunchy, racy and searingly honest about his own life, he gives little attention to his parents' books and their lives. Although he briefly suggests that the books are borne out of the sadness of a life that was not to be – his father had been an architect; but having lost his position, became an almoner to a City company – and the sort of job found in the *Everyday* books, as the Quennells tried to bring alive ordinary people of the past. Later in the book, he describes his parents' regular evening activity of writing, as drawings and manuscripts were taken out to study at the end of the day. Harry Batsford, the publisher, is described as having 'long serpentine tendrils of brownish hair … woven round his polished skull; he kept a damp cigarette permanently glued to his lip.' The books' illustrations are like little cameos decorating a page, often of tradespeople and craftspeople, bearing no relation to the text, usually about a completely different subject such as Queen Victoria or the architecture of the Houses of Parliament. Artistic discretion throughout the course of the books exhibits wayfaring types to be heavily cloaked and clothed, hatted and hooded; one with shoes on, one crippled and bare-footed, holding a T-bone staff and all the while showing the reader scenes from everyday life, while mixing up class clothing, elements and motifs. Nothing is systematic at all. The image of a wayfarer could be a thing of curiosity and desire, and in harnessing the figure to paper, part of an alchemical transformation to another time and culture.

There is one poignant memory of Peter's mother in *The Marble Foot*. He recounts how she once told him of her childhood fear. One day, she went blackberrying with her brothers and for a short while they left her beside a gate. A tramp approached and beckoned her with 'hideous grimaces'. Presumably, as she told her son about it years later, it must have been an abiding memory that lingered. He also writes briefly about their working methods and how his father would leave blank spaces for his mother to add in the drawing, but not until he had outlined the architecture or perspective, if the drawing was of a building. Her role was to be figure illustrator, and they were involved in a shared process, very akin to how a medieval manuscript was made where the scribe wrote the text, leaving spaces and areas for the illuminator to work on afterwards.

Creating images of wayfaring and recording them can sometimes feel like appropriation. Nothing can really capture the past, except by the naked eye, there and then. At least, the walking process keeps some of the walking spirit alive, especially when your physical search is in vain, and you get some idea of struggle, hardship, longing and long-standing pain.

My Belgian journey complete, with a quest unrequited, I returned over the water.

Three

Wayfaring Works 3:
Clothing the Naked

I have been an alien in a strange land.
The Book of Exodus (18:3)

B ack in England, Newhaven, East Sussex. Paradise was in short supply here as well. The month of August. Early summer's green gloss had faded. Another place, a bit edgy, where flea markets and art on old warehouse walls and outdoor display boards seal over the cracks, but where I am reminded of the words decline, deprivation and lack of investment, often much cited by the media. The port of Newhaven, beside the liberal sea, mingles with detritus and dust, where long, soft embedded earth is now hard substance of metal barricades, concrete, fences, and port accoutrements. There are no ships or boats visible on the horizon from where I began my walk. As I went, I tried to stay close to the water's edge.

The plan was to follow in the steps of the Normans who came over to Britain in determined spirit.

Tracing the de Warenne Family

The Norman de Warenne family may have commissioned illuminated manuscripts depicting wayfarers, from the Flemish illuminators discussed in Chapter Two. William de Warenne I (d. 1088) likely came over with William the Conqueror's retinue from France and it is believed the two Williams were close. The family came from Varenne, near Bellencombre, about thirty kilometres from Dieppe. The origin of the name 'Warenne' comes from the river, Varenne, and William may also have fought under William the Conqueror at the battle of Hastings in 1066.

I came, I went, and I chose a selection of walking routes to try and trace the Warennes (Newhaven to Lewes, Lewes to Thetford in Norfolk, Gorleston to Thetford) all of which encompass some of the places where the family built, settled and established authority – and where wayfarers may have walked. Although the family's landholdings extended to Surrey, Lincolnshire and Yorkshire too.

Instead of taking a ferry from Dieppe, I started my journey at Newhaven, directly south of Lewes.

Trying to track the Normans' arrival on the south coast of Britain is like looking for a coin in the desert. We do not have a concrete place that marks the spot of arrival, although this is much disputed and gives historians sore heads. From the air, the south coast of England shows a gentle undulating line, with a sharp left-hand turn south of Chichester and a slightly smaller sharp right-hand turn towards Eastbourne on the right. The Normans would not have seen the shape of the land so clearly. Pevensey, one of the so-called *cinque ports*, lies to the east of Eastbourne.

Here is a castle and here, they say, William the Conqueror landed. Here, too, William I de Warenne (who became Earl of Surrey and Lord of the Sussex rape of Lewes) died from an arrow at a siege at Pevensey Castle. Proud proclaimers in the marketing of a 'first'. The first site of the first Norman landing. The first Norman foot on dry ground. Something to be proud of, but something to be challenged by other places with claims to make about significant events along the south coast. Perhaps historians don't want to agree though, as disagreeing a claim maintains energetic historical discourse.

The de Warenne family would have come in boats with many others as part of a determined cortege: knights, courtiers, servants, chroniclers, even ecclesiastical heavyweights and many a hanger-on curious about new shores. The family may have disembarked somewhere along the stretch of coast from Rye to Newhaven, from where they went inland and north to Lewes, where, in a place they had never been before, they built a castle for a home and a home to say, 'we are here to stay.' The castle could affirm their strength. As if that was not enough, they also founded Lewes Priory (constructed 1078–82). Before too long, they started to possess land further north. In securing land and authority, it became the 'done' thing to look down at the feet of the wayfarers whose movements and fates the earls now controlled.

Walking Newhaven
It was a rainy day. Finding one of those inauspicious footpaths you are both surprised and not surprised to

hear is at the back of a housing complex. Now, Newhaven reveals the very under-heel of its existence, where along the way there are glimpses of what might have been. Over there, little patches of woodland with the biggest thickets of blackberries I have ever seen, trailing and tugging their weight along; close by, an abandoned low-lying wall; further over, a curve in the road, buildings without roof, broken windows, rubbish undone by ravenous foxes. A cheerful young family with buckets and baskets, calling out and chatting as they walk in boots – to pick blackberries. All around are the town's white cliffs – connecting to Seaford and further west to the famous Seven Sisters. I see a partially exposed section of white hill and wonder if the Normans thought there were rocky banks of white all over the land. Perhaps they saw the white, like the Apostles witnessing the Transfiguration, as a transcendental sign. A sign Divine that they should seize and stay. If only they had taught the resident Anglo-Saxons to speak French.

The residential part of Newhaven is built on a hill, as the ground rises away, the houses stacked up like Lego, from the Channel. From that hill, the land is flat but then rises again at Lewes. Here below are the spoils of a port at the mouth of the River Ouse: containers, some waiting to go elsewhere, some which you sense have not been moved for years. The rust eroding, the metal fragmenting. There is storage for port activity, the odd boat, the sense of the remnants of cottage-size industry, evoking the feeling of a time long gone. Newhaven had been an Anglo-Saxon settlement; but they say that once there was a prehistoric fort here, later fortified again during the Napoleonic wars and which, later, became a garrison position in World War Two. There is a sign in italics to the fort on the OS map. Things marked in italics are often the 'remains' of monasteries or holy wells. These are enticing distractions, although quite often the remains have not remained at all, for you either see ruins of something built later, or even just grass, or a hedge or mound, or the area is so completely covered in undergrowth, you wonder what you are expected to see, other than your own vivid imagination. But maybe that is the nature of heritage – it keeps you working, guessing, and imagining. Though not too hard, as evidence is required, not flights of fancy and speculation. Even so, Newhaven's fort requires a probing mind. There is a path that goes up, from where the sea is visible. Danger at the cliff on the path can start you off on your wild imaginings. Did the Warennes walk up that hill, look to the horizon, and wonder what they were doing? Did they look back, with the wind in their hair, the salt on their cheeks and ask to go home?

As the poem 'Newhaven' laments:

> Why do you lie so black and harsh,
> Frowning over the ancient marsh,
> Straggling under the long, green, crest,
> Giant toad on a gentle breast?

These lines were written by Gerald Durani Martineau (1897–1976), schoolmaster turned poet, whose work was published by Victor Benjamin Neuburg's Vine Press. He was based in Steyning, Sussex, where he was part of a utopian community. Neuburg is probably better known for being associated with the infamous occultist Aleister Crowley where sex, opium and friendships were febrile and fragile things, rather than for his literary and publishing endeavours. The poem comes from a collection called *Way of the South Wind*, incorporating elegy, landscape lost, hills, beer, frothy folklore and people who go 'hush' in the woods for fear of waking the fairies.

Newhaven's terminal for the ferry is well-designed, even if it does not look so. It is all an interlocking of road bridges, one-way systems, black fences and then amorphous urbanisation. More urbanised space than people urbanised. There are few people to be seen; after all, the streets are wet with rain. Maybe they are with the seagulls high in the attic bedroom this Sunday morning. The paths and roads around the town are contoured to conform with the port development that led Newhaven's future. Although the Channel crossing from here to France is long, it is not as long as the one from Nieuwpoort to East Anglia. So, fewer lorries and cargo ships go this way than at the port of Dover.

There are some travel accounts for Newhaven. In the eighteenth century, John Burton (1696–1771), author of sermons, remarks, and even a lamentation over his dying wife, was also the author of *Iter Sussexiense* (1752), a personal kind of travelogue. On Newhaven, he cursed the abominable, impassable roads of the Sussex muddy land. He wrote:

To the Ouse from whence perhaps the town derived its

name, which, as it flows along the plain, cuts the town
in two. It is navigable, and about sixty furlongs off, falls
into the sea, where the mouth of the harbour is called
New Haven. Beyond the river a hill rises abruptly, very
white and steep, but so overhanging and overshadowing
all lying around it, that to a distant beholder, the houses
below seem as if they had been dug out of it. And who
would not admire the street leading down to the river!
Standing on the ridge, you see on the right and the left a
well-peopled valley, vessels going up and down, well-wa-
tered meadows, and workshops for whatever is needed
for navigation.

While he looked around him and further away from his
reach, he was also an observer of what happens below. He
asks why cattle and women had long legs and thinks it
might be on account of pulling the feet out of the mud.
Did he not think that men had the same problem? He
writes about mud in more than one place:

Sussex is a windy, fertile, and pastoral country, smooth
and flat indeed, when seen from afar, but not easy to
ride or drive through; so that, having thereby earned a
bad name, it has passed into a by-word, and any difficulty hard to get through, or struggle against, may, by
a simile, be called the Sussex bit of the road. Not even
now, though in summer time, is the wintry state of the
road got rid of; for the wet, retained even till now in this
mud, is sometimes splashed upwards all of a sudden to
the annoyance of travellers. Our horses could not keep

on their legs on account of these slippery and rough parts of the roads, but sliding and tumbling on their way, and almost on their haunches, with all their haste got on but slowly.

Not all his comments were negative. The weekly market was clearly a source of joy, for, 'as wayfarers, we enjoyed its great convenience.' Like all travellers, he needed sustenance for his journeying.

Nevertheless, Burton did not have far to return to some sort of home, as his mother lived at the rectory house at Shermanbury, between Horsham and Shoreham. He wrote up his journeys to Sussex in Greek, and sometimes Latin. That he wanted to write was not in question, but it was avowedly for an elite audience, which in those days did not have to be justified.

Newhaven also caught the attention of E. V. Lucas, who in 1904, wrote in *Highways and Byways in Sussex*: 'Of little Newhaven there is little to say, except that in rough weather the traveller from France is very glad to reach it and on a fine day the traveller from England is happy to leave it behind.' If I include myself as a commentator on Newhaven as well as Burton and Lucas, we cannot keep the weather out of things. It sets the scene. But I like to think Newhaven offers more than just a barometer, although the degrees of the weather's effect seem to possess the Sussex writers.

Lucas lived at Kingston Manor near Lewes in Sussex between 1908–12. His daughter once reminisced about the local shepherd Jack Tuppen and his brother Charlie. He once confessed to Lucas that he had not washed his feet for thirty years, but 'must … have walked through a good deal of water on them.'[19] We learn that he was often out with his sheep. He was not well educated, 'but knowing whatever there was need to know. Strange, battered hat, bowler like in shape upon his head…' But what of the man's clothes? I wonder how far he strayed with his flock; presumably he was up on the Downs, up the steep hill from the village of Kingston. I wondered if he thought about the people that had come before him. Lucas was also the author of the charming 'pocket-sized' volume of poetry *The Open Road: A Little Book for Wayfarers* (first published 1899), intended, like many anthologies in the late nineteenth century as books walkers and travellers could take with them. They also tapped into the ever-increasing market for recreational books to mark increased leisure afforded to some people. But the book does not make much of the notion of wayfarers; rather, they are those who have the time to read the anthologised poems with themes such as the sun and the skies, lovers and summer sports.

I found the path that led me to the River Ouse and the river spoken of by Burton. I made my way northwards towards Lewes, which is the chalk land of the Downs. Behind me now was the spread of neglected buildings and road and a place that negotiates daily with its watery neighbour. On the left a different body of water, an artificial lake, with little inlets made by rushes and bulrushes, making enclosures for anglers to settle down for the day to fish. There was thick growth, too, on the parallel path that I took, which is not that well-trodden, yet neither well cared for. Weeds and grasses grew high here. I walked on partly embedded brick, or by remnants of buildings or water-side huts now a bit shattered, their proud completion long gone. Just around the first turn of the river, there is an old boathouse, made of cobble and brick, with a semi-circular doorway for the boats to enter from the river shore. Here on the muddy, rather tousled, damp bank, dry in some parts, there is a fringe of wooden slats followed by cobbles, sturdy enough to make a bank to protect land from water, or should it be the other way round? A little way on, a little marina-like wharf, where the long white posts in the sky are the staging markers to shore-up the boats. There, I heard a crackle sound, or was it a cry, a lament from the wind? The wind brushed the water, but it was not being groomed in just one direction. The water went one way, and then the other. It galloped itself up and around. The lament could sound anguished.

The rain had only just stopped. There is no obvious shelter along the Ouse, and I thought of those walking from need, wondering where they might find somewhere with some sort of roof. There are no trees here and it may have always been like this. Yet for the romantically inclined poet, the shelter could be part of the wistful musing on the scene where they walk. In 'Ode to Evening' (first published 1747), the Sussex-born William Collins (d. 1759) speaks to that yearning for both wandering and shelter, working in tandem against potential bad weather:

Then let me rove some wild and healthy Scene,
Or find some Ruin 'midst its dreary Dells,
Whose walls more awful nod
By thy religious Gleams.

Or if chill blustering winds, or driving rain,
Prevent my willing feet, be mine the hut,
That from the mountain's side,
Views wilds, and swelling floods.

The shelter imagined becomes a source of comfort in contrast with the showery twilight evening of falling, failing light. Knowing there is some hope gives the poet something to yearn for. There is also the desire that the description of wandering as a romantic poet and finding things to be melancholy about, becomes contagious to the reader. It must take some courage by a poet to write down what they feel and see, hoping that the reader will, too.

Besides the musing, what of the law? Sussex would have been full of vagrants as elsewhere in the eighteenth century. In October 1744, it was written: 'The number of rogues, vagabonds, beggars and other idle and disorderly persons daily increases to the great scandal and annoyance of the kingdom'.[20] The parish found unlicensed pedlars and wandering beggars nothing but a nuisance and it was ordered that, 'the parish officers must four times a year at least … make a privy search in one night … for the finding and apprehending of rogues and vagabonds'. There is the record of Jane Willis, the wife of a soldier, who said she had always been a pedlar, 'laying in barns'.[21] In essence, vagrancy was then considered reprehensible, and in some cases, it was noted too that it was problematic between October and March, perhaps for obvious reasons. But the reports do not explicitly say what is wrong about the 'vagrancy'.

By the path further on, the landscape changes. Now, a cluster of yellow flowers and thistles that have lost their lustre. Dog excrement, or maybe sheep – the type was indeterminate, but some is of determinate size and some large enough for me to think I am looking at a piece of charcoaled wood, rather than animal evidence, as this was antiquated waste – lain for some time. Here is a land where in places a garment such as a glove or hat often clings to a branch out-grown from the path's boundary; where houses have scrapyards with abandoned cars and motor-vans, discarded prams and shop trolleys with only one wheel, and a few hysteric geese. Here are fences so aggressively built beside public footpaths, framing paddocks for horses with grey-lined winter coats that the paths are under threat of their very existence in favour of householders pining for more cropped space. Large plastic wheelie bins at the roadside lie in wait like standstill robots to be taken back to the yard by the kitchen after rubbish day. Disproportionately large compared to the small, box-like houses covering much of this recuperated, marshy, kale-rich, but brittle land. There, then, are the sloping walls of grey stone banking up against ex-coal-mine housing estates, good for kicking balls against. All around are forlorn-field edges where the crops are thinly sown and where mud, toppled-over cans and one forgotten crop frond come together. Where too you might see a foot-print dusty from dry mud on a discarded piece of cardboard, which will never be cleared up. Disintegrating animal intestines and fragments of people's lives open, bare and discarded. And then the ill-assorted human debris, mixed in with bits from the natural world, which is only replaced when the landscape might occasionally yield to a gentle slope breaking up the monotony.

The little marina whistled as I passed along. And the birds were singing out. There was too, another distant cry. I tried to hold the map and the notebook to write down what I see; I glanced at my watch, and I looked at the map for reassurance. I scrawled a word or two, wondering if they would be meaningless by the time I returned home, for memory plays its distorting part and without good visual recall, the sharpness of seeing things then and there soon disappears. I saw a puddle made from recently fallen rain, a woman in a thick red raincoat walked past me, soon giving way to red as a burning reflection in the low-lying water. In quick time though, both the reflection and the fantasy left me as more rain started to fall.

The odd duck perched on the partly damp wooden posts on the riverbed. There are posts too, silently marking a spot, that also reveal a changed time or mood. At various intervals of the river, there is a gate, or a little fence for a comforting demarcation for the separation of water and land, animal and human, air and ground. This is the power

of the boundary acting for local landowners. Along the
River Ouse, sheep are often seen gathering beside the gate
and I did not want to disturb them, although at times they
moved off the path, as if they saw me coming. Then, like a
cow, they might just stand and stare, for it is their territory,
their gaze seemed to say to me. I had a choice: beside the
water is a path pushed up to create a boundary, which is all
grassy and soft, while on the other side is a gravelly path –
bordered by grass. The riverbed at one point has netting,
which I fantasised about containing fresh and glistening
fish, ready to be sailed down the river to Newhaven and
onward to markets. But I was wrong, for the nets tie stones
in, which help to keep the water out. This is landscaped,
carefully choreographed land – the river has lost its natural
function, or at least what we think that might have been;
and as it gently curves, or bends and burps, a liquid fall
or bubble, it is like the smooth sheen belly of a horse or
whale. Most of the time, you think you are following the
river in a straight line, but you are probably not; for your
understanding of scale and vision becomes quite estranged
when following a river's course.

It is no good trying to imagine the conversation of the
Normans who walked or rode here. It is no good trying
to imagine a conversation between an Anglo-Saxon and a
Norman as the latter exercised their right of coercion and
'conversion' to a new authority. In any case, I doubt it was
as simple as that. That is why the word transition came
into being. Matters of law, rule and religion do not just
switch from one to the other, with utmost clarity. Never
just a Norman. Never just an Anglo-Saxon. The Normans

were following the way of the Romans before them and even the Angles, Saxons and Jutes after that. There were many 'Flemings' in regions of England such as East Anglia and even Sussex. The Normans may have fought battles, conquered, and gained territory in one sense, but they were also followers and had to assimilate with other peoples and nations.

I imagined myself sitting on the bank like a lady in Seurat's picture *A Sunday Afternoon on the Island of La Grande Jatte* (1884–86), sitting there without my legs showing, in a long Edwardian black skirt, all concealed, tucked-in and neat like the woman in the picture. All I really saw though was a black sheep poking its head through one of the gates that mark off sections of the Ouse Walk and, so, dreaming of a lady in nineteenth-century Paris is not as easy as wondering about how many sheep have irretrievably got their heads stuck in gates throughout the history of farming and herding them. I marvelled at their thick coats and told myself how fortunate I was to have the same raincoat that I bought when I went to India over thirty-five years ago.

I saw a man walking towards me, who clearly knew the Ouse well. And both sides of it, too. He suggested that I walked along the side that I was not planning to, as he said it would be nicer and I would end up in a part of Lewes where there was a little pub – the Snowdrop Inn, named after a snow drift that once killed some people in Lewes.

I took his advice, even though it meant not ending up at the de Warenne built priory, which was my initial plan. You see I am easily persuaded, even when the destination is a pub with an unhappy association. Is there a culturally perceived pastoral characteristic of the River Ouse valley – the hay-bales, swollen and cosy for a mouse, the expanse of green grass for the cows, the winding river, the hills around? Does it carry the same artistic weight as, for example, the Dedham Vale in Essex immortalised by John Constable? As far as I know, there is no well-publicised literary or artistic heritage for this valley. What is the difference between this marshy, at times windy, desolate, but beguiling landscape and Dedham Vale, where the riverbanks and old trees offered Constable artistic inspiration? What is the difference between this part of Sussex and the part made so mythical by artists such as Eric Ravilious? One answer might be that he painted on the Downs, where the chalk land is higher and so there might be less moisture. Is this the fateful twist of circumstance, and does the fortune of an artist depend on the locality they choose to paint in?

The River Ouse is famous in one tragic way. This is where Virginia Woolf killed herself and I am reminded of this tragedy, as I see Rodmell's village church in the distance on the other side of the river, which is also gloopy and grey most of the time, like a ditch. Now I see a landscape that is barren, remote and empty, now I am seeing a landscape differently owing to association. And will it be ever thus?

Further along, there was a gaggle of cows and sheep, minding their own business in the same field. Beside them at the river, seagulls grouped to fly together, flying out and around, out and back again and when I sped up a bit, flying out a bit further, maybe for their summer migration. The birds shadow paths with their flight, punctuating the river's thin colour of silver, grey at the edge. Maybe this is why artists did not paint here; the colours were not vivid enough, even at summer's zenith.

Soon, the wind pulled me along. I was nearly sucked into the river channel that is narrow at the source, as it goes towards Lewes. I could see the town now, on the hill up there. I stumbled a bit on knots and bumps on the path. It needs more shoes to smooth it down, and so the going can be slow. In 1303, Alice de Lonesdale, a young girl from York, injured her foot in a fall on the road at Stamford. She was sleeping rough in Southwark; her injuries spreading infection. She was taken to Hereford Cathedral, where she stayed for three days by the tomb of Thomas Cantilupe (1218–82), when he appeared to her in a dream and anointed her with a milky ointment, curing her. People waited patiently for things in those days. I was impatient to complete the walk. Though I was well covered, and I was not yet tired.

Bare, weather-worn travelling flesh of naked legs and feet reveals plight and poverty, and these are sometimes shown in medieval illustrations, executed with a mere brush-stroke daubed with bright colour. In the thirteenth-century *Rutland Psalter* (London, British Library, fol. 47r, c.1250–60, Plate 4), the light clothing of a woman barely covers her body. Her red cloak does not conceal her legs, or her feet; one is slightly in front of the other. Tied to her back is a baby as her hands hold a green painted walking staff and a bowl, a begging bowl. Hoping for more than she would ever have received, she faces a little creature curled up at the bottom of a border, who I do not think is going to be able to help. It looks like he is almost laughing at her, as the mother's eyes are cast down. How much walking to find help and how much hoping has the woman done and how many times has she been scorned? She would never have known this picture, but is this how she would have regarded herself?

Wayfaring Nakedness
The artist of *The Rutland Psalter* had the privilege of painting the female figure on carefully executed parchment. But it is an impression, no more. And all they have done is capture a moment in time. At the same time, the illuminator had the visual power to gently mock. To 'ape' the wayfarer shows vulnerability, as we see in the illustration of a naked man on crutches in *The Macclesfield Psalter*, fol. 168r, (Figure 5). While the crutches protect his private body parts to some degree, he is exposed. Nudity exposes more than just body parts. It makes an appearance in the life of the fictional King Aethelwold in the thirteenth-century romance, 'Havelok the Dane', dealing with the matters and legends of ancient Britain. He who went out of his way to be kind to the poor, and who let chapmen wander around selling their wares without restraint. In envisaging

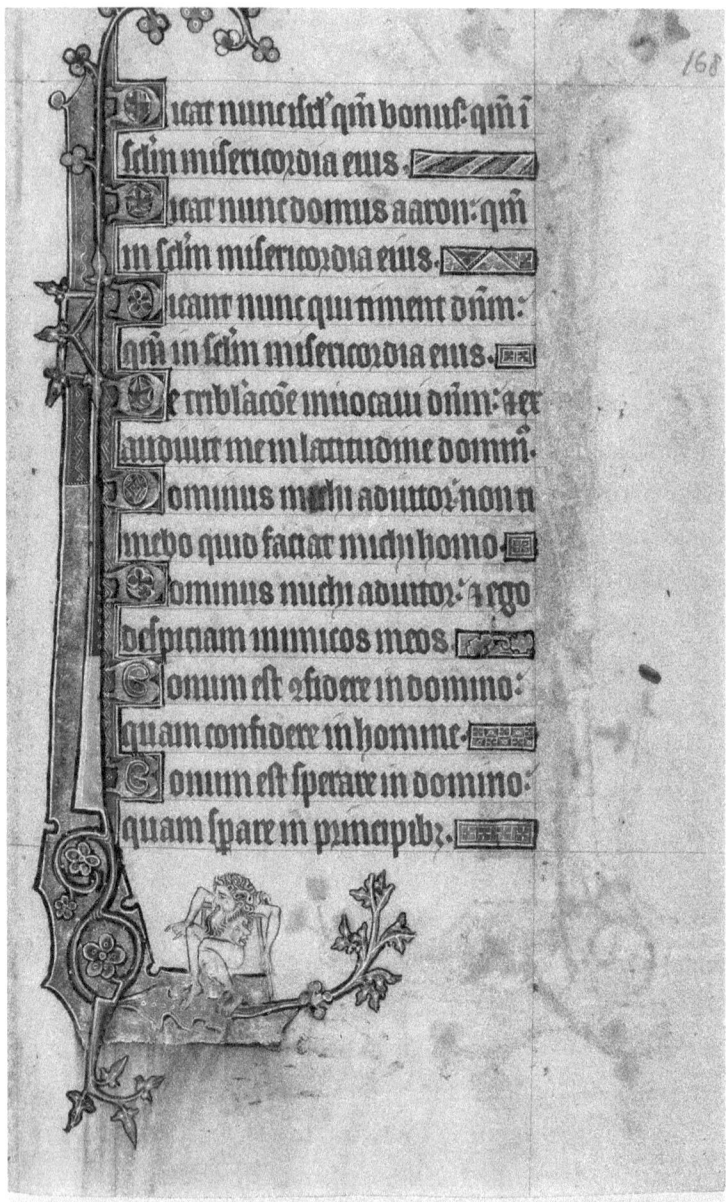

Figure 5: *The Macclesfield Psalter*, Cambridge, Fitzwilliam Museum, MS 1-2005, fol. 168r, c.1330–40, 170 x 108 mm.

how they could exist, the king was also safeguarding roads for passage. As the poem writes:

Then might chapmen fare
Through England with their ware
And boldlike buy and sell...

As he nears the end of his life, he must make provision for his only daughter, who could not yet inherit the throne as she was young. So, he leaves his estate to the Earl of Cornwall, Godrich, who had vowed to give the King's wealth and lands to his daughter when she was to come of age. By the time she turns twenty, she has become a beautiful woman. Unsurprisingly, the Earl does not want to give up what he has gained. She was taken to a castle in Dover, and left there, ill-clad and without enough food, where the narrative continues, 'It is no shame for to sink to obtain food and drink.'

A naked state can be linked to choice as well though. In *The Lausiac History* (419–420 CE), Palladius of Galatia tells us about Serapion, a famous monk. Not, it must be added on account of his prayers or reputation for preaching, but because he wandered around without clothes on. He visited a female recluse in a cell in Rome and asked her why she was doing nothing. To which she responded, 'I am not doing nothing; I am on a journey.' There seems to be virtue in both the monk and the woman. But if he was exhibiting the virtues of spiritual poverty, it needed the recluse to explain things.

We do not really know what the motivations were for

incorporating wayfaring figures, often scantily clothed, into a book for spiritual contemplation. They were either salutary reminders of another's plight, and a call to 'clothe the naked', or they may just have been intended as distraction from prayer and contemplation. While St Augustine said that things are 'solved by walking', so the image of the wayfarer in a religious book might offer balm to a weary soul which needed to renew its own heavenly path. The steps to Heaven had to be sure though, so remembering the poor was a start. But the painted wayfarers were also visual thoroughfares for the artists to show off their skills in painting gestures, positions, bodily movements and variety. And showing figures going from one place to the other enlivens the page.

Apart from the white of the cliffs, Norman families such as the Warennes, making their occupying way through the land, relied on natural light, putting pressure on them to get things done in the day. But when walking had to continue, so, too, did the wayfarers' hardship. In contrast, the medieval painters, who came to East Anglia to paint for the Warennes and other patrician patrons, found their light from candles precariously positioned to the folios they worked on. Through their illuminations, they would capture light and gold enriching the pale pages, once the milky hides of goats and calves. Even after the process of preparing the parchment, the tiny hairs of the animals' bodies could be felt or touched.

The walk then led me further inland. This was quite a detour, as I walked further west onto the Downs, and found a church open, the church of St Laurence in Telscombe village. It is usually closed. But it was open today for a meeting – a gathering of about eight people, all very friendly to me, despite their proceedings. They even got out of the way (this is a small church), so that I could see something I have never seen before – a twelfth-century wheel, which had served as a device to ring the church bell. There they had gathered, devoted people, caring about their church and its fabric and future, discussing plans for a new loo with an architect. His plans were laid out on large pieces of paper, indeed, all for a little loo to go in the existing vestry: the perfect size for another small room. I wondered if this loo would be given a special religious sanction. Churchgoing is made much easier today, with such modern conveniences.

Not far away, I visited the church of St Peter at Southease – gardeners were there: a wheelbarrow, a spade, a fork, a pile of weeds and tangles and a boy dancing and jumping round the barrow while a woman, who I presumed was his mother, cleared weeds. This is the church of the round tower, one of quite a few in this area. Here, inside, another group of people were chatting and discussing; a lady whispered to me that they were speaking of a funeral. One lady said that she needed to go back to help bring in the corn, another that she had known the church for over thirty years. I was hearing snippets of local life without having to ask for it. And I did not even need to see if they were planning any loos here – 'just keep things here as is', they would want to say to any earnest parish council; at least, that is what I thought they would say.

These churches are not far from Monk's House in Rodmell, the home of Virginia and Leonard Woolf. In her diary for Wednesday 17 August 1938, Virginia Woolf writes of the woman of Mount Misery who drowned herself. Local lore holds that a wayfarer is said to have prayed there to bring him luck. As far as I understand, Woolf was not much of a churchgoer. But she must have passed both Telscombe and Southease on her daily walks on the Downs.

My walk continued by the River Ouse and ended on hillier ground, where there were more sheep on the path, sheep at the side of the path, sheep hanging round the gates, as if waiting patiently for the night club to open. The animals bolted as soon as they became aware of me. I like a finite path; it makes me feel safe; but here on one side is a high bank, dropping over towards the water and the train track for Southern trains beyond. Another sort of finite space that felt reassuring. To the right a more open marsh-like landscape, with rushes and corn thrashing through the breeze. The path was gritty; scudded marks made an accidental composition, appearing as stick-like figures. It was also scattered with sheep pellets – I imagined that they could be human eyes, or that of a guardian angel, a hawk, or eagle. Further on, a tuft of sheep fur on the ground – looking like a star. The microscopic is breathtaking when you walk alone. As Susan Owens writes in *Spirit of Place: Artists, Writers and the British Landscape* (2020), nature is so explored in writing that now 'we have become minia-turists.'[22] It is not just the meadow, but how it lies that is of interest, what collects at the river shore; even plastic, coil, rope or shell and the feather, say, of a starling is something to inspect.

One can have mono-vision with a path. Looking down takes one into an underworld of the trodden, the squashed, the unseen, the un-thought-of. But also, the netherworld of the untrodden. A path also gives the walker a distinct space to move through and a direction. This is one of the reasons walking can be so very satisfying. No choices must be made, until you reach a cluster of paths, where you are either following the right one according to the map, or where you might make a choice to change your route, or even to get lost. There is another satisfying aspect to paths – always there, continuous and just long enough. Most of them have a border, which gives a sense that there is shelter and protection. We can look ahead to give walking purpose. Puddles on the ground can be disrupted or rippled. Plants at arm or eye level can be pushed back or twisted or just moved out of the way. We can drift along the path with our thoughts, or wonder whether we walk on flint, or chalk, rock or sand, plant, weed, or stewed and sunken bird foul. The corner where the path might turn a little is inviting, the brushing against branches, sending more seeds pollinating, and the sound of the undergrowth burning, crackling, dripping, altering in the wind. The detritus of nature seems unbounded and untied. We know that this is nature working incessantly to survive. But it is true that humanity marks and reshapes it as it is trod upon.

There was a blowing all about, the crops bursting through with the motion; the bounty of wheat yellowing and quickening, as I noticed the far-reaching view of the white cliffs near Newhaven, where I had begun. Wide, open expanse. No finite path, but still I felt safe. I walked through a farmyard, at the bottom of the hill, with lots of cows, men hanging around, ruddy, rugged faces, mud tracks, calves, pigs in huts. It felt like an ancient Cornish farm, weather-beaten, worn, in decline, but clinging on with the chalk and the security that the farm had been in the family for generations. I was in the land where the surface reveals its bare face, as if it has been parched or white-washed, wash day for the Downs. A land of chalk that can look incomplete, naked even, or bleached, and flushed white by sun rays.

I think of stories about the comings and goings of people. A knight leaves King Arthur's legendary court, Beowulf leaves the Anglo-Saxon mead hall to fight Grendel, people go on pilgrimage and a medieval knight leaves his lover. During the fourteenth century, people left villages due to famine, plague and despair. Yet they left one thing for more uncertainty. They were figures wandering through lands that suffered loss and abandonment by other people departing to go elsewhere.

Body, Place and Space

There is something alarming at being in a place where you know people were before you. I can panic at the memory of thresholds to a room or a building where I have spent time with other people, when we have departed and left the space for our own private rooms. I think about the space and then I think of it now empty and abandoned. It is not that I want to be back in that room; it is just that for a while it was occupied with people coming and going and now it is not. And for some indiscernible reason, that time unsettles me. We habitually plunder a space, but then we leave it, having made a mark, visible or invisible, a memory there, something dropped or lost on the floor, a pen, or a tiny piece of tissue, or a dried cell or particle of ourselves. And yet during the pandemic years, many of these rooms and spaces were uninhabited for longer periods of time. And in office buildings, this is continuing, which makes me wonder if it is unlucky to leave spaces empty.

An image of a wayfaring figure is a thing to exploit in the arrangement of a painted space. Human form helps to punctuate an otherwise empty architectural vista which shows off the artist's artifice.

The Renaissance painter Fra Carnevale used the body in motion to add vitality to his composition in *The Ideal City* (Baltimore, Walters Art Gallery, c.1480–84, Figure 6), which may be Urbino in the Italian Marche region. Here is a figure alone carrying a staff. Look a bit closer and you

Figure 6: *The Ideal City*, Fra Carnevale, Baltimore,
Walters Art Gallery, c.1480–84, 77.4 x 220 cm.

sort of barrel of liquid. So, he is in a city where people
are working to good and thorough effect. The citizens at a
distance are in long robes, while he is in a short white tunic
with a coat over his frame. He is also bare legged. How
easy it would be to miss the personification of generosity
holding a cornucopia on top of the black marble column
towards the far right of the picture. But we cannot say if
it is directed towards the figure or not. The odd thing is
that he also has a red hat on. And he is positioned right
at the painting's edge, a strategy to get him noticed. He is
the closest figure of all to the viewer. Descriptions of the
painting mention the architecture, but not the people. He
is going about his business, but he cannot be inconsequen-
tial. For some, perhaps, he was part of an ideal because
cities had a growing sense of civic pride in the fifteenth
century. And the picture shows a fully operational town
square with both building (edifices completed), water
(fountain) and body (man, coming and going, bringing
and collecting and taking things).

Saints' narratives tell us how active and busy, always out and about, 'on location' sort of people they were. The reputation of a saint could help to ease the poor who were travelling out of need. But, quite often, it is all the places where they were which take on a significance. The church of St Botolph's, not far from Chichester, on a crossing point on the River Adur, became established as a refuge for travellers and pilgrims. It is also known as the wayfarers' church. Botolph (620–80CE) was an Anglo-Saxon of minor nobility who became the patron saint of travellers and wayfarers. He and his brother Adolph had been educated at a Benedictine abbey in France. Botolph returned to East Anglia and was given land on which to build a monastery, likely Iken, near Aldeburgh in Suffolk. But the monastery was destroyed by Danish invaders in 870CE, and his head was taken to Ely, his torso to Thorney (Cambridgeshire) and what remained to Westminster Abbey. Over the course of this complicated journey, his brutalised body parts were transported through the gates of Aldersgate, Bishopsgate, Aldgate and Billingsgate in the City of London. Their physical fabric no longer exists, and the last one was destroyed in the Great Fire. Although Botolph is not that well-known today, many churches all over Britain are named after him, and without these spaces to commemorate him, he might be lost to us altogether. You can still visit the church of St Botolph-without-Bishopsgate, as well as numerous churches all over Britain which are dedicated to him.

I notice my surroundings more when I walk alone. Walking with another, I would be unable to repeat the route we have followed, as I am unable to talk and listen and look simultaneously. Walking and talking are companions. But to be able to see and watch while walking alone is just as inviting. But it does take courage to notice. I remember Hardy again. In *The Return of the Native* (1878), he captures the sense of a silent walk, writing, 'in these lonely places wayfarers, after a first greeting, frequently plod on for miles without speech.' There is that anonymity and the sense of observing from a distance. Later, he refers to a female wayfarer being ignored by a woman who does not let her in. Were there times when the author did not always think about the significance of each word he put down on the paper? In my own experience, there is a strange process when writing whereby a phrase or sentence is dropped insouciantly on the page, but when reading back over what is written, you realise that you did not, at the time, see each word in isolation. And rereading what you have written, you realise that in the practice of writing you need to see words as individual units and then parts of a whole. And each one should be looked at more than once. Each must be carefully seen, with both brain and eye. In the case of the long novel, I suspect that some words were not cherished in the writing of them as much as others.

Without Shoes
Being barefoot as a wayfarer on a path is a more exacting definition than to describe such a figure as somebody who merely walked. Perhaps the barefoot wayfarer has less resonance in our climate of shoe recycling. In Ermanno

Olmi's film *The Tree of the Wooden Clogs* (1978), set in the nineteenth century, a man in a peasant community ingeniously makes his son a pair of shoes out of stolen bark of a tree, so that the boy can go to school. Such is his imagination and ingenuity that the man risks the crime for the sake and love of his son. The act of shoemaking, though, is too much of a risk and the father is cruelly found out. We value shoes in the sense that we buy them, we wear them, we know we do something good by throwing them into those recycling bins with the discreet handles, as if opening the lever to Leviathan's den. Because we can, we dispense with them readily. We buy to throw away. The father in the film values shoes so much that he must metamorphose them from a tree. He is a craftsman. He goes to the purest point of nature. But he is not aware of what he is doing in the way we might be. His sense of using the materials of nature then is so different to ours. And even though we are trying to save our planet, our idea of how shoes come into being is so removed from his knowledge. I bought little blue shoes for my children, which were replaced all too soon with a larger size; it was hard for me to let go of them though, and I haven't entirely. I could not throw all of them into the gaping hole of the never-ending cycle of waste.

I grew up taking my shoes off to play in gardens, in trees, and at the water: streams in woods where the bluebells grew, pools at Cornish coasts where I took my nets and then splashing in puddles wherever they might be. I had no sense, then, that I was wearing a precious and valuable commodity. One of the few battles I had with my mother was over the wearing of white socks; she urged me to wear short ones. As a self-conscious schoolgirl all too aware of my growing clumpy calves, I wanted them covered and I petulantly fought most days for long socks. 'All the other girls at my school wore them, so why shouldn't I be able to?' I retorted.

One day, in the 1970s when summer days were, it seems in hindsight, always sunny, I was paddling in the pond at the local Common with my younger friend. We used to talk to one another through the barbed wire fence that separated the bottom of her garden from the top of mine. On this afternoon, Nina cut the sole of her foot on some glass which must have been in the pond, and she began to cry. Her mother was frantic as she had to go to hospital, and I felt responsible – perhaps as the elder, I had encouraged the bare-footed larking about. Yet to go barefoot as a child is the summit of freedom. The shoeless traveller through time made their mark on a land, maybe as both child and adult, where the rocks were just a little bit younger than the land I had touched with my childish limbs. And which, without me having to think at all, moved so much, enabling my childish pleasures and whims.

It is the minute movements and steps practised and perfected, too, that bring a ballerina into repute and glory. As they leap and pivot, twist, reach and turn, ballet dancers make no tangible marks in the air. But when they move their arms, legs and feet, in fast or slow, or nimble, eloquent movement, they make shapes which in themselves make new shapes: a U or a V or an O, or half an O and so on – and those shapes make further spaces in-between their bodies. Lowering to the ground from a great height, the fall of the shoe, that is, if the move goes well, makes a gentle padding sound. Delectable. Look under their feet though when they are elevated, shaped like caterpillar legs or a contorted Buddha, or a splayed-out new-born lamb and they make a space. Look through the arc of their arms as they move, or those enfolding them from their dancing partner. And as they dance, the spaces within the frames of their bodies and arms make new spaces giving them instant borders and containment. All the time, as they dance, their bodies reveal new intersections and dreams of infinity with where the body might go, which pushes to break the limits of what their balletic poses can do.

As I walk now, largely in a straight line, my body shapes to accommodate the way. But I think of my heart. My blessed heart which pumps when required, acts according to its creation, performs the rhythms of beating in finely tuned accuracy. Its systems work within me as I go. It has, like all, a shatter and a shard here and there from broken love, but the organ keeps on going. I believe it is now proven that one can suffer psychologically from a broken heart; but its processes are so perfectly primed that I rarely think about it just beneath the three layers of my skin. Wayfarers, too, would have felt the pangs of love, even though their survival to keep a love alive was not a given. What was in the hearts of the Normans that made them fearless about the turbulence of starting new lives in new land by the rough seas of the English Channel? The de Warenne family would go on to acquire or be given more land. Perhaps they had less time to think about their hearts, for their mission was dynastic claiming. And so, a barefoot wayfarer, creased from love or pain, like a well-used map, wore a simple unshaped garment, without sleeves or cuffs, loopholes or neck hole. In images, such a piece of clothing folds in on itself, like the wings of a Bateleur eagle battling in the sky. The eagle, though, soars high for hours on end, the wayfarer had to lie low for shelter. Then St John's eagle, as a religious symbol of St John the Evangelist can share the page with *babewyns* and strange entertaining creatures in marginal imagery. The word *bateleur* in French means acrobat, tumbler or tightrope walker; such people were itinerant entertainers who walked to the next castle or court as they were commissioned to perform. The Bateleur swoops and zooms, dives and rolls, just like an acrobat and it travels much further than any wayfarer could do – as much as five hundred kilometres per day. The bird has speed on him. But I don't think he travels as much as the Arctic Tern migrating to various mating grounds. The Bateleur might even be found flying over us in Britain. He could easily get noticed in a landscape painting dominated by browns and greens as he has a long pointed red beak.

Without buildings as anchors to commemorate families from ancient history such as the Warennes, charting and reflecting on walks made, evoke, by contrast, just how fragile humanity can be. Hilaire Belloc's *The Four Men: A Farrago* (1911), depicts four characters walking about ninety miles together in Sussex. This use of the word farrago, as a random assortment, might sound like a jolly jaunt out with friends, on a five-day journey. The characters are Myself (and here, I do not mean this author,

but possibly Belloc), Grizzlebeard, the Poet and the Sailor
who go on a sort of pilgrimage from Robertsbridge in the
east to Harting in the west. Beyond the seeming joviality,
conversations (sometimes in the pub) transmit a sadness
that life is transient, and we are just passing through. The
character Myself reminisces about a book he had read in
which a man was crossing a wild heath, weathered by rain
and wind. Glimpsing the light of a fire, he found himself
moving towards it until he found a chapel where people
were singing. The traveller was moved by the light, the
warmth, the stone, the altar, the joyful sound of singing
voices. But the congregation was 'hooded', so he could not
see the worshippers' faces. For him it did not matter, he
felt what was going on through the sight of the textures of
things and the might of the sound. But not for long. He
fell asleep during Mass, and when he awoke, he saw that
the building had become a ruin, with broken panes of glass
and he was on his own. In that brief time, something had
changed. Time had refreshed itself, leaving him a diminished sense of hope as he went on his way. The account
evokes that ungraspable feeling when, from one moment
to the next, our mood disperses, dissonates, but we do
not always know why. When the sense of walking is the
sense of moving, a journey can dishearten and unroot us
in inexplicable ways.

That is what I felt when I once followed a seven-mile
self-guided walk around Hilaire Belloc's village of Shipley
in Sussex where he had bought a windmill. I found myself
on a rewilding estate, as part of a soil and land regenera-
tion project. The leaflet mapping out the walk around the

village was now out of date, since the estate has developed since the walk was written. From what I saw, while seeking to give free and open land to animals such as deer, the space was surrounded by car-parking signs, bars and railings, none of which created a sense of freedom from manicured and over-managed lands. In meddling to make nature cleaner and greener, we do not know for sure to what state of authenticity that should be. Which was, I presume, the point of the estate in 'rewilding'. In encouraging this way into nature and in fostering the notion of reclaiming the land again, we are in just as much danger of losing our way. Wildland footpaths show you where to go, with maps of trails and signs in different colour codes giving you time and distance. So, you can map all you do and where you walk here. You can camp and 'glamp'. And like gastro pubs today, the website promises the now commonly used three-word enticing phrase, which is 'Stay, Eat, Shop', the sort of things you want to get away from when you 'visit' the countryside. Good intentions for guardianship of the land turn inevitably into commercial gain. To justify care, a business venture is born, where you can go on tours and attend yoga workshops in the cabin or the yurt. There is a shop where you can buy plastic-wrapped deer meat, a commercial website, book spin-offs and a café selling coffee in wasteful paper cups. I was dismayed to see this managed perspective, where animals are being encouraged to have lordship over the land, while you gingerly walk around perimeters or on designated routes, all the while, as gawping voyeurs, getting a piece of manufactured 'peace'. Although, the inverse could be that humanity is being left out of the animal kingdom. It just didn't feel like that. For in inviting us to visit felt like the expectation of going to a safari park, with the promise of seeing animals in their own environment, existing in the way they have always done. But are these places really 'natural', as humanity has still intervened to create that place for the animals? And in any case, do we have the ultimate ballot on what sort of landscape animals should be living in? Old oaks are surrounded by fences to stop the deer from eating or destroying the branches and roots. This is 'Nature' park territory with signs telling you where to go. Rewilding is a reconstructed condition of what we think has been humanity's deconstruction of authentic land. Then again, perhaps the word rewilding has been erroneously applied; it sounds like a fixed and controlled entity, the very antithesis of how we view 'wild'.

We find ourselves today looking for countryside trails sourced from aggressive marketing and media outlets, rather than finding them inadvertently, where we might find something altogether a bit purer. Today, nature is explained to us as if it is a commodity that we must understand; yet perhaps that is a myth that I am romantically creating, for when was nature ever wholly pure? It just seems that in our desperation to make people more aware, we are tracked and traced through rural areas, just as we track and trace animal and plant and woodland species. Today, the natural environment is to be witnessed as an ordered thing, not something that we experience for ourselves. So, the 'experience' we are being encouraged to seek becomes all the more fraught by reminding us of rural fragility. We seem to be at the point of paying for nature, rather than stumbling upon it. I think about what we have lost when there are now more people in 'Nature enterprises', such as a concrete path around a reservoir in deepest Sussex, than there are walking along a scrubby footpath at the back of somebody's house, which really has a much older history.

Of course, feeling encroachment when out walking is nothing new.

As I go, I see things blocked and squeezed in wherever I look. I see a house wedged in between two walls. The house where the large dogs that I have seen there live, perhaps. This is a house in Blackheath called 'The Wedge', squashed in between two bigger houses. It could also be called the Narrow House. But like any invader, or encroacher, it seems resolutely determined to stay. We have a propensity to stretch things as far as we can to create stability. Sitting on a bus, I notice the 'filled-in' buildings, a space made by fire or needless rebuilding, only to be quickly replaced. Scrappy land encourages wildlife such as the nightingale. But we cannot refrain from intervening.

Walking in search of Belloc reminded me what lengths we go to, to conquer and reclaim land. As I got lost, I nearly stumbled into traffic, going at least sixty miles an hour on the A24, as I had to cross from one side of the road to the other. By then, I was a bit angry that what seemed like aggressive behaviour had hindered my way. It was only at the end of the walk that I saw the windmill and a plaque to the author. I was the only person there. It is suggested that Sussex is to Belloc what Cumbria is to Wordsworth. This felt a bit far-fetched to me, since Wordsworth's literary claim on the land attracts many thousands of people every year.

Enclosure
John Clare (1793–1864), that meticulous observer of rural labour and life, detested the idea of borders and land being sealed off. In writing about the landscape, he shows how painful wandering is when it is curtailed through the creation of barriers owing to enclosure (which began in the early modern period) – the conversion of common land and the abolition of the open field system, changing to enclosed units. Glimpsing alterations to community and landscape, he writes of the path in 'The Village Minstrel' (1819):

> There once were lanes in nature's freedom dropt,
> There once were paths that every valley wound, -
> Inclosure came, and every path was stopt;
> Each tyrant fix'd his sign where paths were found,
> To hint a trespass now who cross'd the ground…

Roaming free became less viable. The poor were marginalised and fenced out. The effects of such measures are noticeable to us today, as we can walk on the ambitious footpaths that were since created to give the public a sense of the right to roam, a way to give paths back to the people. But that is essentially all we have known. Clare knew otherwise and felt bitterly the lofty authority of landowners to be able to divide and apportion land. The pen was a writer's privilege then, but walking, Clare observes, was not. It was words, too, that enforced the changes:

> And be it further Enacted, That no Horses, Beasts, Asses, Sheep, Lamb or other Cattle, shall at any Time within the first Ten Years after the said Allotments shall be directed to be entered upon by the respective Proprietors thereof, be kept in any of the public Carriage Roads or Ways to be set out and fenced off on both Sides, or Laned out in pursuance of this Act.[23]

Clare's poem, 'The Mores' (1820), has often been called *the* poem about enclosure:

> Inclosure came and trampled on the grave
> Of labour's rights and left the poor a slave
>
> Fence now meets fence in owners' little bounds
> Of field and meadow large as garden grounds
> In little parcels little minds to please
> With men and flocks imprisoned ill at ease…

Clare the poet was sad. So was Clare, the man who wanted to walk.

For Clare, enclosure was an act of destruction passed on humanity which he saw not only as a major impediment to walking, but also a leading cause of people needing 'poor relief'. He also saw land obstruction as the end of freedom, orchestrated by those who had little understanding of the poor. The poem is also a lament for what the birds, trees and flowers will witness, and a wistful cry for his bucolic childhood which represented complete freedom. Elsewhere, in a short piece of prose, he writes that 'childhood is a strong spell over my feelings, but I think so on and cannot help it.' While he railed against what he called 'lawless enclosure', he also admired the country's own boundaries, as in 'Pleasant Places', where he writes of the 'Old narrow lanes where trees meet overhead'. I, too, feel gentle joy when walking along a lane enclosed by a tunnel or arch of trees that have met in the middle.

For Clare, the paths are the predicament. They offer joy, choice and things to 'view' and they 'wind', forgetting perhaps to see that they have essentially been moulded by humanity in some way (stepping stones, footprints, a mown meadow, a church, a lake), if not complete aggressive containment. But they were under threat. He does not want to stop what he sees as he goes in 'The Moorehen's Nest':

> Then I walk and swing my stick for joy
> And catch at little pictures passing bye
> A gate whose posts are two old dotterel trees
> A little footbrig with its crossing rail
> A wood gap stopt with ivy wreathing pale
> A crooked stile each path crossed spinny owns
> A brooklet forded by its stepping stones…

Power writ large over the poem. Then speaking through the clay and clod of the land, as if each particle in there mattered.

Yet we could be beguiled by what he says. Is Clare

responding in deep sorrow to a countryside that has changed for him in a subjective way as he grew older, rather than what enclosure itself had wrought? For he also finds joy in many aspects that are essentially man-made. Much of nature has some sort of imperceptible margin, and his poems might be characterised as a bid for complete freedom, even if that is relative. In 'Autumn', he writes, as if calling out, 'In solitudes, where no frequented paths / But what thine own feet makes betray thy home.'

There is likewise an association with Clare as the wandering, tramping poet. His grandfather was a schoolmaster at Helpston, Northamptonshire, who likely roamed the countryside, tired and footsore in search of work. After seducing the parish clerk's daughter, he left the village, leaving her to bring up John Clare's father – Parker. Wandering for destiny may have been in the family genes.

The Scottish-born Andrew Young (1885–1971), who spent most of his life in Sussex, knew too that a walker can trespass and feel most constrained when walking in the countryside. He writes in 'Private':

> Trespassers will be persecuted –
> How? By whom? Who has the right? –
> Hush, go your way; let lip be muted
> With finger' greens will screen from sight –
> Then who has placed this noticeboard? –
> No one; myself; what matter who?
> The one who claims to be landlord
> Of this hill coppice and path through,
> Each cracking stick loose flint and all

Wild flowers, untenanted snail shell.
White butterflies that rise and fall,
Round holes of rabbits and all else.
But why dispute? Thick crowd the leaves;
Deeper sleeps the moss across the trunk;
Wayfarer notes on thorn-stabbed sleeves
Green caterpillar's arching back.
Ten years from now at most a score
This tangled pathway will be lost,
And where its owner walked before
Moonlight will stumble like a ghost.

The sea, though, gives us the illusion of freedom. The sea that unites the travellers from Normandy with those going back and forth to France on a ferry today. The sea gives us the best chance of hope and freedom, its perils and its consequential rising inch by inch every year, to be forgotten as refugees and immigrants bravely cross the English Channel for new hope. As one drop of water touches the side of the ferries, could it be the perpetual drop, that just goes round and round on its life cycle, its shape and size the same as it ever was into eternity?

Mothering Eternity
Motherhood has a perpetual life cycle. One winter, I drove along the ridges of the Wealden district in East Sussex. There was a cold shield of air, hanging as fog, as if it had lost its bottom to prevent it coming down too low. There was the frost I had not seen for a very long time; it was frost forming perfectly on thin branches at the hedgerows. No

more, no less, so that it looked like the frost had measured itself out precisely on each branch. For no obvious reason, an image of the Madonna and Child came into my mind. One of the more tender images that you see in Renaissance art, but also in modern depictions where the baby is enveloped in the voluminous folds and curves of the cloth and flesh of the Virgin Mary. She bends her head towards his and they are as one. And as I was listening to one of my favourite carols, 'In the Bleak Mid-Winter', I began to understand the point of the Nativity. It is about mothering, tenderness, love and care. For centuries, the carols and images have been used to underscore the under-rated, but hugely important, model of motherhood on all of us. The deep winter was all around and on an annual wheel; at a time of cold, we remember the Virgin birth. Its roots lying in the dead of winter in a country so far from here. But with a yellowing light dimly emerging where the fog was, I began to see, almost for the first time in my life, to understand the poignancy of a poor mother and child at Christmas time, offering hope for all. Leaves on the ground were edged in a frosty outline that had not yet melted. And where usually thin branches on spindly trees were tremulously outlined against the dark winter sky, the force of the cold was so strong that they held fast. The frost endured, not just for a morning, but till noon and night, and the next day and after. Somehow the tenacity of the hard frost helped me to understand the endurance that religious belief can give us in our darkest days of winter. And it was true: the air was crisp and cold and even. Even the frost continued to be crisp and cold and even. And as I walked along a footpath on a blanket of left-lying autumn leaves, the frost had become like glue adhering to them all, so that the landscape looked like a huge fishing net where the threads had become wet and fused with one another.

Those who took to the road on foot for different reasons may not have known their mothers. Maybe it was motherly neglect that had caused them to walk in the first place. Maybe it was motherly wretchedness that could not feed her child, forcing her young to seek food elsewhere. How to be a good mother then? You only know as you mourn the loss of their biddability. You only know in retrospect. You only know how you might have done it, later.

William de Warenne I's wife, Gundrada, a woman born in the 1040s, knew what was expected of her as a mother, that is to say, to produce offspring, keep the line alive and well. After all, she signed herself 'Gundrede, wife of William de Warenne'. She herself was from noble Norman as well as Flemish parentage, and of an 'advocate', meaning secular lords, essentially a position synonymous with brutality. Her brother Frederick was given the now ruined Castle Acre in Norfolk, in c.1090, while another sibling, Arnulf, became a tenant-in-chief in East Anglia. So far apart, but East Anglia and Sussex were connected through one family who did not find land distance an obstruction to their mission.

William and Gundrada had visited Cluny, in Burgundy, on a pilgrimage to Rome and thereafter decided to found their own religious institution. And so, Lewes Priory was built between 1078–82. Gundrada's effigy (she died in 1085 during childbirth, at Castle Acre, Norfolk), is in a prized place in her own special chapel at Southover Church (St John) not far from Lewes Priory. Her remains and those of her husband William were originally buried near the high altar of the priory church. Her tomb slab disappeared at the Dissolution but was rediscovered in 1775 in Isfield church and then the stone cists with her and her husband's names on them in 1845, when part of the Lewes to Brighton railway was cut through the priory grounds. These contained mixed-up bones which have revealed that she was less than 5ft, while he was 6ft, so the tomb makers would have needed a long tomb to accommodate them both. The inscription makes clear her role: 'O Holy Pancras, keep with greater care a mother who has made her sons thy heir.' The church was a '*hospitium*' or hospital for travellers linked to the priory, marking the place as well that travel had had in the couple's life. Yet the narratives of those associated with these holy places become fragmented and tossed about in their afterlives.

The domestic dramas, emotions and the ordinary lives (and like all of us, they had them!) of medieval dynasties and legacies are sacrificed by the history of their rule: whose side they were on, battles won and lost, or in the power struggles between King and Lords of the Manor, or different families and supporters of the monarchy. And one way of holding and maintaining power, even if just symbolically, was by a family extending its territorial prowess and reach. And the de Warenne family did this to good effect. Reaching out to the poor or seeming to in your personal Holy books was another way.

From the start, the Warennes showed an awareness of the

poor. On paper, at least. Yet in castle building, where the stones of the land were made into stones for permanent settlement, they could exert a routine aligned with sunrise and sunset. Without a regular habitation, the wayfarer would live by the daily rhythm of nature without the comfort of day and night. But that was hard. Uncertain and presumably endless. In their destitution, they were no sleeping beauties in the tower. But the nobles also knew that preserving their souls would be an important part of God's life plan for them. For the nobility, the need to repent of sins, while displaying kindness towards the poor, was an obligation that could not be ignored. While the poor may have had unchecked entry into the Kingdom of Heaven, the nobles had to work that little bit harder. The depiction of those destitute in their manuscripts was one way for the elite to get close to them, but not too close. As Jean le Bel wrote of the poor in the fourteenth century: 'Little did it matter to us.'[24]

Those who did care might have invoked local saints to guide them in their spiritual instructions. A Sussex peasant was, so the story goes, approached by St Julian in disguise offering him shelter; he was a sixth-century Hospitaller saint who became the patron saint of travellers, boat keepers and innkeepers. His kindness had a legacy, though. A stag had prophesied that he would kill his own parents. And that prophecy was proved correct. Julian subsequently travelled to Rome for forgiveness. At the crossing of a large river, in seeking penance, he began to operate an inn for travellers, the sick and the poor, even providing a ferry service, and, fortunately for Julian, a person with leprosy who stayed there was a messenger from God. All was to be forgiven, and Julian was saved.

Clothing the Naked

St George's parish church, Trotton, in Sussex, is the location of *The Seven Works of Mercy* (Figure 7), a medieval wall painting, uncovered in 1902, after years of slumbering under a white-wash layer. The obscuring of the image was a cleansing metaphor for the sixteenth-century adapted form of Christian instruction which required far less from a worshipper than the medieval Catholic practices. Here, we see how to clothe the naked, as one of the Seven Works.

Figure 7: *The Seven Works of Mercy*, West Sussex, St George's, Trotton, 14th century.

A figure is helping a beggar put a shirt on ('I was naked and ye clothed Me'). At the last bottom panel on the right, Christ looks on and the person with mercy credentials is a woman. What is less clear is whether the command was to carry out the works weekly, once a year, or only once in a lifetime. While you were not being watched by the parish priest, I suppose the point was that God was keeping an eye. His was an invisible one too. And that is how you knew how you would fare at the time of death, where your destiny was determined. And there were no exceptions not to get close during plague times. Mercy was still your mission. When Christianity urged first and foremost to care for neighbour and the 'other', people stayed physically close. As any person in their homes would have been reminded: 'charity suffereth long, and is kind, charity envieth not, charity vaunteth not itself, is not puffed up (1 *Corinthians* 13:4). Your whole physical and mental being was a default sinful sting to be cast off by labouring to preserve the soul, even if you had killed and needed to plead for forgiveness.

Lack, or valuing lack, was a good quality to have in the Middle Ages, as described in the poem 'Wynnerc and Wastoure' (from a miscellany of writings by John Lydgate, fourteenth century): 'For if thou wydwhare scholde walke and waytten the sothe Thou scholdeste reme for rewthe in siche ryfe bene the pore.'

'The Seven Works of Mercy' had practical encouragement as well. At medieval hospitals, workers were encouraged to carry out good deeds. Since the level of destitution and disease was very high, Humbert of Romans (c.1190–1277), a French Dominican friar, said the greatest act was that of looking after the sick in hospital. While those working in the hospitals were expected to be chaste and obedient and act as if poor. Looking after the other was a conduit to the beneficent eyes of God in Heaven. The message of an after-life at Death was so strong that good works were seen in this light. In giving, something spiritual is returned to you. That was the highest gift to strive for, but which also comforted you in anticipating your death and afterlife. A little fifteenth-century Latin treatise called *Instructions for a Devout and Literate Layman*, probably written for an elite audience by their priest or confessor, was intended to be carried around in a purse as it was not bound into a book. On parchment, it was written: 'Say a prayer and include the words, "Thou who hast made me, have mercy upon us and upon me."' So, mercy was applicable to the giver, as well as those who have been in receipt of material help or care. Furthermore, when they were due to go out, they were encouraged to say, 'All the men of this city or town from the greater … to the less are pleasing to God, and only I am worthy of hell.'[25] Self-worth is rarely measured by a fiery pit now. Rather, through constantly changing media visualisation, image here now, gone the next, you can forget crime or conscience quite quickly. *The Seven Works of Mercy* cycles, like the building and the fabric of the church, were designed for posterity. The pigments made and mixed to stick fast to the church's wall, made to last for ever. One single image that reminded people every time they went to the church to think of others. One set of images that you would memorise so well there would be no doubt you would not forget.

So, to the end of the path that I have taken. The things I have seen. The pebbles, like footsteps, leave marks, but these are more permanent. Turn them over and the pressure has left some sort of groove or stain on the surface. Chalk paths, when the mud flows, yet not always squelchy and soft, can feel a bit municipal. But when the rain has cleared, the going can be tough. And there is a sort of arid look, like a bleached marble frieze which has lost its colour. For Belloc, in *The Old Road* (1904), the characteristic chalk of England is the best preservation of the road. He wrote, 'it therefore invited the wayfarer who was not permitted to trespass upon tilled land. But unlike other waste soil, it was admirably adapted to retrain the trace of his passage.'

I walked into Lewes. The ruins of the priory. The castle on the hill. The up and down of Lewes, its people and its history. Substantial remains of the de Warennes' existence in part, in places, in bone and text. Solid medieval walls, if a bit less substantial than before, still standing. A way in which we can remember them. The wayfarers, though, have long gone. They have already passed through.

FOUR

WAYFARING WORKS 4:
SHELTERING THE HOMELESS

When I sent you forth without purse or wallet
or sandals did you lack anything? And they said,
'Nothing.'
The Gospel of St Luke (22:35–6)

Frontier land can drift and weave between two counties, or between water and solid ground. I travelled to the border of Suffolk and Norfolk. An area that, long ago, would have been sea. The paradox of 'now', where we hear about rising sea levels and how countless seaside towns and houses will be under water in Britain in time to come, recalling the time when the coastline of East Anglia was subject to alteration and shape-changing. A higher water level now means homelessness and dispossession. I am thinking about whether, before too long, land will be reclaimed again from the irrepressible waters and, rather like the morning after it has snowed in the night, imagining how differently things might feel. For this land is, I suppose, always marshy and watery in places. And in-going betwixt land and a bit of estuary here and there, disappearing, returning, eliding; there is a sense of uncertainty where water ends, and land begins. When the Romans were here, there was water all around. But that didn't stop them moving further inland; in fact, it would have made their ambitions to conquer that much easier, if there was water to travel through in small boats.

St Christopher

I planned another walk, this time to Gorleston on the Suffolk–Norfolk border starting at Fritton, heading west just off the road to Great Yarmouth. I parked the car and pretended to myself that I had walked from Norwich. Here, at Fritton, is a so-called Norfolk round-tower church. That is, a church with a round tower. There are many in Norfolk. Nobody quite knows why, although since decent stone was available locally, flint had to be used, which is not an easy or malleable material to build with. It is thought that many towers dating from the medieval period housed bells. But they could also provide accommodation for the parish priests.

A heavy door, and inside, facing you, a faded but still visible mural of St Christopher, larger than life, carrying the Christ Child. A journeying giant, but all tender. He is taking the boy across the water. Living alone by the water, he watches travellers pass. At first, he does not know that the child is Christ. Murals of St Christopher were designed to protect medieval travellers when they were on pilgrimage or wayfaring. They would open a church door and there he would be, painted to greet you, unmistakably watchful. In this version, Christopher's short tunic, a bit incongruous against his large frame, looks blue at his chest (wateriness? a jumper?) to reveal his long, strong, legs and fleshy sturdiness. The right leg is slightly bent, elevated from the faintly painted fish in the water, while the Christ Child sits all in line with the crown the larger saint wears. The crown sits on a hat, like a jewel in the sea, so maybe it is cold. Both crown and the halo of Christ that might once have been powdered with gold, are ranked side by side. Christopher's head is tilted slightly upwards towards Christ, who blesses with his right hand. While Christ is perched on his Atlas-like shoulders, Christopher holds a staff nearly as long as his body.

My brothers wore what my mother called 'St Christophers': medallions with the saint engraved on them, attached to a necklace. She knew he was revered as a saint of protection and, as they went to boarding school at the age of just eight, St Christopher, she had hoped, might help in her absence. It wasn't until shortly before she died that I asked my mother why she gave my brothers these amulet-like protections. As a Catholic, my mother knew something of her saints, and she knew their attributes as well. However, Christopher could not lull you into security for too long. Leave the protecting giant and you often had to face the Last Judgement on the east wall, or on the chancel arch, where you needed grace to receive the Eucharistic giving and blessing you were told was there for you. Lurking there and displayed more prominently, were demons and devils assaulting, grabbing, and pushing sinners into the mouth of Hell. For some people, their time was up. They had not prepared for the afterlife, performed 'the Works of Mercy', prayed for the dead, or said confession, and all those other things expected of you. Life, then, was like a very sharp, studded collar, poking your conscience; it was not a laurel leaf giving you easy credit. That came later, if you had done what was required. Preparation for death wasn't for some distant tomorrow, or next Wednesday week. All of this makes St Christopher benign and comforting in spaces that were often brimming with fear-inducing imagery, so hot on-message that the beholder knew they could burn in Hell-fire pits. There used to be images of St Christopher, as well, on house exteriors, so that those passing by could stand and stare at him, with perhaps a nod or a prayer to petition his protecting arm or leg.

Time Here Matters

I had been advised by somebody at the pub where I left my car to get a bus at 11.05 a.m. from the main road. Since another one was not scheduled for a few hours or more, I needed to get that bus. Unable to see the bus stop ahead, I started to run along the side of the road, in the absence of a pavement or verge; it was a dangerous thing to do. St Christopher may have been on my side, though, for I soon heard the bus approaching. I hailed it down, half expecting the driver to ignore me. But he stopped; he let me on, hot, breathless, and fumbling for my purse. I may have apologised for my existence at that point, aware too, of the others already on the bus, who you could tell had been there for a while, as there is a gaze that becomes bus travel that is one of dazed boredom, even though people still look at you. As I faced the long day ahead of solitary walking, I was reminded of a line in Hardy's *The Return of the Native*: 'in these lonely places, wayfarers, after a first greeting, frequently plod on for miles without speech.' How true that turned out to be. I have wondered if this would have been a very different book if I had met more people and recorded their conversations.

Once at Gorleston, my plan was to walk north to Great Yarmouth and then join the Angles Way to begin my walk proper. Now, I was not far from the River Yare's great mouth at Great Yarmouth. The land feels fragile. Thousands of years ago, there was no clear-cut border between the wet and the dry. If the predictions are right, that absence of demarcation might return. But we want a clear, strong, heavy line drawn between land and sea. With the planet under stress, we want strong land protection from the water to keep both land and people secure. In certain irony, perhaps, while people complain about the United Kingdom's geographical borders being porous we want them safe to protect our land from rising water as well. Here now, in this part of East Anglia, remnants of towers and defences are seen. Height might soon have an intensified role here. As in parts of the Low Countries, this reclaimed ground means that channels weave in and out of the land. Nothing feels permanent, even today.

During the Middle Ages, Gorleston-on-Sea, near Great Yarmouth, was full of salt and wine merchants, salt collectors, wooden boats, fishing nets and artist immigrants arriving from other North Sea lands to show potential clients their shiny, sacred art. And books such as *The Macclesfield* and *Gorleston Psalters* – both with de Warenne connections. Well, I fantasise, but scholars have established this link and so will I. Now though, Gorleston is a place that you might choose to avoid. As a coastal town, it no longer serves as a route to anywhere; it is a destination to avoid. Like many struggling seaside towns, its destiny is hazy, flat, uncertain.

A ridge of cooling towers, modern wharves, cargoes and containers mark what is now a suburb of Great Yarmouth, further north, but a small spur of land juts out into the North Sea, from where the River Yare snakes up towards the town's centre. The railway lines have been dug into what was once water and mud and spit. The herring trade connected this area with the Low Countries. A 'Free Fair' for herring and other types of fish took place on the dunes by the River Yare up until the fourteenth century. For a long time, there had been tracks and drovers' roads as part of a trading route through the hump of East Anglia and the land on the other side of the North Sea. Now, though, lively coastal activity has been exchanged for passivity. This is the silent cloister of the forgotten. The containers conceal all, and like Nieuwpoort, I could not see the sea, and there were few people around: they know better. Further down south at Oulton Broad, the tread of the Angles Way moves up and down steadily like the monitor of a dull heartbeat, because it is not doing anything out of the ordinary. It is just beating methodically, reliably, steadily. The path is all straight. And the paths created by humans criss-cross the land levels created by them. One activity that seems unceasing in our time is the building of new blocks of flats on what you might think is the fragile anchor of land where you can go out no further, even though you cannot see the sea. But the estate agents will sell them as properties with a sea view. There will be gulls with their aerial acrobatics to capture something of living by the water, but that is all. Gorleston is not set up for pleasure at the beach; instead, here or there, a scrappy piece of paper, a discarded nappy, a broken wheel, a rusty bike. Time and the perils of industrial and maritime change and plunder have wrought neglect and amnesia on places like Gorleston. This is the ground for ditches, marshes, mud, dirt and paddling and squelching, but not for the childish squeals of delight at the seashore. No, Gorleston is about survival. And now, it seems to be surviving partly as it was, and as it will be to come. Perhaps it is in hopeful transition, but who knows. Meanwhile, the town waits.

Along a paved path going north, there is a man-made ridge, as Gorleston protects itself from the windy rages of the North Sea. Further up at the coastal edge, a Morrisons, more containers, thick grassy clumps, the colour of the shiniest Pre-Raphaelite painted blades, depots and disused ground. Devoid of plenty, at least this is a place where wildflowers, too, grow insouciantly. These flowers are in a hostile land where you would expect pollination to have migrated. As ever, it was challenging to read a map and navigate, carry all the accoutrements for walking, write notes as well as checking what was before and beneath me. Where hard material bulks of industry were working, I saw people in orange hard hats, bolstering themselves against the weather.

When medieval illuminators from the Low Countries came to East Anglia, Gorleston would have had religious matters at its heart. Once, the town possessed a priory, a friary and a leper house. Homes to accommodate those who prayed and preached, as well as those who were ill. The Austin Friars came to England in 1249, and they were called to preach and hear confessions. They provided care to strangers and even, it was said, 'Flemings'. The Order was also established at Gorleston (from c.1267–1538, that is until the Dissolution of the monasteries). In the fifteenth century, a monk called John Brome established the priory's library, known for its quality collection. It is said he put indexes to all the books in the library. It is said, despite there being books everywhere, that the contents, the books, the words have now dispersed. It is said that such a tragedy was the consequence of storms, and in 1813 it was recorded that in a terrible gale, the tower of the priory collapsed: '100 feet high, it has stood and been a mark for ships passing through Yarmouth roads from time immemorial, was on Thursday night, blown down in the gale with a tremendous crash.'[26]

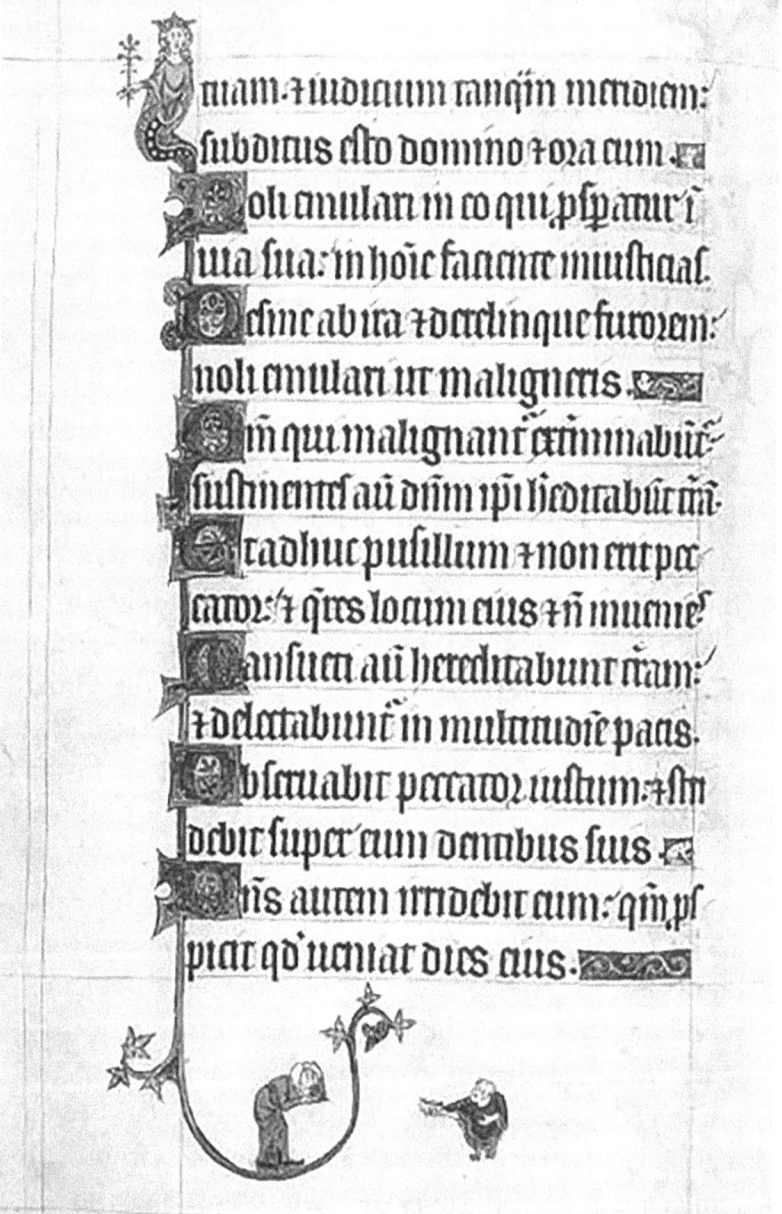

Figure 8: *The Gorleston Psalter*, London, British Library, Add. MS.
49622, fol. 48v, c.1310–24, 374 x 235 mm.

Plate 1: *The Macclesfield Psalter*, Cambridge, Fitzwilliam Museum, MS 1-2005, fol. 98r, c. 1330–40, 170 x 108 mm.

Plate 2: *The Macclesfield Psalter*, Cambridge, Fitzwilliam Museum,
MS 1-2005, fol. 85r, c.1320–30, 170 x 108 mm.

D dominum cum tri
bularer clamaui: ⁊ ex
audiuit me.

D omine libera animam mea
a labiis iniquis ⁊ a lingua dolosa.

Quid detur tibi aut quid appo
natur tibi: ad linguam dolosam.

S agitte potentis acute cum
carbonibz desolatorijs.

H eu michi quia incolatus
meus prolongatus est: habita
ui cum habitantibz cedar: mul
tum incola fuit anima mea

C um hijs qui oderunt pacem

Cy sen noint vers egypte

Plate 3: *The Taymouth Hours*, London, British Library,
MS Yates Thompson 13, fol. 95v, c.1325–30, 170 x 115 mm.

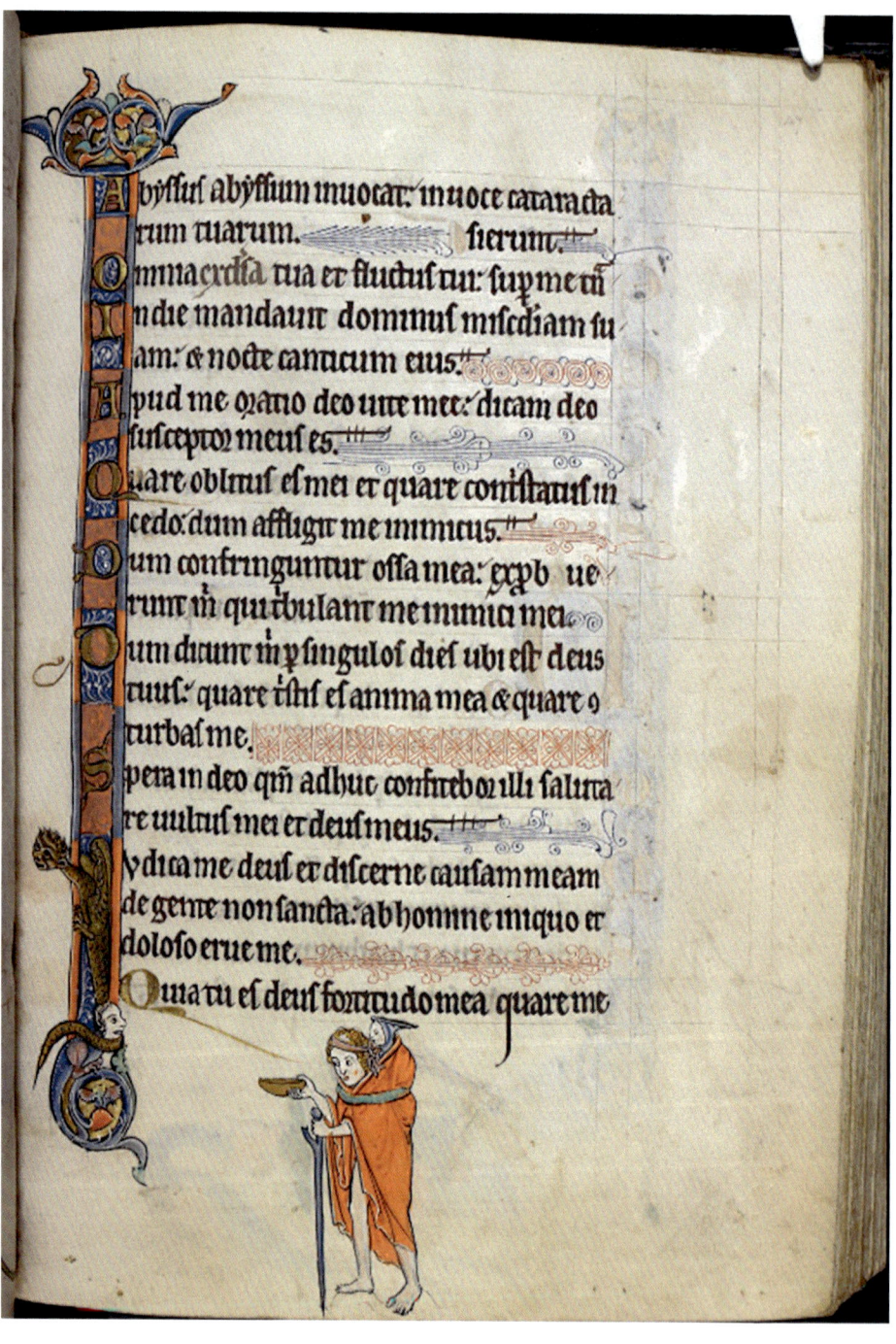

byssus abyssum invocat: invoce cataracta
rum tuarum. fierum.
mnia excelsa tua et fluctus tui: sup me tu
n die mandauit dominus misediam su
am: & nocte canticum eius.
pud me oratio deo uite mee: dicam deo
susceptor meus es.
uare oblitus es mei et quare contristatus in
cedo: dum affligit me inimicus.
um confringuntur ossa mea: exprob ue
runt m qui tribulant me inimici mei
um dicunt m p singulos dies ubi est deus
tuus: quare tristis es anima mea & quare 9
turbas me.
pera in deo qm adhuc confitebor illi saluta
re uultus mei et deus meus.
y dica me deus et discerne causam meam
de gente non sancta: ab homine iniquo et
doloso erue me.
Quia tu es deus fortitudo mea quare me

Plate 4: *The Rutland Psalter*, London, British Library,
Add. MS 62925, fol. 47r, c.1250–60, 285 x 205 mm.

Plate 5: *Ghent Book of Hours*, Cambridge, Trinity College Library,
MS B 11 22, fol. 23v, 14th century, 18 x 45 cm.

Plate 6: *The Gorleston Psalter*,
London, British Library,
Add. MS 49622, fol. 132v,
c.1310–24, 374 x 235 mm.

Plate 7: The Wayfaring Tree
(*Viburnum lantana*), 1796,
Wellcome Collection.

Plate 8: *The Wayfarer*,
Hieronymus Bosch,
Rotterdam, Museum
Boijmans Van
Beuningen, 1516,
71 x 70.6 cm.

Plate 9: *Our Mother*, cast iron, oil paint, string and cloth, Grayson Perry, Victoria Miro Gallery, 2009, 84.5 x 65 cm.

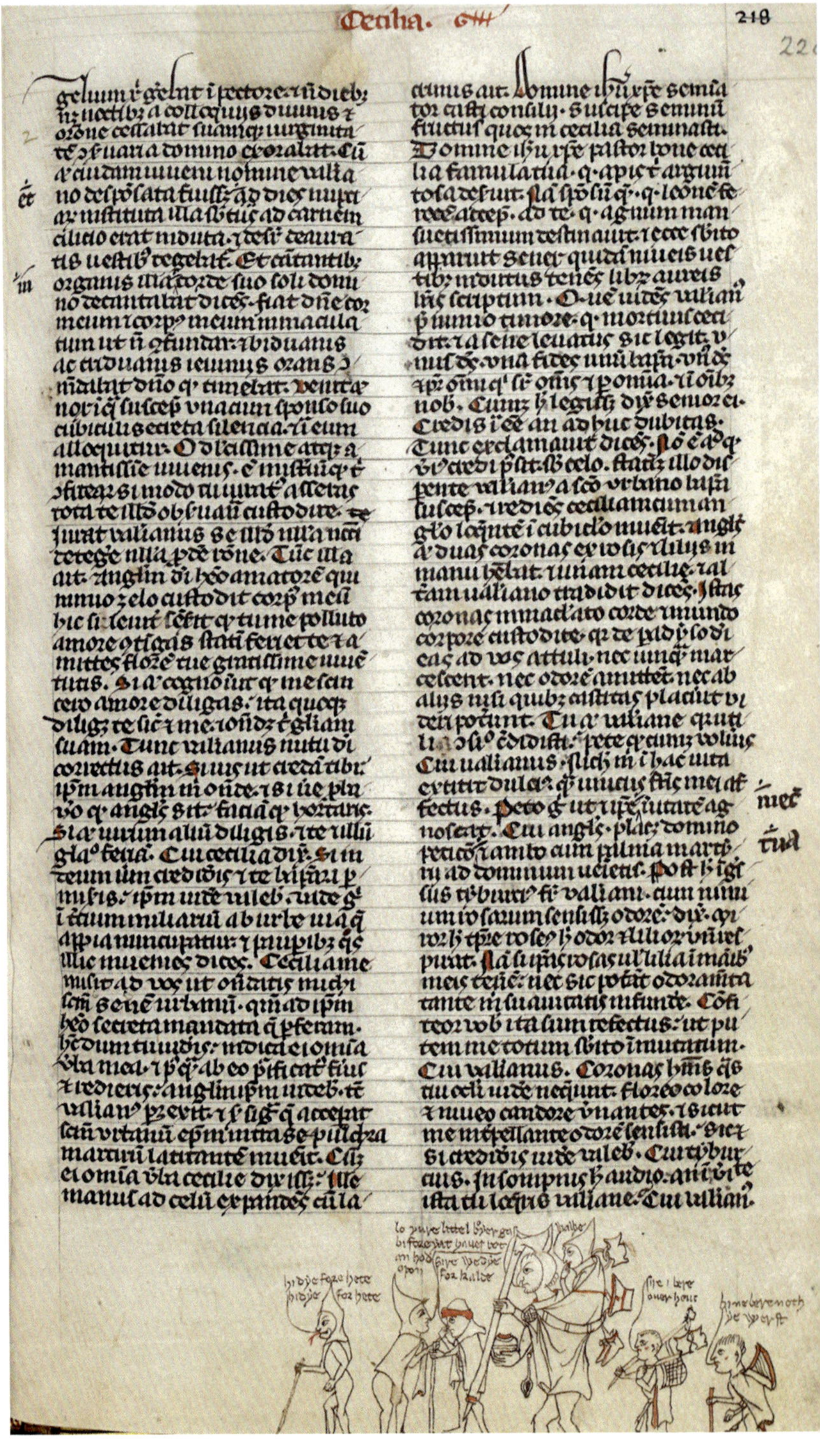

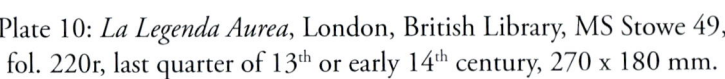

Plate 10: *La Legenda Aurea*, London, British Library, MS Stowe 49, fol. 220r, last quarter of 13th or early 14th century, 270 x 180 mm.

Poverty. Decline. And decorated manuscript pages. In *The Gorleston Psalter* (London, The British Library, Add. MS 49622 fol. 48v, c.1310–24, Figure 8), near the bottom right of the folio, a figure stands alone. He has a round head, no hat, a shapeless tunic thrown about; he holds out a bowl and his feet each displays three toes. He is looking towards a figure to the left who is partly protected by a curling tendril, like a foraged hedgerow cut away, which he stands on. It is a decorated structure, separating him from the man. All the same, he is vomiting at the sight, which seems like a radical response to somebody in need; yet as we know so well from Shakespeare, melancholy is all the more potent when accompanied by a bit of comedy. Such a vignette may seem like an odd thing to include in a solemn, precious and luxury book. But with a few brush-strokes, the painter could show you were a good Christian, but in the knowledge that a bit of distraction would not go amiss.

Gorleston and the de Warenne Family
The de Warenne family's coat of checky (no, not cheeky) azure arms appears in *The Gorleston Psalter* from time to time, impressing the family name in a personal book dedicated to being prayerful, while reminding them of the weaknesses of humanity, the very things that, in our less than faithful world, we still hold dear. I wish I knew why it is called *The Gorleston Psalter*. But we do know the family owned land further north from here and some say the manuscript was associated with the church of St Andrew in Gorleston. It may be that the book was commissioned

by John de Warenne, seventh Earl of Surrey (1286–1347),
who belonged, as the generations went on, to that heady
mix of Normans, French, Anglo-Saxons, Angevins and
Flemings. The mixing of families and arms, in both senses
of the word, ensured dynastic longevity, while a beautiful
book would secure their memory.

John's father, William, died when he was only six months
old, in 1286. He was seven when his mother died in 1293,
and then his grandfather died in 1304. So, John succeeded
to the de Warenne earldom in that year. Marriage was
swiftly arranged for him in 1306 when he was only twenty
to Joan (Jeanne) of Bar, daughter of Henri III of Bar, and
granddaughter to Edward I as her father had married
Eleanor, King Edward I's eldest daughter in 1293. She
was only ten at the time. John and Joan's liaison, apart
from sounding like the title of an Alan Bennett story,
must be one of the few marriages we know about from
this period, since it was not a happy one. The problem
was John. He wanted a divorce so that he could marry
his mistress Maude de Nerford, who came from Skeyton,
Norfolk (1292–1346), the Nerfords being knights under
the Warennes. Maude was already married, but John tried
to argue that she was pro-contracted to him before his
marriage to Joan and that his wife was his cousin.[27] John
the adulterer; excommunicated by the Bishop of Chichester, John, a sinner, who needed to repent. The Archbishop
of Canterbury, Robert de Winchelsey, wrote to him on
11 May 1313, criticising him for leading a 'disorderly life
for guarding and retaining Maude Nerford.' Think more
about your soul, he was urged, and the preservation of

his lineage was brought up too. A Court hearing account described John as: 'imitating the obstinacy of Pharaoh and closing his ears like a serpent, degenerate from his high ancestry, regardless of his salvation, and prodigal of his fame and honour, while he lived in notorious adultery with another woman'. In the spirit that one allegation is never enough and stronger in a battalion, on 23 May 1314 Walter Reynolds and eleven of his 'suffragan' bishops admonished John to end the affair 'without delay as otherwise they could no longer suffer such contempt of holy church.' What Maude and Joan thought of all this talk about the man in their lives, we don't know. John and Joan never got that divorce, but only a legal separation, and he had several illegitimate children with Maude, but none with Joan.[28] John surrendered most of his estates to King Edward II. But the King granted them back, so that his land could be inherited by John's illegitimate sons with Maude, who had been given Conisbrough, his Yorkshire estate. Much is made of John's personal life, but such marital goings-on cannot have been uncommon then. Lacking fewer primary sources than other periods, this is a rare insight into the fragile affairs of the heart for the medieval period. John, we know, had his encounters with strangers too. On January 27th, 1331, it was recorded that some men were named in a complaint by John de Warenne including William Nywe, chapman who had 'carried away his goods and assaulted his servants at Sefford, co. Sussex.'[29]

John's sons, it is thought, were resident religious at the hospital of St John of Jerusalem and it has been suggested that *The Gorleston Psalter* was commissioned for them.

In *The Macclesfield Psalter*, there is a recurring image of a young man in some of the margins. Looking holy. And maybe wondering about the sins of the fathers; there is even one illustration of a young man in bed, waking up, as if it is morning, looking as though he is struck by some sort of need, or is it an awakening conscience?

Walking Over the Ancient
What possessed me to think that I could trace a wayfarer's steps or feel their swollen sorrow as they stumbled and plodded; blistered, thirsty, dirty, exhausted, even leprous and diseased in search of food, warmth and shelter? My life does not resemble theirs in any way. These figures are completely invisible to me, but some of the paths they walked on are probably the same; they walked the same way, they looked out too and they peered through apertures of shelters or churches, where the light fell on the slit casements which beamed through a narrow-lit moon at night. The dark, the sun at solstice. At dawn. And at the day's end. In summer, stems of foliage caressed their sore and nettle-poisoned legs. The dock leaves may have soothed their stings as well. In winter, though, the rain and the wind would have been crushing, the longing for shelter unbearable.

I had prepared for torrential rain or thick heavy cloud. One or the other, but I got neither; instead, a ballooning sun, intense, insistent on Gorleston high street. So, all the extra layers in my rucksack were redundant and I had uncomfortable walking boots, bruising toes and breaking nails. When you lack, you cannot be frustrated by what clothing you have packed, for you do not have that choice. Choice gives you too much to think about. I tried to imagine nervous artists arriving to work for some of Norfolk's elite. The audacity of the visual choices they made, painting indigents.

Gorleston has made valiant efforts to recognise some of its eighteenth-century luminaries on the houses where they lived: blue plaques identifying doctors, or ships' captains for example. One is dedicated to a man called the Rev. Forbes Alexander Phillip (1865–1917), an author, dramatist and vicar of Gorleston. I wondered if he had heard about the de Warenne family and their commissioning of religious manuscripts; but there is little here that recalls a medieval past and a place where foreigners disembarked to start new creative lives.

I climbed over a wall to visit the church of St Andrew's, but it was closed. There are also the priory gardens, which have replaced monastic ruins. The distance in time between medieval church and priory building then, with the advance of large, shapeless containers, marks the inescapable onset of modernity, and the anonymity of our towns' fabric, and while the flint that is the robust material of the church looks indestructible, the containers look as though they are shifting, as the mist and cloud settle heavily beside them. I see the future for stone in an advert for a 'stone improvement company' inscribed on the side of one container, such that I concluded that the passing of time in Gorleston is emphasised by building materiality.

Now, the people of Gorleston wait at the bus stop, where hope is mingled with the tax on time and tasks to achieve, rather than in a medieval sense, that of the liturgical hours for prayer and the hope of salvation by waiting at the church door. And when and where Heaven will provide the eternal. Faithful fervour is not within apparent reach in Gorleston; but beyond the harbour wall to contain humanity is vague infinity, the colour of a shroud.

In the physical search for a monument, a stone, or just a destination, you realise that the quest can turn into something else. And that the looking for the destination becomes secondary. When medieval pilgrims were urged to go on a pilgrimage just once in their lives, it was probably hoped that the pain of the journey would enable them to think about the physical and spiritual sense of Christ's suffering. Indeed, pain was positively encouraged, for if you experienced pain, then it would transcend to spiritual suffering, just as it had with Christ. His pain was a model for all ensuing suffering that he knew would just go on and on. Friars left their homes to remind people about discomfort. They even chose bodily suffering with hair shirts, spikes, pokey things and rats under the bed. The grislier the better, and the power of that message worked for many years.

When friars wandered to speak to people, they relied on the pleasure of arrival; their legs weary with the hardship of the way. St Dominic would walk as he preached, and when he came upon travellers, seized the moment to speak. Humbert of Romans (c.1190–1277) tells us that the friars would preach outside as church attendance by the poor was low. And they knew they might find people by market squares.[30] The Dominicans also carried a staff, and a hood draped over their head as part of their habit. Etienne de Bourbon (1180–1261), preacher of the Dominican Order, said that he saw noble ladies so affected by the Word that they put on the humblest clothes to follow the preachers from town to town, so that they became beggars. Etienne cleverly turned this gesture into a fashion statement, urging people to imagine themselves in beggary. What a wondrous thing he must have felt he had done with his words in the metamorphosis of his followers.

And just as the laity in the locality were encouraged to believe in healing and miracles, the poor were also told about their local saints: if they 'followed' them, it was said, they might get cured. The more people followed a saint, the better the saint would be known. The better he / she was known, the more money the site in their name would gain from those who worshipped them. It was a mutually beneficial system, seemingly flawless, where faith could make what you heard feel undeniably true. Disabled people, the blind, the leprous, the plagued would bring their faith with them as they walked to chapel or church and lingered at outdoor crosses and holy wells. It was this power of belief through walking which kept people going.

Norfolk Saints

It did not seem to matter if there was no living proof of a saint who had cured or healed. What was said had the potent ability to 'stick'. The people of Norfolk invoked St

Walstan who spent his life looking out for the poor and infirm, though his renown remained largely local. *The Lives of St. Walstan* (975–1016) tell the story of a boy, born in Blyborow (now Bawburgh), the son of Benedict and Blida whose life of renunciation started when he left his parents' home aged thirteen. Meeting two poor men on the road, he gave them his garments. It was said that he was 'in the manner of Priapus, the god of their fields in Norfolk and guide of their harvests, all mowers and scythe followers'. He worked in the fields at Taverham, often in bare feet, even though he was given shoes by the farmer's wife, which he then gave away. In anger, she made him tread on the thorns of briars, but they transformed into rose petals, and in giving away his clothes to the poor, he forsook all to follow Christ's message about poverty by God's vow that he should be a pilgrim, and going to Walstan as his naked servant. First, he is tested in reaping wheat, as part of a series of tests to show he could please God:

> Barefoot on ye stubble both sharp & hard,
> he goeth meekly & suffreth patiently,
> trusting hereafter to have a reward:
> his Mr & dame thereof had pity,
> & Ordained him shoes to save surely:
> A bottle & a bag with victuall him to feed,
> passeth forth to field.

Challenged to walk barefoot, he bore without hurt, 'punished and pricked with thorns all about'. Later, he is warned by an angel of his imminent death – following which he seeks *viaticum* (from the Latin *via*), meaning provisions and / or money for the journey and anointing. A short time before his death, he threw away his scythe at noon, close to lunchtime, while working in a meadow, asking that any labourer who comes to his shrine driven by any need be given help and healing.

As a paradigm for his life's good works, his soul rises to Heaven. His body was put in a cart with oxen (he had a special concern for animals). Some accounts say that, at the river, the wagon and body fell into the water at the deepest part of the river, but both body and wagon passed over as if it were solid ground, and so the imprint of the wheel of the cart appeared on oxen's faces. Reinforcement always helped, just as Christ's face appeared on St Veronica's handkerchief as she followed him up to Calvary and soothed his hot and troubled brow. Others say that springs appeared on low land when Walstan's wagon passed, from Taverham to Costessey, to its destination at Bawburgh and then the wagon entered the church opened by a blaze of angels. And because of the miracle, a well sprang up; because of this, visitors duly came, including the lame. Because of this, miracles began. One visitor, the knight Sir Gregory Lovell, fell gravely ill. Bedridden with aching bones, lying naked, with nobody to heal him, he went to St Walstan's well and was swiftly healed with the water. Walking to water was seen by the Church as a source of enlightenment, calculated to remind us that, before Christ, all was dark. For some years after Walstan's death, the bones of the boy of hope and miracle were visited. For some years, the boy was miraculous.

He is still remembered at Barnham Broom. Inside the church are dado panels painted beside the chancel arch to let you into the most sacred part of the church, *en route* to the altar. He was painted alongside other saints in these wooden spaces, framed by tracery, all capped by cusps and crockets of Gothic arches, a screen, itself rendered transparent, where carved wood twists into curls and coils, arches and points. A structure, rising, as if it is a ship on the sea with blithe sails, where it is broken down to make little pointed apertures, decorative and delicate, as if they had become their own little vessels. The screen, even though shorn of its once bright medieval colours, means that you would have noticed Walstan even more then. There he is in the saintly ranking, some with their towers and their palms, their books, falcon, a trodden-upon devil, a sword, sometimes even their spectacles, their long robes and capacious sleeves. Both hat and halo, both shoe and wrist. Clothing fit for Heaven, but also the horse.

Itinerant friars told stories, known as *exempla*, when preaching, which using allegory or the theme of disguise, spoke of the perils of not following the accepted Christian codes of conduct, which would include giving to the poor and beggars, so to fulfil Heaven's entry requirements. 'The Three Travellers', who had one loaf between them, narrates the story of three friends on pilgrimage discussing how to share just the one loaf.[31] Knowing there was not enough, they discuss whether to abandon the loaf or not. They decide to sleep 'upon the way', and whoever saw the loaf in a dream would win it. So, pitching the goodness of one against the other, one got up, ate the bread, and woke his companions to ask them about their dreams. The first said that a golden ladder reached up to Heaven where angels took his soul. The second said he was tempted by devils in Hell. The one who ate the bread said that an angel visited him and asked about his companions. Fearing they had taken the bread, the angel said, 'oh no', and took him to the bread. He said that he was taken to Heaven, thinking he saw his companions there surrounded by food. The angel assured him that his friends had all he could wish for. Then the angel took him to the gates of Hell; yet, even there, there was bread. He said to the angel how sad he was, to which the angel responded that Hell had been what he deserved. A medieval audience would have known that the literal tone of the story was masking the important moral truth not to deceive, reminding people of the stark choice between Hell and Heaven.

There was work to be done to avoid Hell, by means of spiritual healing. For they all knew then that when death was close, it might be less anguished if they had prepared. At Horning on the Norfolk Broads was a pilgrim hospital of St James, founded by the monks of the abbey of St Benet Hulme. It was also one of the many refuges for the sick travellers and pilgrims going to East Anglia in large numbers. The hospital of Hautbois, north of Norwich, was founded in 1235 to 'receive both wayfarers and poor of the locality'. By 1257, it had a chapel, so the inmates could be comforted in a spiritual sense as well. When life was tough, the hope for Divine reassurance was expected to sustain people, particularly when medicinal cures were few and far between.

Socialising Poverty in the Nineteenth Century

In the nineteenth century, stories engendered a social awareness of poverty and the dismal working conditions of the poor. Charles Dickens wrote about wayfaring out of need in a story entitled, 'The Seven Poor Travellers'. He used a hospital location for travellers in Rochester, not far from where he had a house, that is Gad's Hill Place. The hospital building, which still stands today, is known as Watt's Charity. In his will, dated 22 August 1579, Richard Watt founded a charity for 'six poor travellers', specifying it 'should provide furniture to harbour or lodge in poore travellers or wayfareing [*sic*] men to harbour and lodge therein no longer than one night unless sickness be the further cause thereof...'[32] In the story, the storyteller (alias Dickens), sees Watt's notice on the door and knocks with curiosity. A woman answers and responds to his request to visit the travellers, saying: 'Nobody ever asked to see them, and nobody ever did see them.' The writer continues that he 'pictured them advancing towards their resting-place along the various cold roads ... I made them footsore; I made them weary; I made them carry packs and bundles; I made them stop by finger-posts and milestones, leaning on their bent sticks, and looking wistfully at what was written there; I made them lose their way...' For Dickens, the wearied travellers have little but the blessing of anonymity.

Fragmented wispy shrubs bordering the road beside a pond are the only structures of any weight to support the two figures walking along the road in the Victorian artist Frederick Walker's painting *The Wayfarers* (1868, private collection). A man and a young boy with a red garment tied up in his arms walk at a slight angle to the picture plane. The man carries a stick, the boy walking, perhaps against his will, his eyes cast down, his lids nearly covering his eyes. The man places his hand on the boy's shoulder, a telling sign to us that he is blind, which may explain why his staff is pushed out perpendicular to his body. They walk on a lane bordered by a leafless shrub. Beside a pool, with a thin line of trees above them. In the soft light, perhaps that of a late winter afternoon, a yellow light. The colours take on a damp hue, and the road glistens a little from recent rain. Nevertheless, they do not look altogether poor: the man is dressed all in black with a hat, and the boy wears a green satin shirt and brown trousers. So, the clothing and the warm glow in their midst, a juxtaposition made by a painter who wanted his composition to beguile. The work was made at a time when 'genre' paintings by artists such as Frank Holl and Luke Fildes were intended to depict despair, poverty and difficulty. But painters could not completely sacrifice their skills in painting light and shadow, warm colour, mood and atmosphere; for their talent had to be expressed as well. We do not know where the father and boy are going, but the composition is the road that shows them the way.

That sense of wandering without having a purpose is audaciously described by Dickens in his account of tramping life, where hedges are shelters and roads offer vain hope, and scraps in London the only possible succour. This is 'Tramps', from *The Uncommercial Traveller*, 1860, with the opening line: 'Whenever a tramp sits down to rest by the wayside, he sits with his legs in a dry ditch...' He interrogates the bundle – 'what can be the contents of that mysterious bundle, to make it worth his while to carry it about?' Enter a woman with 'her legs in a ditch' and in his precise descriptive way, Dickens offers the reader a passage of amusing satire, but which is also a wry comment on how the poor were treated and reduced to the threat of the workhouse at the time. The road, meanwhile, becomes a metaphor for those without hope.

From Gorleston, I could not, at first, find the path going north. I ended up in the labyrinth that is the out-of-town shopping hub; all I needed was a hole in a hedge to lead me to the water alongside the River Yare, which I knew marked the continuation of the walk. All the while, I walked along noisy, unattractive roads; odd glimpses of a door lintel there, an egg and dart moulding, a Doric column by a doorway, even more of the odd blue plaques (for example, that of Mary Sewell – a washerwoman, who was the mother of Anna Sewell – the author of *Black Beauty*); and all such architectural details, from when this area, once a thriving port, had fine houses all around. All the while, I still found things to look at. Eventually, I gave up my search, took a taxi, and the driver drove me further down the river, so I missed the marshes walkway, built to accommodate feet on concrete, rather than the squishy surface of the shoreline.

Burgh, Castle, Tower, Church

Gorleston and Great Yarmouth are at the furthest reaches of the Broads, where the roads run in unceasing parallel with the gentle hills beside. The river then turns in west, becoming broader as it moves towards Burgh Castle. Once there was a footbridge connecting Gorleston to the lower part of Great Yarmouth. And at this time of year, late June, all was tingling and twitching on the roads' verges. The poppies on the roadside, the petals looked so fragile, yet they resisted being blown off as the cars sped by. The flower is equally at home, quite often solitary, in fields and pastures, while the fields of corn look as though some spirit has flecked them with gold. Seen from above, it looked as though they had little haloes.

The Roman fort of Burgh (pronounced Borough, with the Saxon name Cnobheresburg) Castle, has a far-reaching view of the marshes, two windmills and cows grazing in water meadows. This land was originally inhabited by animals who roamed free, but who then became the hunted ones – horse, deer, bison and even elephant. And now, the paths are lined with dogwood, hazel, maple, the odd small oak. Nature abundant does not necessarily mean there is more authenticity, for what was once the playground for animals is now just the odd dog walker far away on the desolate marshes.

In 1813, the Gorleston gale destroyed three sides of the fort's tower, which had been a beacon for ships sailing by. I sensed this is the sort of landscape that would have inspired Turner, where quickly moving intervals of light required rough and furious sketches to capture every alteration. Further on, barely seen from a rough track, but visible through a small grove of trees, I found an old church dedicated to St Fursey (a seventh-century Irish missionary), who founded it in 636. If the illuminators had walked this way ... I dreamt on. These isolated churches may once have been viewed as islands of safety. When grazing lands were created, the church became a central source of strength so that people could survive in communities here. Although, if artists had walked this far, they would have been walking down from an estuary further up at Caistor. There would have been a small island, bearing the weight of division between those in the north land (Norfolk) and those in the south land (Suffolk). During the reign of Edward II, there were ferries for both animals and humans to transport them over the River Yare.

Open paths become woodland paths. But the land, low-lying, still stretches endlessly outwards. Arable field, a quay, a mini harbour or an isolated church, all seemed close, as if within reach. It reminded me of seeing a full moon from the window, and feeling it is graspable, that it could be as little as half a mile away. Another fantasy short-lived.

The sandy path and soil make rivulets like puddles streaked with oil out of the ground that is ridged, so that the sand does not sit flat on the path's surface. A path that felt like I was walking up and down mini sand dunes, and where I soon discovered that the Angles Way is not a well-used path. The landscape is low-lying, gentle, at times desolate, and at times the guardian of ugly view-points. It has marsh, prairie, winding creeks and hollows.

Some might find little beauty in it, but I am drawn to the mystery of fragile land near water. You can also find wheat fields bordered by grassy paths and with more and more banks of wildflowers, presumably left by a farmer to tick off the land regenerative classification that orders how we use the land these days. After enclosed paths, the open horizon gives me a greater sense of how the sea connects this bit of land to another.

Walking for Stories

As I walk, I continue to wonder just why I do. For I surround myself with sights and quests, but also some trepidation. Poets and artists walk to unleash imagination and romance. What came with that, though, was often fear and an imagination that spiralled. 'The Fakenham Ghost' (first published in 1802), written by the so-called labouring class poet Robert Bloomfield (1766–1823), is a ballad based, they say, on fact. It tells the story of the Dame of Fakenham, once walking into a dark copse: 'The lonely footpath, still and dark, / Led over Hill and Dale.' She meets a deer who cleared the way for her, but she was fearful and in spirited haste could not stop, as she felt the presence of something following her. And as it got darker, so she became more frightened. Hearing steps, she turned around but saw nothing. Convincing herself that there was something on the path, no prayer would help, and she thought she heard a 'spirit'. Her thoughts quickened such that she then believed she was sharing the path with a ghost, which then became a monster. Thinking that she needed to ask for forgiveness, she prayed for her sins and arrived at the entrance of the white gate to an estate – but the wicked ghost followed her, even though the gate closed loud against the post. Without much ado, the ghost becomes a goblin and then, as if the reader needs more suspense, her husband and daughter appear. Despite a fearful beating heart, it turns out that 'An Ass's Foal had lost its Dam / Within the spacious park.' Of course, mistaking a donkey for a ghost makes quite a funny story and the poem is short but carries more wit and weight than its balladic brevity suggests.

Bloomfield, born in Honington, not far from Bury St Edmund's in 1766, to a tailor father and a mother who ran a dame school, set his poem in Euston Park where the church of St Genevieve still stands in West Suffolk, close to the Norfolk border. Although it is not framed in this way, the fearful woman seems like somebody who has the restless mind that we might associate more with the Romantic strain of wandering poetry. While the woman's inner thoughts are not central to the mood of the story, this poem is a metaphor for imagination. Her mind is the shadow, the demon, the monster, not the reality. I remember what is written in Jean-Jacques Rousseau's *Confessions* (1790). He observed that it was walking which 'animates and enlivens my ideas', and 'I can scarcely think when I remain still, my body must be in motion to make my mind active.' In the case of the woman of Fakenham though, walking intensifies her emotional and fearful state.

In his collection *Rural Tales, Ballads and Songs* (1803), Bloomfield's poem 'The Miller's Maid' tells the story of a miller who became rich, but whose wife looked out for the poor. One wet night, they hear a voice sounding like a screaming child, who 'begg'd for Mercy at the door'. The miller lets in a girl dripping wet, and, as they give her dry clothes, notices 'weals' and 'blue wounds' on her body. She tells them that having lost her parents, she and her brother were sent to the workhouse. He subsequently went to sea, while she found servant work, but was beaten until she escapes, and the comfort of strangers is her only refuge. Here, the ballad form transcends mere song; its very directness to remember others' plight is the point.

For all the paucity of material facts about the Middle Ages, storytelling thrived, especially in ballads and tales about hardship. Many of these narratives feature characters who endure life's hardships with a spirit of resilience, often undertaking ordinary acts of goodness – such as the simple yet unrecorded action of walking to help others.

St Goderic, another local Norfolk saint, born in Walpole in c.1070, exemplifies this sort of act. He learnt the chapman's way of life by 'wandering' around to sell small items, taking them to villages around his locality. Ambitious or not, he became a big-scale merchant. In his life of the saint, Reginald of Durham tells us that the man, all thick-bearded, with bushy brows and rough skin, spent four years in Lincolnshire, living by his feet. From there, he then went to St Andrews in Scotland and Rome, and later Jerusalem and Santiago de Compostela, ultimately settling in Finchale on the River Wear. He showed his status through the things he had to sell. Having a conscience about giving has longevity and reminds us of the Three Magi who brought their gifts to Christ, born as a pauper in the manger. The Magi may have been in the thoughts of a woman called Katherine, who left her Suffolk manor of Mettingham in January 1337 to spend some weeks at the family residence in Norwich and arranged a daily dole for thirteen paupers to receive herring and bread, from her own stores.[33]

That same sense of giving is stressed in the comfort of the village preacher in later narratives such as Oliver Goldsmith's pastoral, 'The Deserted Village' (1770), a lament to village depopulation, the cause he condemns of woe and suffering. His house is described as dear to his country flock, humble and not unwelcoming:

> More skilled to raise the wretched than to rise.
> His house was known to all the vagrant train,
> He chid their wanderings but relieved their pain;
> The long-remembered beggar was his guest,
> Whose beard descending swept his aged breast…

These lines evoke the ongoing ambivalence between noticing and noting and wishing that the wayfaring poor would not walk and beg. Yet how could they be ignored? Goldsmith, originally from Ireland, had travelled around visiting settlements and communities and saw for himself the effects of society's fragmentation on the individual, partly through enclosure.

If the idea of pilgrimage, the emblematic scallop shell attached to bag or hat, while for some, in part, kneeling some of the way, takes one through life to death and, in Christian terms, hopeful redemption and salvation, so wayfaring, the simple act of walking, marks resilience and survival. These journeys are the hidden histories of the pedestrian, as wayfaring's very movement is elusive. But in both types of journeying, sin is chasing you like a long black leggy shadow not far behind. Where today we might have mapping and tracking apps, charting exactly the number of minutes and steps to get to a place, then backtracking our journey with the number of steps taken, a medieval person had handbooks which showed travellers meeting sinful personifications such as gluttony and luxury. This is manifest in the late medieval account *Pilgrimage of the Life of Man* by Guillaume de Deguileville (English ed., 1426), a kind of journeying for the soul, not dissimilar to *The Pilgrim's Progress*.[34] Such books, primers of moral etiquette, became commonly well-known, once the printers' blocks started to ink and spread the world's words. Pilgrimage equipment is often a staff, a wide-brimmed hat and a satchel. The wayfarer, certainly in the Middle Ages, might have walked only with a staff. A satchel was a way to distinguish the pilgrim from a wayfarer. Accoutrements define you.

Borders in Need

As do borders; we create mental and actual borders to survive. About other people, places, times. It suits us to construct a difference between those in need and those not. There are construction lines of defence everywhere, reminders too of how we shut out the vulnerable, those wanting shelter and support. Borders on land and pathways have been made by humanity over time, pervading our very existence. While those on land and lane have been stirred, ravaged; in gentler weather, whisked, rearranged or tangled, continually reshaped by wind and rain. So much of how we speak and what we think is governed by limits – geographical, political, local, or even by people in transactions over just a small section of land. Garden fences carve out a corner of possession. Sometimes ferociously. Every section matters.

We are always constructing borders. Even about the mud.

When I run, I move in and out of the white sections that mark the road junctions, showing you where you should stop and look. There was a residential road where I grew up whose marking I remember well. It is still there, with a large house on the right, belonging to a family we knew. Whoever was driving would stop the car, to turn right or left, or park outside said house to go to parties. I have absorbed that junction in my memory, without ever knowing why. Yet now, realising that there could be a connection between junctions and poems, I always loved A. A. Milne's 'Lines and Squares' from *When We Were Very Young* (1924). The poem is about a boy who is told to watch for bears and watch his feet and to keep them in squares as a precaution. For the boy thinks that those who tread on the lines will get eaten by the bears. I would notice the lines round the squares demarcating the concrete slabs on the pavement and so would avoid the lines, and then I would use them to try and play hopscotch, or I would make my own squares with chalk outside. I wish I had asked the pavement square painter or the white 'box' painter who must have come periodically with their cans of paint whether those lines they made meant anything to them.

Border Metaphysics

On the other side of the border of mud is the grass. Then the grass makes its own border. Every corner and slice matters; to have that slice of the cake where the icing is never stripped off, or remove the outer edge of the bread, tougher, less inviting than the squidgy bit within. There are borders on pieces of toast, at the edge, between the grain and another grain, borders on pages, the spine, both physical and metaphorical. Perhaps less obviously, bowls create borders with what they contain. The tangle of tomato stalks hanging out of the bowl's rim looks ever more forlorn as a tomato is plucked off. They are breaking borders, as they are carelessly arranged in the bowl. And oblivious that soon they will be discarded to make a new border with bags of rubbish in the bin. Grapes in a bundle are attached to the stalks that curl round and back and under. Look too quickly and they resemble worms. They have no borders but slide in everywhere.

In the early morning, darkness to light creates its own fuzzy border. A gate with a section at the top that contains its own little space frames air and light and makes a transparent finite space. A crack on the road has made a margin between one side and the other. The crack zigzags along as it breaks the straight line of the frontier. Like an unploughed field where the clay fissures in the heat and does not repair. And this line will crack even more as the land lays waste, water-starved, with no crops to lay down. The road's crack is not yet wide enough to fall. The surface is hard just as the clay is hard; it ceases to crumble. Seizures of clay dismantling years of pressure. A branch waving gently in the wind touches the surface of the brick wall of the garage, but only with its flickering shadow. It breaks its border in an illusionary way. The monster machines that emerge as I run past a gate, or a field edge carry on as if they know no borders. They are taller than the tallest hedge, have arms and limbs that stretch, contort, pull and push, and which have towering and agile frontiers. They could pick me up in one fell swoop like an eagle with its prey. Their monstrous power is all over me. The wild garlic leaves I pick collide with each other: they are wider than a quill, but nearly the same height. I could dip them in a stained puddle and then write with them. I could make a sepia soup by crushing twigs and fallen leaves, mix and swirl with a stick, as if I were making marbled paper. Each boundary: above, below, all around, everything has a demarcation, which is also blurry and without true permanence. You might think, too, that really there are no borders at all. For if you look out as far as you can see, you might not see any. Even so if you look again, the bits in-between are not impervious or spacious. Somewhere, something invisible to the naked eye will define them. The sense of a border, where it begins, and ends, is limitless and all at once: you can conjure it with a wand or stick or thought.

My childhood home was approached by a steep drive. When I was a very young child, my brother would walk with me up the drive to the post box at the top where it had been installed. This was to save the postman walking all the way down the drive and back up again; it is the sort of thing my parents suggested as considerate, thoughtful people, always thinking of others. Back then, 'he' was everywhere: in conversations, classrooms, or, on the playing fields of the media and the telling of history. As a girl, I was the 'she'; not told to 'shoosh' more, but I was the girl, so I was quieter by expectation. Brother and sister we were, and we held hands, as my mother would have told him to look after me. I was the baby of the family, the girl, the one that needed protecting. Then he became the one, as he struggled with every aspect of his life. There was always the anticipation in the walk up the drive to the post box, particularly on the day when I got my 'O' level results – but on that morning my father drove me up instead. Later that day, I flew to Crete. I have never forgotten the afternoon heat which hastened sleep after lunch. That sleep was just impossible to resist, as if I had been given some of Titania's eyelid intoxication by Bottom in *A Midsummer Night's Dream*. I doubt if I have ever slept as well since. I was sleepy, too, on happiness for surprising that teacher who had dismal expectations of how I would perform in examination. That was exquisite intoxication as well.

Imaginative Surviving

In the heat of Italy, where I lived with my children for a while, we would walk barefoot. In early January when the Italians were walking along the Ligurian seashore promenade in boots and fur coats, we had the sand to walk through. *Gli Inglese* wearing no shoes was a source of shock and disdain, which was verbally expressed to me one day when the children were playing at home in the garden with no shoes on. There were insects with poison and oozing dangerous secretions to tread on and sting, alongside the snakes and the boars in the wood adjacent to the garden. I must have been deemed an irresponsible mother. I wanted my children to know freedom. Danger, too, maybe. Just for a while. And so, I think it worked, as only recently one of my sons told me that he now looks back on that time as one of 'enchantment.'

We see how things survive the laws of probability, and I must have subconsciously weighed these factors up, as my children grew up. We survive our mental roving as well. When the flowers thrive despite the polluting particles of speeding cars at the road's border; when the sound of a phone is mistaken for a moaning bird in the sky; when a voice that I think I hear is a cry of laughter or a scream for help; or the mobile phone on the train that I think is ringing for me. When the grinding sound of a farm machine groans once, twice, a third time; a pause, then repeats; when the sky looks like a large uninviting shroud, unable to fold itself. A grey horizon line with grey boulders of metal, steel, and cranes reaching upwards into the sky. Flecked with red, there are large white ships bright against the sky. The shore's edge is surrounded with the detritus of humanity. We can walk in gloopy white froth, not water these days. We glide and slurp in oil, rather than through a wave. Like walruses in a heap on the shore, amorphous and heavy with bursting weight, we continue to overstep.

Humanity has long shown awareness of the path as a metaphor for fracture. It can be invoked as the place for tread and track, destiny and wandering, but scuffed with difficulty. Poets can sound quite sick with the thought of beauty and seeing something as they walked. While what has become known as 'the thisness' is the thing of interest, the going on the path often becomes a metaphor for a longing, intangible though it is. In 'The Saw-Mill', the Irish poet James Clarence Mangan (1803–1849) starts: 'My path lay towards the Mourne again; / But I stopped to rest by the hillside'. He looks on the water and saw-mill churning and 'humming', lulling him into a reverie, but which then became a matter for his discontent. The poet addresses the abstract, anonymous wanderer to reflect on his changed mood, until the end when his destiny is the going 'yonder dark vale!'

Seeing something unusual or out of place prompts reflection on your circumstances, which can then vanish when you see something else. But then those thoughts, with equal rapidity, return. This often-inexplicable feeling is found in Wordsworth's 'Resolution and Independence' (1802). The poet's words are capricious with fluctuations: rain becoming sun, night becoming day and while a hare runs, 'I was a Traveller then upon the moor' which helped the poet forget his sadness. Yet in the last stanza, he illustrates the chasm between happiness and dejection where the latter, unbid and ineluctable, brings feelings too that he cannot name.. So rhapsodic joy in travelling can be harshly modulated like a major chord in swift dissonating freefall. Relentless walking on cleared ground with no path in sight hollows out the heart. Twentieth-century poems evoke the many difficulties encountered on roads and hostile land.

In Alan Jackson's 'The Grim Wayfarer' (1969), the heart of soldiering man is used to signify our mortal transience: 'A low wind rose and tuffied their ankles and fluttered their rags so that from a distance they looked like a line of trees bending into the wind.' Conversation comes, not from other men, but from a tree which says, 'You are the grim wayfarer. You are no man's nothing.' At this point, the tree has the final laugh, despite the agony of the men in combat. Other images evoke a bent, creaking, shrinking body. Towards the end, in the spirit of a fairy tale where a knight or damsel is tested, a baby appears from a flash of light, Moses-like, and the narrator is asked to take the child. 'Sing and walk light', another imperative. If you walk to survive, what else can you do, but hope for light?

Today, I walked on marinas, staithes (landing places), quays, harbours, staging posts, walkways, fields, paths. All gave me a structure, but all I did was conjure them in my mind them as potential hazards. The best thing I can do is think of the quality of the surface upon which I walk – whether it is cold, or dry, or wet, or even hot. And think about what is further beneath the surface and consider the rock. It is sandy, of sandstones and clays and a distinctive building stone known as Carstone. At Great Yarmouth, buried beneath glacial deposits 180 metres down, is a stratum known as Crag. While I walked on surfaces – dusty, muddy, pot-holed and ravaged – I tried to think about whether I could be walking over an invisible footprint made by an anonymous ancestor. Despite years and centuries of modification, relayering and shifting of the land's surface, it is possible that a tiny scar or groove or mark is left untouched. The dramatic changes of roads over millennia must have left some infinitesimal small smudge of something. Squashing the earth with feet. What is beneath now, might have been there then. A tiny eroding stone, shredding sediment of chalk or clay, the tiny grain of sand that moved miles along, returning. One could be sentimental about sharing the same shifting ground. How does one track foot marks? How can I see a foot mark fossil? And would the Romans have thought about the itinerant smiths of the Bronze Age who integrated field and track as they went about carrying their ore and tools?

Most things change and change imperceptibly. But you never know. Something may not have changed at all, some microscopic, unrecorded thing.

I Walk On
Returning west, leaving the estuary, the land changes from grazing marsh to scrubby heathland and a landscape, that was once marked by manors, their lands and the habitual parish church. Along the way were churches in de Warenne 'hundreds' with fresco cycles of *The Seven Works of Mercy* in the family's holdings – remnants are still found at Moulton St Mary, Edingthorpe, Potter Heigham and Wickhampton, churches which are not on the usual Norfolk list of

'Churches you must see before you die.' Oh, thank you, I say to myself.

So sodden and waterlogged was the land, so often under water were the crops in the fourteenth century, that to walk in wet meadows and paths must have been like further torment from a wrathful God.

I ended up at Thetford's Holy Sepulchre Priory (founded by William III de Warenne, c.1139). Something of its structure still stands, a place for wayfarers to congregate and shelter. From November to March each year, three people were looked after, with the order that they should receive nightly 'a loaf of good rye bread and a herring or two eggs', and 'provide three beds and hot water for washing.' I noticed something with my untrusting eyes, left there on the ground: stale bread thrown out, soggy mulch from the pot, carrot scrapings, or were they tiny bones left from a corpse? Even by the eleventh century, Thetford was a fancy place for merchants to meet and people made things there too – cloth pots, metal goods, coins and then walls, lots of them – as defence, for castle, ramparts, arches, doors and ecclesiastical barriers. Norfolk Castle Acre Priory, also founded by William de Warenne (c.1070), whom I have already discussed, was then inherited by his son, another William, when in 1090 the site was given to the monks. It is reported that in 1351 some of the monks at Castle Acre had 'spurned the habits of their order and were vagabonds in England in secular habit'. One of these miscreants was named as the prior William de Warenne, half-brother of Earl John. They had successfully bought their arms, and indeed the arms of the de Warenne with those of the Fitzalan family who were later conjoined with the Warennes can be seen on the north face gatehouse entrance at Castle Acre Priory. For at the death of the seventh earl of Warenne, the property passed down to his sister Alice's son, Richard Fitzalan (1313–76), deemed a better bet to secure the lineage than leaving it to one of his (many) 'illegitimate' sons. What mattered for families struggling to survive through dynastic knots and ties was to ward off being thrown asunder by bonds that could come unstuck. The de Warenne family knew all too well that a dynasty's survival had to be shielded against the odds; sometimes joining to another family was the only thing to do.

The base line of survival for the homeless is fragile, less is protected and nourished, and often the only way is to move on. Religious shelters may have given wayfarers a semblance of stability, but these were merely temporary fixes, much like my voyeuristic imaginings of their plight. I found myself admiring those who built monastic institutions, thinking about all religious and domestic needs – from the church and cloister to the refectory, the dormitory, to the infirmary and the warming house. I could pass through now, as Thetford Priory is a ruin for visitors. With my English Heritage pass, I became a temporary resident and then, after a while, I began to think about going elsewhere.

FIVE

WAYFARING WORKS 5:
TENDING THE SICK

We ar men of pes, sekyng auowery,
Wey-farende men at wolde haue gryp,
We ask e leue to speke þwyp…
Robert Manning of Brunne,
Chronicles and Memorials of Great Britain and Ireland (1338)

The Brecks: Sand and Track

From Thetford, I stayed a while in an area south of Norwich known as the Brecklands – comprising part heaths (sandy fields), commons, fens, woods and moors (borne of managing that sand). The very large pine trees grown to maintain the sandy ground are not inviting; the heath's colours are often tawny brown; when there is green, it is often prickle. The heaths here contain the rougher features of nature in tracks, gorse and furze. This is not land tended to by tourists. They say that most people going to Norfolk drive right through the Brecks (as it is commonly known) as they go north to the coast; parts of it are glimpsed from the straight road that is the A11 on the stretch from Thetford to Norwich. The Brecklands evoke mixed responses: for those just driving through, it is a kind of sick, afflicted land, dull, oppressive, without attraction and outwitted by what is considered normal for Norfolk elsewhere. The land has been manicured and managed over the centuries. Yet it is no more managed than somewhere like the Yorkshire Dales, where the sheep have done their own managing. Still, you do not visit the Brecks for hills. But you might like to go there to drift.

Even so, in Caldecote, north of Oxborough, there was once a shelter for wayfarers and animals.[35] So this implies common land settlement, or a place to return, where wayfarers might have been alongside the sweating, sulphurous bulk of the warm-skinned animals.

Standing there, out on the open heath, feels somewhat like standing at the porch of a house, waiting for the door to open, when an east wind blows and assaults one's bare legs instead. Indeed, wind is a feature in *Lavengro: The Scholar, The Gipsy, The Priest* (1851), by the Norwich-born, George Borrow (born 1803 in East Dereham in Norfolk – died Lowestoft, 1881, penniless and unknown), which is an account of tramping life. In the book he refers to the wind on the heath. And one Jasper Petulengro says: 'If I could only feel that, I would gladly live for ever.'

Pines and Purples

Tall Scots pine, deciduous trees less visible, open ground, but few paths, bushes but few hedgerows, cars, but few people. Vole, partridge, hare, rabbit. You think about retreating but something impels you not to. You can stand on bumpy, scarred, sandy or uneven ground without wondering what direction to take. For this is not land that has been augmented with footpaths, field edges and hedges to single out communities and their arable land. As Brecklands expert W. G. Clarke wrote, 'the magnitude of the outlook makes man feel his insignificance.' As an exclamation, what a timely reminder that we have over-stepped the mark with our own sense of importance. In the Brecks, you are reminded of that.

Even so, when the sun shines, you can take your shoes off and imagine you are walking on a beach and on land untouched by humanity, even though that is not true. Sand, desert-like, in the eye and hair, was in fact hugely problematic for this territory. There is less sand here now because trees were planted to suppress what were once described as 'travelling sands', which often formed sand dunes. The planting of pines from the nineteenth century, particularly by landowners, was intended to give structure and solidity. Still, some sand remains. It travels while you stumble. It shifts with your step and weight; there is little differentiation between the sand and the sandy path. As John Evelyn (1620–1706), the seventeenth-century diarist and woodsman wrote, 'this land makes you roll from place to place. So bad were the sands that the Little River Ouse was blocked. And in all of this, it is harder to leave a trace of yourself.' The sand on the paths is broken up by a tuft there, a clump of grass here, a tiny mound, but mostly it is not hard to imagine sinking through it. In the deeper sand, though, there is chalk and flint. I am walking in a large sand-pit and in a place lacking essential beauty. I have returned from time to time. That which has no draw, draws me back. Where there is evidence of people in the surrounding areas, there are the sickened and worn shreds of what we make ugly – the edges of billboards and signs, boards for Paintball or combat centres, signs on houses doubling up as fish and chip stores, shops on the edges of things, wound-up cloth lying on the pavement winding-sheet-like, buildings that look as though they have just ended up there by accident, yet persist in surviving.

Gates mark thresholds between sandy heath and woodland verge. And woodland verge fades into water. Without clear markers, you can lose your way; the ponds and the River Ouse are almost invisible in high summer, obscured by foliage. The water is kept in check by water-loving plants all around: rush, marsh woundwort, waterdock, and high comfrey. Sometimes, the water is bordered by pines, an incongruous juxtaposition. Sometimes the pines and firs are almost bent double like a leaping fawn whose legs are airborne, a feature I have seen before, somewhere like Canada. I understand this can be the result of trees growing towards the light, or a traumatic reaction to being cut, or becoming sick, from bad weather hitting the part that we now see is bent. Although you might not think it, as the woodland is plentiful and thick, stretching across from A road to A road, skirting round RAF barracks and stopping short of a town or two. You can drive on roads surrounded by woods for a long way, with no horizon to comfort you. If it wasn't for the roads, this land would seem without definition. In 1698, the traveller Celia Fiennes noted in her travel diary around Britain:

Thence I went to Windham a Little market town 5 miles, mostly on a Causey ye Country being Low and moorish, and ye road on ye Causey was in many places full of holes tho' its secured by a barr at which passengers pay a penny a horse to the mending ye way, for all about is not to be Rode on Unless its a very dry summer…

The openness here gives us some idea of what non-forested land looked like before barriered land. Heathland was a vital landscape for sheep and rabbits, before corn and wheat made people rich. The forbidding plant-life inhibits grazing but also provides some sort of shelter. Much of the land has been uprooted and disturbed by hares and rabbits and by planting and felling over time. However, in the Bronze and Iron Ages, there would have been long trackways connecting place to place. The Icknield Way, for example, was a conduit between Norfolk and the south-west of England, but perhaps surprisingly, the Romans did not use it.

There is more to look at here than one might first suppose. A variety of flowers flourish on the heathland. There are plants specific to the area such as Spanish catchfly, which seems to like the dry and sandy conditions. There are various types of campion on the paths and on the 'forest rides', the poppy gently sways in the sandy wind. On the banks, purple heather blooms, and the spiky speedwell, violet when flowering, marks the passing of time and is, so they tell me, special to the area. Viper's bugloss is another purple-hued flower, alongside forget-me-not, field wood rush, blue common bugloss, purple hound's tongue …

each distinguishing heath from forest and land as early summer unfolds. Another purple flower peculiar to the Brecks is the grape hyacinth, a contrast to all that sand and dark green. The Brecks might also feel like a place where you want a kind of covering, as a refuge from a stark landscape.

In pre-enclosure time, those seen suspiciously walking about were often labelled as 'outlaws of the heaths'. Cast outside the bounds of law, they were considered almost like animals, and, under a sentence of banishment, forced to roam as exiles. Often they lived in forest, moor or mountain and were known to help the unfortunate. They lived precariously, purportedly robbing churches, loitering around monasteries, while hoping for food or care. Described as wearing mantles or hoods to keep them warm, their mobile houses, their only garment, which was also their livelihood. In *A View of the Present State of Ireland, a Dialogue between Eudoxus and Irenius* (1596) by Edmund Spenser, Irenius (a New England settler who has returned to Ireland), says the mantle is:

> a fit house for an outlaw, a meet bed for a rebel and an apt cloak for a thief. The outlaw, being for his many crimes and villanies banished from the towns and houses of honest men and wandering in waste places far from the danger of the law, maketh his mantle his house, and under it covereth himself from the wrath of heaven, from

the offense of the earth and from the sight of men: when it raineth it is his pentise (shelter), when it bloweth, it is his tent, when it freezeth, it is his tabernacle (tent). And when all is done, he can in his mantle pass through any town or company, being close-hooded over his head as he useth from knowledge of any to whom he is endangered.

Turning in at the Brecks is to sense a strange, almost prelapsarian, amorphous blend of wood and open heath, tuft and bump, branch, bracken and heather and track, where wild animals once roamed. Amidst these remnants of the past, one ancient feature stands out: for this is the land of the pingo ponds. Sunken ponds, relics of the Ice Age, formed when melting permafrost (frozen ground beneath the surface) created small lakes above, at first as 'ice lenses', then as the water settled and the ice melted, the pingo ponds took shape, creating little hills or 'pingos', and at times covered by shifting soil. They are fascinating and are still visible in the Brecks. Sometimes, they are seen in people's back gardens, and sometimes up to five all close together.

Narrating the Brecks
Virginia Woolf, the writer we associate with the Sussex Downs, once spent time in the Brecks. Staying at the sixteenth-century moated Blo'Norton Hall, between East Harling and Thetford with her sister Vanessa in 1906, she wrote to Violet Dickinson on 4 August: 'Nessa paints windmills in the afternoon and I tramp the country for miles with a map; leap ditches, scale walls and desecrate

churches.' Touchstones for what she sees and does. Pre-sumably, the vandalism is a figure of speech to emphasise her exhilaration in exploring the fabric and contents of a church with meticulous attention. The house, we learn, is a façade of red brick, pink plaster, quirky chimneys, thickly embedded and 'layered' inside – wood panelling and patches of stained glass here and there; the sort of interior where Woolf would have found a richly inspirational presence for her writing. The house also has two staircas-es, and we can just imagine her laughing with her sister about which one to take at night. The hall of the house was the inspiration for a short story called 'The Journal of Mistress Joan Martyn', about a woman who discovers a manor house and decides to investigate its history and the people who lived there. And when back in London, re-flecting on her time there, Woolf said: 'Often I shall think of Thetford and wonder if it is still alive.' The Brecks does feel a frail land and is not generally what visitors want out of a landscape. Whatever it is they think they want, so far as I see, people do not find it in the Brecks.

In addition to writers who did visit, the Brecks was an inspiration for those who moved and lived there. Mary E. Mann (1848–1929), a novelist, born in Norwich and buried at Shropham, captured the essence of Norfolk dialect in a series of stories called *The Fields of Dulditch* (1902). Her voice, however, is not that of celebration, but rather hardship, the daily striving to survive. Mann's stories depict working women, drunkenness, debt, desertion, brawls, fines, petty crimes, cheerless cottages and the anguished sounds of the local poor. Among her

characters are Our Mary, Queenie, Brome, Depper, old
'Granfer' and Mrs Littleproud, and girls with beautiful
hair. Alongside the characters are the grim descriptions of
dirty hands, misery, hunger, abuse, dead babies, the over-
whelmingly huge number of children, – and all sourced
from Mann's community. She writes of the local black-
smith, the doctor's widow having to rely on charity and
Penelope Bye, murdered by a 'gentleman' with whom she
had had an affair. There is the grocer's wife, left penniless
by her husband's death, and Cyprian Every, the local vicar
who did not think he had to convert anyone, resolute in
his misplaced wisdom that the dignity of the Church of
England was 'to do nothing'!

In *Ben Pitcher's Elly*, the protagonist Elly tries to escape
from her violent husband, burdened with the task of
feeding her many children. Rabbits look at her from furze
bushes, and she wonders if their lot is better than hers;
her face is disfigured with a swollen lip and bruised cheek
and she is hungry, with a whining child on her lap. Many
men in her life had 'knocked' Elly about. The story begins
with an account of her beauty, 'her hair as golden as sunlit
corn, skin like roses, eyes like a May-day sky.' This is Elly,
the daughter of an objectionable, oppressive father – Ben
Pitcher. She wears a coarse brown apron extending down
from her neck to her heels. But she is weighed down by
two babies as well as younger siblings at breast and feet and
dreads the wrath of her father. He hardly has any money,
but he needs a shilling a week for tobacco and beer. There
is need for meat daily, as well as renewing shoe leather for
eleven people. For this is the plight of a father, mother,

eight children and Elly, who are all sharing one bedroom. How do they survive? Only through denial and getting 'inter' debt, so the reader is told.

Elly's parents decide she needs to go into service. Elly cries: 'I sholl miss the baby and my little brawthers,' for which lament, the father unlocks his brutal trouser strap. She goes to Runwich to work at a public house there; but escapes as she was being treated so badly. Upon her return, her father asks her if she has been a bad hussy and Elly says yes, even though it is not obvious that any misdemeanours occurred. The strap, again. Her mother tries to intervene, but to no avail. Elly is rendered unconscious and ordered not to be there when he returns. So, Elly goes to the workhouse, a place regarded then as 'living hell' as 'we should loathe and dread the devil.' A mere three weeks later, carrying her baby along the road, she goes back home. Some time later, she goes out again, only to return, this time as a travelling pedlar with tins and skewers to sell, as well as saucepans, all of which she has stolen. She says that she has been mistreated by the man who owned the caravan where she stayed. She goes back and finds her baby has died. Subsequently she is imprisoned. Elly is a tragic figure, who may have been based on a Brecks local, known to Mann herself. Elly's enforced comings and goings, not out of wish but hardship, encapsulate many a wayfarer's similar travails.

Rabbits, in Sickness and in Health
I tried to find a path. Yet the Brecks is not somewhere to go if you like plotting a route. With a gentle sensation,

the tip of my left shoe touched a tiny speck of earth, like the whisper of a wispy plant stirred by the wind brushing into an exposed ankle; or the first felt flutter of my baby moving in my womb, tickling the lining, as he wallowed in the warm liquid cocooned within my flesh. Like a drop in the sea, has this earthly speck travelled over centuries only to return? Has it been touched, too, by a rabbit or warrener in the land where they roamed? The rabbit ravenous; the warrener insatiable for daily kills. Yet spotting these creatures now, is like wandering through a museum with big empty rooms, the objects completely disappeared. All that remains are the display cases.

Humans have not tended to the rabbits in their sickness. Quite the opposite; farmers have purposefully culled them in recent years to restrain rampant breeding, and curtail Myxomatosis, which is usually fatal to European rabbits. It spreads through a virus that can jump species, that was intentionally introduced in countries like Australia, France and the United Kingdom to control rabbit populations. Rabbits become unwell with scratches, swelling, and skin lesions, causing painful welts and scarring, nodules and depleted areas of fur. And they usually die within ten days.

The OS map shows the location of many 'warrens', where rabbits were bred for hunting, redolent of a time when the area was teeming with the species before disease took over. There is Lakenheath Warren, Thetford Warren, Wangford Warren and Elveden Warren, converging on parts of woodland marked with red flags, supporting danger areas where walkers are not allowed to go. But the military are. Driving along, a sign says (no, not hedgehogs, or for that matter rabbits) – 'soldiers crossing.' I did not see one soldier. I did not see anybody.

The predilection for rabbit fur and meat dates back to the Norman period, and it continued well into later centuries. There are records of rabbit theft from the nineteenth century when the punishment for stealing one could mean solitary confinement or community service. After warrening declined as a thriving Brecklands industry, the area was divvied up, planted and barricaded. And so were the rabbits. By the eighteenth century, as many as 20,000 were culled annually. They were there once, in military style abundance – those rabbits. This is also evident in medieval manuscripts, such as in the Book of Hours, (*The Ghent Book of Hours*, Cambridge, Trinity Library, fol. 23v, 14th century, Plate 5). The presence of numerous rabbits is hardly surprising, as they do not really do solitary living.

Warrens and de Warenne

By the fourteenth century, the Warennes, recognised for their stewardship of land, were given control of more and more of the land 'hundreds'. With this expansion came not only priories, castles and houses, but also those warrens, the cultivation of which was another skill and source of revenue brought over from France. The East Anglian roads northwards where the de Warenne family had land were, luckily, navigable. Routes connected Cambridge to Thetford and Norwich, and from Norwich a road extended to Great Yarmouth, while the River Yare, accessed at Gorleston, ran east to Norwich. Produce was carried on high-sided boats: corn, wool, minerals, hope, expectation, and general busyness. The Warennes had found roads paved with gold.

In Norfolk alone, there were 10,000 acres of warren land in thirty-five parishes. The well-known Thetford Warren was eight miles long and consisted of three thousand acres. In *An Essay towards a Topographical history of the County of Norfolk, containing a description of Towns, Villages and Hamlets* (London, 1808), Francis Blomefield wrote: 'In the 14th of Edward I, John Earl Warren and Surrey was Lord and claimed free warren', a significant privilege then for exclusive hunting rights. I have not misquoted 'warren' for the family name, by the way. On their lord-held, lofty land, these men bred rabbits for meat and fur, and the dry and sandy Breckland habitat was best, here was home. The Warennes were given the so-called 'free' warren of Methwold alongside Thetford, Tunstead and Gimingham, and associations were forged between their holdings in Norfolk and Sussex; the church of All Saints in Gimingham for example was granted to the priory of Lewes. In 1340, it was reported that a hundred acres of arable land had been destroyed by rabbits 'of the Lord, Earl Warenne', at Ovingdean.[36] The family may have also owned Meeching Warren near Newhaven in the fifteenth century. Through land, priory, rabbit and warren, the Warennes maintained their grip. This lucrative business of rabbit warrens provided fur for the elite trimmings of coats and capes. The meat, too, was brought to the lord's table, both the flesh and skin. Rabbits provided in other ways too. They became an amusing, even flirtatious diversion for the illuminators, who, perhaps tired of serious prayerful illustrations, scattered them on some of their manuscript pages. In *The Gorleston Psalter*, we see the de Warenne coat of arms often on the same folio as rabbits. Together they might celebrate male vigour, or even masculinity. So, it is hardly surprising to see rabbits juxtaposed with lineage in *The Gorleston Psalter* (fol. 132v, Plate 6). However, the *raison d'etre* for these wriggling eared creatures in the illuminated Psalter does not always stem from the rabbits themselves, or indeed, the family who owned the book. The images serve to transform the Psalter into a picture book, or a form of mnemonics, or visual aids for those having to remember the words of the *Psalms – Psalm* 104: 18 for instance states, 'The high hills are a refuge for the wild goats, and the rocks for the conies.'

But while the rabbits were restless, skittish, and in boundless fertility burrowing down into the soft, brown and root-laced soil at the day's close, the male members of the de Warenne household rode out on horseback: strident and bold. They hunted with hawkish enthusiasm, plundering the land with vigour and determination.

I travelled to a village called Weeting in a remote part of the Brecks. It was mid-morning, and mothers were picking their children up from school. The village has devised a little circular heritage trail, which is signed on the green. It soon peters out, though, despite the sign's reassurance that the route is marked all the way. I consulted the OS map, which is largely dominated by the Breckland

forest including a marked Pilgrim's Path, once the route
to Walsingham for the shrine of the Virgin Mary. In his
guide to Norfolk, Robert Blomefield wrote 'that north of
the town (Weting) is a greenway called Walsingham Way
… a Madonna of such repute that the Galaxia or Milky
Way was called by people of these parts the Walsingham
Way as pointing to that angle…'

I took an unmade road towards the ruined castle, located
near the village church, once inhabited by a tenant of the
de Warenne family. The castle, once moated, now has only
a dirty ditch nearby, along with a few blocks of stone, the
last remains of the estate house. In the forest, dew had
collected on plants, the odd foxglove too, with insects
flying from one sunlit leaf to another. On the outskirts,
I encountered a pig farm, which I was advised to skirt,
either to avoid disturbing them, or to avoid germ contam-
ination. Into the silence and loneliness I went. I walked
with caution and questioning again, as I do, why I was
here. I sensed that I would not see anybody on this walk.

I was held up by quite a few diversions – this time, an
arable field, but also a covert (there are lots of these animal
shelters marked on the map). I ended up in thick plan-
tation forest, the towering trees like overpowering gods
raining fury and vapour down on the woodland mortals.
The dew continued to collect on leaves on the path edge,
not yet worn off by the sun. Delicate puddles, small
enough for fairies, were made in the middle of a plant like
silvery filaments of thread. I ducked southwards, but too
soon, merging with one of those A roads. The verge was so
overgrown by weeds and grass that I struggled to find my

footing. My walk from Weeting, severed. And at regular intervals the verge was channelled, so I was in danger of tripping and falling onto the road. The odd foxglove marked the way. I read that this walk would immerse me in an enormous amount of biodiversity, the most in England so they say. So, I was not expecting to be in a forest seldom walked, which is also bisected by a busy Brecklands road. After at least an hour of most unpleasant trudging, I found my way back to the village, passing a petrol station with an overly spacious forecourt, also serving as the village shop. A man smiled at me from his car; I think he could tell I was a stranger in these parts. Poppies and yellow flowers grew around gates that were barely visible through the hedge and late summer growth; things survive on their own here.

As I stayed close to the verge, my walk interrupted, I mused on how rabbits are often visible in or near hedgerows bordering field or path, never too far from a hole for home. The rabbit is more of an ambler than a wayfarer, although there are striking similarities between them. They can be rootless and fearful, quick or slow moving, hovering between things, and have long been met with an equal measure of both hatred and intrigue. Perhaps the main difference is that a rabbit can build a permanent home for themselves, making them self-sufficient and self-reliant. As the nineteenth-century poultry expert Bonington Moubray observed, a rabbit 'travels, tinker-like, from place to place, and is, like those wandering smiths, usually but ill-clad.'[37] And if the anonymous writer who once said: 'They have such lost, degraded souls, no wonder they inhabit holes', could speak to us today, perhaps they could explain whether these words came from affinity or disdain.

Just as wayfarers were deemed a menace, needing food and lodging, when breeding rabbits went into decline, people began to see what a nuisance they could be. Eating, nibbling, breaking off plants, hindering growth and clamouring for nature's diverse attractions. Here was Beatrix Potter's Peter Rabbit *en masse*.

Compare the rabbit to the cat. While one scores highly because it scuttles and bustles and often shows its white bob of a tail as it disappears, the other, because it sits on laps, buzzes and stays soothingly still. They share similarly long back paws, designed for clambering, standing and holding on. Cats can be long, but elegant, sleek but tough. Watching my cat as I do, sleeping most of the day, her paws are arranged as neatly as the lid on a box: her front paws perfectly aligned, or when she is curled up, arranged in a neat little grid. Pictures of rabbits show the same arrangement and neat decorum. Still, the front paws of a rabbit are put to more use than a domestic cat's. Rabbits are put to hard work supporting themselves, using their teeth to gnaw through roots, while their hind legs clear the soil for underground dwelling. Then there are the ears. My cat's ears, shorter than those of a rabbit, prick up when she hears somebody moving in another room, or even outside. Do we admire rabbits from a distance with their intense vision, turned to face the sound that they know might mean danger or something of interest? My cat, though, usually goes back to sleep when she is sure the sound poses no threat. On the rare occasion when I see a rabbit's ears pricked, they continue to hop in the meadows and fields, weighing up the danger. As they can stand upright from day thirteen, it is also likely that if we do spot a rabbit, it is going to be young and frisky.

Historically, rabbits in the Brecks attracted writers who note the aliveness and presence of things. Eighteenth-century travellers like William Gilpin described the Brecklands as a place of blowing sand, rabbits, bracken and bustards, but also said it was 'absolute desert'. In *A Frenchman in England* (1784), F. Rochefoucauld noted the Brecks was 'an arid country full of rabbits ... we saw whole troops of them in broad day light. Only a few patches of scrub broke the skyline.' So, the wind and dust, sand and storms made for precarious living. Debris-laden gusts threatened the rabbits' very livelihoods.

One warren, many interconnecting burrows, and plenty of soil between each, like the thick walls dividing rooms in an ancient house. To each hole, there is a connecting tunnel, one space insulating the other. Rabbits live in large hierarchical groups in these underground burrow systems. Wayfarers might have been envious at the thought of such a habitat, as they unwittingly trampled over warren edges and holes in the search for some kind of shelter. Sometimes, burrow entrances were run over by a horse, so concealing them. Sometimes they were protected by a hedge, bank or wall. That is why dogs were needed for hunting and poaching.

But if you were a common grey, throat-white medieval

rabbit, the warren was the place to be. That is, until aristocratic axes got the better of you. Warrens belonged to special set-aside land for a medieval commodity where all sorts of intricate and unpleasant ways to trap the creatures were employed. Monks also hunted in warrens, as the rabbits provided flesh for their monastic meditating and miracle-telling tables.

From about 1135, warrens were found in estate parks or common pasture. They consisted of high banks of turf topped by vegetation such as furze. Such is soil's malleability, it can be tossed around to make heaps, known as a mound. A pillow mound was a low, flat-topped arrangement, often with a surrounding ditch. The rabbits made good from nature's elements; humans gave it all a vocabulary. Each warren was defined by earthen banks up to two metres high and ten metres wide. The warrens were sometimes near the sea, where hillside locations were good, to help the water drain away. Rabbit burrows were gouged out of what had been untrammelled land. Rather like a modern developer today, drilling ever and ever bigger holes for building. Starting small, the alien families became prosperous from holes and burrows.

The warreners needed a home too. The quite sturdy remains of a warrener's lodge, dating to the fifteenth century, still stands in Thetford Forest. It was a place to sleep after a day of killing, culling and moving rabbits, and a building that served as a sort of watch post. The lodge is approached by a path all sandy with patchy gorse, as well as the common Brecks colour – a purple flowering clump fronting a beech wood. Still, inside, the building reveals its flint-weathered walls and the remains of a fireplace. It once had a thatched roof, and a well in the little courtyard. On the ground floor, racks for drying the rabbit skins would have lined the walls. The tall trees, late developers, show the changing land of the Brecks where wood and heathland converge. Stumps, and sticks for dogs everywhere, small bush-oaks on the ground dispersed with pine leaves, fallen pinecones, light on a blade or two. Bracken, late afternoon light catching it. The bumps of ground uneven from years of hounding over the heat and frost and ice. I walked from the lodge and towards the light at the edge, hear a calling, then, more voices. Falling, rising, disappearing.

A young couple were looking at the information panel and they told me they had walked from Thetford and were fascinated by this building, and I agreed. Similar enthusiasms over one building, one moment, one afternoon. All around the wood, the lodge being the only visible evidence of warrening, so I concluded the wood is evidence of later Breckland management.

Catching Rabbits

Since rabbits were highly prized, the Warennes would have wanted the warrens to be maintained. Hunting was a business that required order and choreography. The scenario is almost like the dance of the animals in a Christmas ballet. Ferrets were sent in, the rabbits netted as they fled from their burrows. Once caught, a quick clobber over the head, a catch and a death. So, you had to know how to trap. It was more complicated than this, though, as the ferrets were pushed down one hole and then another in quick succession, as the process only worked if the rabbits were huddled somewhere in the middle. In Gaston Febus's *Livre de Chasse* (1387–89), the author describes how they can also be flushed by smoke or caught by dogs. There were probably a lot of rabbits in earth-smoothed warrens, giving a reliably rich resource, that is, until humans struck. The warrens were stalked, too, by stoat, fox, weasel, wildcat and polecat, a small-scale threatening territory.

In his book on *British Quadrupeds* (1820), the naturalist and engraver Thomas Bewick wrote that it was the norm for a rabbit to have seven litters consisting of about eight young a year. That sounds like quite a lot, but when your home becomes a target, what chance have you got? Better to breed to be safe than sorry. There was a fair amount of guessing as to how to tackle the rabbit then, but robust words reveal a hunger to conquer them. In *A Compleat Body of Husbandry* by Thomas Hale (four volumes, 1758–59), he said that the rabbit bred as quickly as hog.

Watership Down
Was it the lifestyle of rabbits or seeing them that made Richard Adams (1920–2016), the author of *Watership Down* (1972), give the creatures kindly rather than rapacious attention? He endows them, and indeed us, with names, histories, narratives, knowledge of rabbit lore and land, and characters including Hazel, Fiver and Cowslip, who have clear voices, and with them, a great adventure. As a child, I loved this book, but it did not fully occur to me that Richard Adams was trying to get into the minds and thoughts of rabbits. He lends them so much more than

twitching ears. I was just transfixed by their characters and the sense of them as sapient beings. And he gave them the location of Nuthanger Farm in the county of Hampshire as their home to fight for. Now, as an adult, I see just how movingly Adams personified the rabbits. 'It seemed to Hazel that he would not be needing his body anymore, so he left it lying on the edge of the ditch but stopped for a moment to watch his rabbits and to try to get used to the extraordinary feeling that strength and speed were flowing inexhaustibly out of him into their sleek young bodies and healthy senses.' Or '"You needn't worry about them," said his companion. "They'll be alright – and thousands like them."'

Except they are not all right.

They have to move on to survive.

Only when I recently reread the slip-cased, unusually sized edition I had as a child, with the gently brushed watercolours by John Lawrence, did I realise that Adams writes about the rabbits at times as if they, too, were wayfarers. Not only did I recognise a wayfaring language, but also another distinctive language for the animals them-selves. Bigwig uses the word *hlessil*, applied in the story to describe wanderers, scratchers, vagabonds. It describes a rabbit living without a hole. Just as the wayfarer has been lent appellations for homelessness.

And in the tradition of ancient fables and fairy stories, Adams created a rich rabbit language, for telling tales by the fireside that pass down the generations. It is the power of the narration by the rabbits, and their fear and exhaustion, though, that Adams so persuasively conveys.

There is El-ahrairah, the bigamist king, Frith the God, Fu Inlé the moonrise and Owsla, the group of strong rabbits. Sometimes the imagery suggests they are like humans in danger, longing for comfort in the mist, their dreadfully wet (Dandelion) state and with startled eyes and full of light. So flexible are Adams' rabbits, they can be animal and human simultaneously. They are described in similes: like a cat, neck raised or like a ballerina when alert. So, the reader can decide whether to read the adventures and escapes of the rabbits in fear of their territory as animals or humans. And sometimes the imagery crosses over into anthropomorphism, as if the rabbits contemplate being human. Even the woods and the warrens weave fear into the rabbits' instincts. Their fears and quarrels mesmerised me. And I was gripped by their survival techniques, such as having to leave one home for another. Adams used the language of trouble and hardship, describing Hazel at one point as a ragged wanderer, leader of a gang of vagabonds – but what a hero he is, too. Adams had an innate sense of what makes a good story. Its power lies in how, even to a child, the author evokes not only the rabbit's awareness of nature's moods, but how cunningly they respond to its cadent flow.

As R. M. Lockley wrote in *The Private Life of the Rabbit* (1964): 'In a wild and free state they ... stray sometimes for miles ... wandering until they find a suitable environment.' Wayfarers could not be that specific; they did not have the privilege of finding the ideal location. The medieval wayfarer could not ask for much, but the rabbits, with their well-evolved instincts, did not ask. Hospitality would be nice, but they were good at making their own. They sought, saw and settled. As Adams shows, they are precise and sure, knowing exactly what they need. Unlike humans, as Adams says: 'No human beings, except the courageous and experienced blind, can sense much in a strange place where they cannot see, but with rabbits it is otherwise. For if the ground is too woody, they feel "menaced" by the undergrowth.' They would know when to cross a field safely or not. They would not have liked the Brecks once it had become largely wooded.

The rabbit's association with twitching ears is not a decorative amusement for rabbit watchers. Their heads are all furry, jowly, and whispery in the paintings that illustrate Adams' words. Their heads bolting as they strike into the air; both painter and author catching us out with the briefly glimpsed tactility of the rabbit life. Just enough time for us to say, 'look there's a rabbit.' The sheer energy and exuberance of the animal is caught both in word and in paint.

Another favourite childhood author BB – author of *The Little Grey Men*, alias Denys Watkins-Pitchford (1905–90) – is consequential for me today in a different way. He was also a countryman writer, known for writing and illustrating *The Wayfaring Tree* (1946). And he used his restless state to begin the book: 'In the early spring of the war year (1943) I became restless; like a migratory bird I longed to be away among the meadows and woods of an unknown and uncharted country.' His book is a series of observations and descriptions of encounters in the natural world, where fishing and birding trips help to weave his thoughts, but without much sentimentality. He observes, too, from home, lying in bed listening to the cuckoo, inspecting the sound of a trickling spring from a moss-grown wall, then striding out to see woodland paths, 'bald and fringed with Woodbine packets'. Rather than search for the sublime, he finds enchantment in a path, a riverbank, or corner. Looking for snakes, through marsh, thick underwood and grass, where tangle and sunlight filter, he has an eye for the minutiae of the land. If not a snake, then ants – observing their brilliance at protecting their young, moving their eggs when disturbed. In a series of wandering notes, he writes of the moth hawk, the buzzard, the colours of a bird, the shape and form of others, their flight and speed, the thickness of reeds, willow thickets, corrugated roofed barns, the sedge and goose. Boyhood memories surface of staring deep into a pool to watch the fish, disturbing wasps' nests, passing signal boxes and a barn where he had heard of a groom who had hanged himself. He recalls prickly heat, nettles, and hiding in high weeds that could camouflage him. For him, it was beauty in the turn of a lane, not a perfect sunset, or a crevice and not a changing sky on the horizon. Watching ants protect their eggs with a little help from woodlice, making a pond in his garden – all these things were Edenic, brimming with juiciness and jubilation.

He was unafraid to observe an aspect of nature that today we are rediscovering as important, that is to study things in miniature. And to study the thing, the top or bottom of it, the side, the underneath, the very 'this' of it. It all matters. It all adds up. The everything, the tiny particles – often recorded together, where the marsh marigold blooms, or the peewits breed, where the wild carrots grow on the fenlands, and where you might find the black caterpillars of 'machaon'. By the marsh, riding and path, in the woodland, at brick-works and in open field; all of it mattered. Slugs, earthworms, counting swifts, watching the hawk eagle and searching for wild geese in Norfolk. There are the larvae of caterpillars, the water dock plant with the wide-open spaces of Wicken Fen or the woodlands of the New Forest providing just a backdrop.

BB writes too of the delight the countryman has in possibly chancing on a rabbit in the cool evening. He refers to the activity he calls a 'walk round' as a form of relaxation and has an almost visceral joy in speaking of the infant rabbits as the best. He describes how the sky, on one occasion, was 'salmony', the clouds high and the field still uncut. A sultry evening, where quietly he went, to find some 'lifting heads', imagining the delight ladies would find in their sweetness. 'And they did look cuddlesome I must admit, but the larder was bare, and I thought of fried rabbit legs and bacon.' No nonsense for this countryman, when hunger is at stake, and something is needed for supper. Infrequently, he comments on things that are lost – the old stone milestones: helping the traveller, horseman or tramp to give them a sense of distance. But he says they have sunk from sight, now obscured by moss and ditch weeds. 'The man who rushes by in his car sees nothing of the million grass blades, he cannot realise the bounty, the prodigality of nature ... The tramp is becoming a rarity, so is the pedestrian,' offering another insight into how he mourns the loss of a walking figure, even one that is bound to suffer.

BB also nurtured sad premonitions of the future – the skies will be full (he means the aeroplane), and the countryside will no longer be peaceful. The excitement of the catch – from fishing for the biggest carp to wild fowling and other watery sports that we might hear less about in these, at least superficially kinder, times. He wrote in ways which to our modern sensibilities today would be considered unacceptable. 'Those who know Scotland will know how quickly she changes her moods. She is like a capricious girl, one moment weeping, another radiant and gentle.' We may like *The Little Grey Men*, but we may not like the character who created and possessed them. But that is to judge BB according to our own set of parameters. He was also prophetic, once declaring that he thought in his own lifetime nearly everyone who now possesses a car will own an aeroplane. Sardonic or not, a statement of somewhat embarrassing panache, but of course written in the early years of aviation when the earth may have seemed like a bounteous place for humanity to probe and alter. His writing is a painful disruptor to us today, but his deep understanding of the land is hard to match.

He wrote about how people used the streets in the post-war world where people longed to return to them, rediscovering freedom again. 'They reminded me of birds which have been so long in cages that they are unhappy and dazed when released. They can only hop back into their prisons again.'

The gleam of water, the tinker's ghost, the darkening sky, the sheep pen, but where was the wayfaring tree? I think he used it to denote his restless, travelling stance. He would have known his trees though. The wayfaring tree, *Viburnum lantana* (Plate 7), was often found along waysides and frequently by hedgerows. So, the name, for the wayfarer, who might have seen them as they went.

Delicate brushes, gently washed paper from watery colour extracted to make the oval-shaped leaves and the striking white, flat-topped, scented flowerhead that is the tree in summer. Plants with wayfaring connections. Mugwort, thought to have protected the traveller from fatigue, even sunstroke, wild beasts and evil spirits. But a plant for a home?

Without a home, your body becomes your house. Grayson Perry's figure of the mother is lumbering and laden with the trappings of itinerant life. In his cast-iron, oil paint, string-and-cloth statue, *Our Mother* (2009, Plate 9), she is virtually bald, her eyes closed, cast down, and terse-lipped as she holds satchels, baskets, pots and all she possesses. Her home is her back, and her back the burden of her life.

She even carries a sewing machine, with nowhere to put it. Bound in hessian, a bound-up miniature figure – what looks like a Mummy – hangs alongside, while a pilgrim-like badge decorates the basket. One foot slightly in front of the other, and there is, too, what looks like a parody of a bishop holding a tall lozenge-shaped stick resembling a holy card with a haloed figure in it. With hands held out, not prayerful, but beseeching. Then, most poignantly like a Pietà figure, near her breast, an emaciated nude baby, with mobile phones and a shoe above. The mother is on a little plinth, embodying what Perry calls pilgrims on the road of history. Crafted from iron recalling industrial archaeology, Perry exaggerates the itinerant state, burdening her with a vast number of possessions. In that, a paradox of her materiality. With enough accessories to fill a shop, the mother represents the desert of misfortune and the vapid pursuit of material satisfaction. And yet what is so brilliant about this work is that we do not know or even need to know what the artist's intentions were. Perry created the figure without the religious burden that writers and artists of the Middle Ages were asked to honour, if not in a thinly veiled critique.

As we see, for example, in the medieval writer of the Malvern hills. He is William Langland. In his fourteenth-century satirical poem, *Piers Plowman*, he echoes the Church's message that poverty is an admirable thing:

> Or none sooner saved or surer in their faith
> Than plowmen and pasture-men and poor
> common labourers,
> Shoemakers and shepherds: such ignorant dolts
> Pierce with a Paternoster the place of Heaven.[38]

It is wandering people, those he encountered as he

'walked wide in this world', not those on pilgrimage, who provided the inspiration for his poem. Although they might be searching generally for Divinity's Christian grace, they are primarily bodies, moving through space to become what Langland calls a 'fair field full of folk', and 'human beings of all sorts, the high and the low / Working and wandering as the world requires.'

He is satirical too about the criticisms of those who were just wandering about: 'Then Waster wouldn't work but wandered about, / And no beggar would eat bread that had beans in it.' In truth though, his sympathies probably lay with those 'misshapen', 'old men old and hoary', and 'broken-limbed people / Who take their misery meekly leper-men and others.' These are rare glimpses of the lives lived outside by people removed from the Church's brightly beamed radar. Later, he writes that beggars 'walk wetshod' in winter and 'the poor presses ahead with a pack on his back; / For their works follow them.' People walking for work. Walking for the next day, too, and what that could bring.

In a fifteenth-century illustrated text of the poem (Oxford, Bodleian, MS Douce 104, fol. 51r), one man is pictured in a loosely attired tunic, revealing much flesh on his left leg. Wearing a hood and holding a staff, his arm across his chest, and looking back, in a sorrowful way. He appears at the end of Dame Study's discourse on the abuses of the rich, enhanced by the image of the crying, thirsty and hungry at the portals of a rich person's house. He is, by contrast, battling with the elements.

The open road is also characterised, as if it is another

dynamic character, where forces of both good and evil meet, collide and clash. Sometimes the poet suggests that some believe we are all the same in Heaven – 'I will dress in pilgrim's clothes and travel with you until we find the Truth.' But the poet's voice is also admonitory about bogus wandering hermits and itinerant gospellers without the requisite preaching skills. The poem is a catalogue of weakness, errors and human temptation – with theft, suspicion, and deceit as multitudinous mirrors onto the travails and evils of life. But, in keeping with 'the Seven Works of Mercy' and the Church's teaching, it is also a moralising instruction on educating the rich to look after the poor, in writing, 'Have you shown compassion to the poor when they are forced by sheer need to borrow?' The Church's message is taken out of the arch and the chancel into the field and the street.

Bosch's Wayfarer

That is also the case in a later work of art painted by Hieronymus Bosch called … well, that is the question. What is the title of the painting? The pedlar? The Wayfarer? Everyman? The Pilgrim? The call of the unknowable. The interpretative speculations of the scholars who have written about this painting.

Currently it is known as *The Pedlar* (1516, Rotterdam, Museum Boijmans Van Beuningen, 71 × 70.6 cm, Plate 8), in other contexts, *The Wayfarer*. He, who walks alone and like Perry's *Mother* has some possessions about him. And he is with a dog, who has a mean and menacing look, facing the viewer. By contrast, the man looks behind him.

His colouring, a bit grey, a bit tan and beige, but white too, though not a gleaming white – the same as that of the house, the inn he has just walked past, where people romp and pee, and where a woman bares her breasts. They say the man is fleeing society's undesirables: the people cuddling, the man urinating, the beer barrel and the woman looking out of the window. To find a new path away from the dissolute. A brave one.

A shutter, a bit derelict and broken, and the roof is breaking. But he is only half looking back; we don't know if he has been at the inn, wishes he had, or if he is simply passing by, removing himself from a tempting predicament. Bent and ragged, a man all jowly, unshaven, lean, with bony knees and ankles. He carries the things that might characterise a wayfarer – a long spoon, a travelling basket, a rabbit skin attached and a knife or dagger in a pouch. In his left hand, he holds a hat out, while his right trails a stick that looks a bit like an overgrown golf club. Bosch keeps us guessing and wondering, he might be sore and sick and, no doubt to the irritation of many scholars, we will never know. In some ways like Perry's *Mother*, Bosch's man has no context, allowing the viewer to concentrate on and interpret his plight, without another's filter. Perhaps he is just a man walking. But he is not a sidekick at the edge of the canvas. He is the fullness of the picture. In step, in pace with the viewer's eye, he is soon to go into an uncertain, distant time. Bosch's *Wayfarer* prefigures the modernity of Perry's walking *Mother*.

I think it is fair to say that Bosch died, leaving us to guess about the meaning of most of his works. What a brilliant way to go. That cannot be said of the mortal hopes and fears of the so-called Suffolk itinerant or pedlar poet, known as 'an unfortunate being' – James Chambers (1748–1827). His acrostic poems, threaded with humility, reveal a man whose meekness becomes his very subsistence. In the introduction to the poems, we learn that at times he was in the workhouse, at times surviving in barns or stables, fields or pigsties. So abject was his situation that a Mr Cordy of Worlingworth wrote about his case in *The Ipswich Journal* (1810), asking his readers to watch out for the poet, and answer to his needs. He asks for 'compassion on the suffering wanderer'. And that 'it is astonishing to see such capabilities of mind under the garb of extreme wretchedness.' He adds that he has written many 'fugitive pieces of acrostic poetry':

> James Chambers is my name
> And I am scorned by rich and poor
> Many a weary step I came
> Enduring hardships very sore…[39]

Economy in being becomes the way for him to express economy with the letters of his name. In his fragmented state, he reshapes it through words. He leaves out the 's', but it does appear as the start of 'sore'.

Once ensconced in the workhouse at Soham, in self-referential fashion, in 'The Poetaster' (a poet of inferior means), he writes of what it means to rely on others:

> I have walk'd till I'm weary, and worn out my

clothes
And my stockings are torn as I walk in the dirt,
And some month I have existed without any shirt
My feet they go wet, and my neck takes much
cold.

Of his anguished state, he writes as if he is being treated like a recalcitrant animal in the farmyard; with contempt 'ston'd and 'harness'd bout'. What determination he had, meanwhile, for word making: by day writing in sheds, reading his Bible, having been robbed and insulted by boys, and looking at medicinal plants such as wood betony and what 'cephalic virtues' there were in chasing 'dire disorder from the brain.' Then by night sleeping in wagons, open fields, hedges, barns. His motto though must have kept him going – 'kind heaven will provide.'

It is at strange times of day where needy figures become even more anguished.

In Gerald Maa's 'The Blighted Star Fruit' (2007–08), it is early morning when the strays and vagrants might still be roaming, and where the poetic voice does not distinguish human from dog. 'Hand', 'unclipped nails', 'crude haloes', let forth words to 'a three-legged dog' and 'a one-legged man – wordless sounds'. A sharp light where star fruit is found, imagined and made real. By contrast, a shabby abundance of what is on the ground, where the sun can obscure as much as reveal. The words of the dogs:

The mottled one coiled back like the dog that
badgers

Bosch's wayfarer, bandaged, poor bastard, with his
   gnarled stick,
Not looking at us, but rather caught looking back,
And above his head a doorway – no, the gallows?

   The poem viscerally charts the use and the grubbiness of
hands to feet and the ground of detritus where the human
spirit belongs.

All Those Pedlars
Even though the pedlar is also a wayfarer, he could be
seen as the baddie. In the anonymous ballad 'The Bold
Pedlar and Robin Hood', the pedlar is joshed and ribbed
by Little John and Robin Hood, who urge him to reveal
the contents of his pack:

   There chanced to be a pedlar bold,
   A pedlar bold he chanced to be;
   He rolled his pack all on his back,
   And he came tipping oer the lee,
   Down, a down, a down, a down…

   And when he reveals that he has 'gay green silks' within,
Little John declares that 'it's by my body', and that half
the pack will go to him. The flash of swords is shared till
'blood in streams did flow.'
   Go for tea in the beautifully decorated café, with the
chatter among the tiles and the cake and puffy scones and
the wooden panelling at the Victoria and Albert Museum.
Sit down and take tea while looking at a stained-glass

window of a pedlar. Likewise at the Garden Museum in Lambeth, once a church. Here is a pedlar in a window of commemoration, for he had made his fortune and given a piece of land to the parish.

Walking to make your fortune is also commemorated at Swaffham in Norfolk, in the Church of St Peter and St Paul, with a bench end of the Swaffham Pedlar figure, carved in wood. Hatted, booted, carrying a pack looking more like a mini coffin than a sack, strapped and tied to his back. The story of the Swaffham Pedlar is the man who dreamed of walking to London Bridge. Standing on the bridge, he met a shopkeeper who asked him what he was doing. He said he was waiting for news. It so happened, as it does in all the good stories, that she had a dream the night before of treasure buried under a tree in Swaffham. So, deciding that he had the good news he wanted, he went back and found the treasure under a tree in the churchyard. As it happened, fortunately for him. In the carving, the pedlar, pack on his back, is shown with one foot slightly in front of the other. It may have come from the family pews of one John Chapman. The fifteenth-century *The Black Book*, now in Swaffham Church Library, says he really lived, and that a chapman is a type of pedlar. Here is a chapman who would have 'made it', leaving the rough-sleeping, walking, sickly, vagrants all around. I found a record, a removal order 'from Norwich St Edmund to Swaffham, 3 Jul 1767, for Trundle, Elizabeth, vagrant, removed'.[40] Sometimes, the records give the ages of wandering people. On 3 May 1839, 'Thomas Jones (signs Thomas Butcher) of Northiam', Sussex was an offender as 'being a common vagrant and an idle and disorderly person for that he did ask alms at the back door of the house of Miss Frewen at Northiam and on being refused did use abusive language and swore at her'.[41]

And while the pedlar's lot, on the surface at least, was more stable than just a vagrant wandering without purpose, people who sold things were often deemed suspicious. Thomas Wallentine (or Vallentine) was a 'dealer in ribbons'. His offence (5 Aug 1816) though was 'vagrancy.' His sentence was 'convicted of being a rogue and vagabond and wandering from place to place'.

While we might think of a pedlar as a commercial traveller, with advantage and hope, but who probably knew how to dupe people, that is not how he is portrayed in Wordsworth's 'The Pedlar' (composed February–March 1798):

> Him had I seen the day before, alone
> And in the middle of the public way,
> Standing to rest himself. His eyes were turned
> Towards the setting sun, while, with that staff
> Behind him fixed, he propped a long white pack
> Which crossed his shoulders, wares for maids who
> Live in lonely villages or straggling huts…

He is observed, alone, travelling through woods, the stars' light exposing his state, 'Not from terror free.' His senses quickened to remind him of his youth, where roaming the hills with the sheep he tended made him realise he could roam further away from the Cumbrian hills he wandered in and see the minds of others. Being outside intensifies his existence.

But for Wordsworth, this was living in love with all that is outside, and what was intrinsic to his art. His poetry valued a sort of solitary saunter outside, the main preoccupation and inspiration for his poetry. Seeing other forms of walking, such as that impelled by need, gave him other creative impulses, which included the expressive potential to convey people's travails as well as their emotions. Perhaps rapturous poetry as a vagabonding aesthetic has been exaggerated; after all, most people were still walking out of dire need even in the eighteenth century.

Wordsworth drew inspiration from the reliably giving land in his poems, and as well as viewing nature, he was in search of the truth, not the pastoral, the ideal poets and artists often recreated. In 'The Female Vagrant' (1793), Derwentwater is the backdrop for the story of a woman who goes from riches to rags. It is written in nine-line stanzas, as if the odd last line is a harbinger of what is to come. The girl's father is a fisherman, and she has few cares or sorrows. Books in the house give her lots of pleasure; mint and thyme, peas and roses and lilies grow in the garden, a 'hen's rich nest'; while swans would come to see her. Father and daughter's fortunes change when an avaricious newcomer buying a manor offers gold to the father to knock down the cottage, but since he says no to this proposal, his fishing rights are refused, and they must move anyway. Marrying a weaver, three children on, his loom gives no work, and the family go off to the American Wars of Independence, but they all perish of the plague, except the girl, 'Where looks inhuman dwelt on festering heaps!' and where is witnessed, 'The breathing pestilence that rose like smoke!' Facing her solitary state, she is thrust 'from earthly port to roam'. Hungry, but not daring to knock at doors, on she went. Dizzy with pain and hunger, she is found and taken to hospital. Later she finds some relief: she sees the glow of a fire in the woods. Journeying in the dark, she finds herself unsuited to this sort of life. This was not the life she knew. 'Three years a wanderer'. And years thereafter carrying around the memory of a happy childhood.

In another part of the woods, I met a couple, prepared with walking implements: boots, thick socks, packs, map in laminated sleeve and staffs. Shorts on. Expectation, even a bit of wonder. We exchanged greetings, as they noted I would walk on ahead of them. I asked if they were going on a long hike, as it looked like it! They said, 'oh no, just a loop, but we like to take the flasks anyway.' Wayfaring, I think, must derive from the same root as *ferre*, the Latin for both suffer and ferry. Walking can be synonymous with carrying loads. Ahead, a narrow path had been carved out between two fields leading to the heath. From there, I could see no more – just a shadow made by the two green edges of the path looking as though they meet.

The Brecks will suffer with the sand if the low-lying land of Norfolk succumbs to rising sea levels. The sand will be mud, and the water will get muddier. The sea will make channels mixing weed and root, slurry and froth from outlying industries. Touch will feel slippery, erode, flirt with fingers. It prophesies the future of low-lying land. For now, touching the ground is precious.

The Australian poet Sarah Holland-Batt writes of feeling and touching a textured land in her poem, 'Thalassography' (c.1982), essentially about the fish in the Pacific:

> I have skimmed that muddied slurry,
> felt the nip in the throat
> where the salt in the air is the salt of the coast,
>
> I have tacked where the tide is incomplete:
> no rollers and breakers,
> only an ebb that rocks the wayfarers –

That poignant end dash. That poignant abrupt end to the verse, where again, it is those travelling who will be affected the most.

Later, she writes:

> I have spent half my life in low tide –
> nights where I have not known…

By the end, she sees the movements of the water, the ever-widening waves as the chasm of life. That may divide us all for ever.

We might go back to primordial landscapes where animals roamed freely, where to be naked with the animals did not divide us. Written before we knew the immediate dangers we are facing now, as we come to terms with the way we have treated the land, becoming sicker and sicker, the poem mirrors the feeling of instability with the land, the very thing we have always relied upon, the thing we will be desperate to cling onto when the destructive roars take hold.

The beauty of poetic words is that they can match the sensibilities of a time yet to be. In 'Rugby Chapel' (1867), Matthew Arnold's words speak to an angry sea of change:

> The track, the stream-bed descends
> In the place where the wayfarer once
> Planted his footstep – the spray
> Boils o'er its borders!

We witness a sick and poisoned earth, a vision of storm, dislodged snow, danger and havoc, so poignantly placed in this poetic prophecy. And as the earth drifts, so we are in danger of losing our foothold. And we see this in Bruce Springsteen's lyrics in 'The Wayfarer' (2019), where he personifies a loner who is nomadic and rootless on the streets, while others sleep.

Danger is now the weight of humanity's long relationship with nature and the land. The needy medieval wayfarer stumbling through time and hunger is becoming a universal bewilderment as we all walk on a land that we know we can no longer expect too much of. We might all be wandering aimlessly on rootless ground, spinning in devastation and confusion. No wonder the apes mock and parody us.

Six

Wayfaring Works 6:
Visiting the Prisoner

The wayfaringmen, though fooles, shall not
erre therein.
The Book of Isaiah (35:8)

Picturing the Ape

Apes are often depicted as mock humans in medieval manuscripts. They are also sometimes redolent of the wayfarer. The ape, with trestles on all fours looking like a cripple, carrying a basket, walking with a staff, carrying their young, holding a begging bowl. Images that gently mock the 'lowly' poor. Half beast, on a human boundary. A delight in the in-betweenness of things. The apes are often cheeky: stealing a pedlar's goods, playing with boots, acting like a *jongleur* or fool, wrestling, selling goods like a dodgy pedlar, carrying rabbits in a bag. And apes are frequently shown interacting with others: pulling wheelbarrows, training bears, sitting on a goat or horse backwards. In some instances shown tied or chained.

Figure 9: *The Ghent Psalter*, Oxford, Bodleian Library, MS Douce
5, fol. 74r, c.1320–30, 86 x 63 mm.

These are satirical vignettes, cartoons for an elite audience. A creature that cavorts, squats, jumps and frolics. A creature all lithe and sinewy. A stock-take of apes imitating humans. In depicting them in this way, the illuminators tacitly acknowledged humanity's proximity to apes; uncomfortably so. But in that, we might take the point. They echo us. And we echo them. So, we can be part human, part flesh of 'beast'. And the images might reveal a truth or two about what it is to be human, for it was believed that Barbary apes (those shown in the manuscripts – often with no tail) were unworthy, degenerate humans. And those humans deemed unworthy by the elite could be likened to apes and ostracised like the wayfarer.

In a Flemish Psalter, probably made in Ghent (Oxford, Bodleian Library, MS Douce 5, fol. 74r, c.1320–30, Figure 9), there is a barefooted figure on the folio's edge. He holds a brightly painted orange staff. He walks: one foot in front of the other as if he is headed for the centre of the page. The figure carries a basketed baby, the load of which makes him bend over. He is alongside a path which is a curly blue tendril weaving into the border where the text begins. Being on the edge is not so bad: elegant decoration enfolds the figure. Below him, another figure with an ape face holds up a page of text, maybe something liturgical. Maybe not. But there is nothing certain about such a drollery.

The significance of apes in human guises or clothing, or even in their raw, naked state remains something of a mystery to art historians. While there was a lot of visual joshing by the illuminators, and indeed by woodcarvers, we cannot be sure if this visualising was about moralising behaviour, or images intended for hilarity or derisive distraction. Or perhaps a bit of both? As little drolleries as marginal images, could these be doodles intended to poke fun at the book owner? The ape, at once reviled, but amusing, frolics and flirts on the pages of medieval manuscripts, from Psalters to Books of Hours, where the illuminator delights in the creature's imitative abilities. Often, the ape provides more entertainment than the human figure. In short, we will never know why they are there.

In the medieval Bestiary, the illustrated book of lore about animals domestic and mythical, there are descriptions and characteristics of each animal with an accompanying illustration. They were often copied and illustrated in monastic settings, as possible teaching tools for the clergy. In the book, it is written, 'Animals are known as wild because they are accustomed to freedom by nature and are governed by their own wishes. They wander hither and thither, fancy free, and they go wherever they want to go.' One of the Bestiary's descriptions is of the ape with boot on one foot and one held aloft in his hand. While he might be having fun, the ape is confronted by a hunter, who puts on boots, then takes them off in the animal's presence and then leaves them behind. The creature tries to do the same; after all it is fun to imitate.[42]

As you might have noticed, last chapter's walk was shorter. We are running thin on wayfaring routes and as we have heard so often in recent times, we are running out of road on this earth – in more ways than one. Yet artists have always found visual and virtual ground on which to make art – and in this context, there is the carefully preserved parchment and there is the weather-beaten stone that makes the cathedral arch, vault, or portal. There is, too, observing and imagining. Never ceasing and always reaching beyond. As the apes know us better than we think they do, this chapter walks with the illuminated apes, since they walk too, and who, of course, can be captured on parchment better than in the wild.

Figure 10: *The Ghent Psalter*, Oxford, Bodleian Library, MS Douce 6, fol. 136v, c.1320–30, 87 x 62 mm.

And as you can see in an image from a Psalter (Oxford, Bodleian Library, MS Douce 6, fol. 136v, Figure 10), apes carry humans – often fools who are begging, or who cannot walk. The apes in these vignettes walk and have purpose. One grips his staff with both hands. Alienation and exile were painted in mysterious, cryptic, perplexing ways in the Middle Ages, and the apes seem to have walk-on parts to express some of this. The artists seem to reveal both the distinctiveness of the ape, and their uncanny resemblance to humans in ways the Church would not have sanctioned. There were numerous ways in which to distort and trans-gressively adapt the human shape and form. After all, this fool in the image does not look as though he knows where he is being taken. He also has his back to the immediate destination which is the next page and because he is on the 'verso' page, the 'recto' page is right beside him – if the page is opened out. So, he is ignorant, blind, and looking in the other direction. The pages seem to work against him.

From afar, the ape's foot can appear identical to ours. I remember being struck by Fran Lebowitz in *Pretend It's a City*, who talked about her wanders around New York without wearing shoes. In a manner of speaking, I was not sure how to follow the ape on my travels in search of the wayfarer, apart from doing the same. But I think I might be nervous about the dirt, the gum and the glass on the pavements. Perhaps, if I look down at my feet, that is enough to imagine I have walked alongside the apes. As they do with humans in the manuscripts.

It was not so strange to see apes in art, or even out and about in the Middle Ages. They could be pet animals, and often the chosen one for clerics in Britain where they were taken out on a lead – the ape I mean, not the cleric. Hugh of St Victor (1096–1141) wrote that: 'Even though the ape is a most vile, filthy and detestable animal, the clerics like to keep it in their houses and to display it in their windows, to impress the passing rabble with the glory of their possessions.'

Medieval Animals

Ape remains have been found at Cromer in Norfolk. While animals were hunted and hawked, the medieval countryside and towns were full of oxen, cows, pigs and sheep. Apes too we might assume. Markets such as those held under rights, as for those under the de Warenne family, were places for the gathering of people, as well as collections of wool, linen, corn – and animals. Strict rules, though, were imposed on the movement of animals such as pigs, and, for that matter – humans. Long before the age of enclosure, there were restrictions on the right to roam, despite the *Charter of the Forest* in 1217, which was supposed to make it easier for people to drive swine through woodland without fear of reproval or penalty. Woods reminded people, too, of the wildness of animals such as wolves, their sounds igniting fear. Equally, there was the fear of the animal and their wildness. And then, the 'wild' wayfarer. Yet at the other extreme, some took comfort in the company of animals. Godric of Finchale (c.1067–1170), a chapman-turned-hermit, from Walpole in Norfolk, insisted he preferred the company of wild beasts.

Animals have often been imagined as belonging to another world separate from humanity. Yet in the Middle Ages, they were also seen as unsettlingly familiar. More so than was comfortable. So emphatically did this ring true that moralising fables warned humans not to move around like animals. This correspondence with the qualities and natures of animals brought parodies of humans in word and art, to disassociate from animals. The ambiguous boundary between animals and humanity ensured that people would find ways to divide them more. Animals were metaphorically placed in the pulpit as exemplars in sermons, with fables construed by preachers to endorse a sense of distance between humanity and the animal kingdom. Perhaps to our eyes, to a vulnerable, open-eyed, susceptible humanity, who deferred to the priest and his words. There was a fervour, then, for making folklore and fable, just as God's Creation had erected a hierarchy for all types of creatures. But that alarming likeness between human and beast, and the crossover between them, was a dividing line faint and permeable. And, at times, it was redrawn altogether in keeping with society's edicts and mores. The punishment for the sin of bestiality was going barefoot for the rest of one's life, as wrote Thomas of Cobham (d. 1327) in *Summa Confessorum* – making you closer to the creatures, the source of the crime you were accused of.

Ape Commentary

The tradition of giving imaginative expression to the ape goes further back to the halls and groves of antiquity. The Cercopes, a mythical species of diminutive humans with tails, were turned into apes by Zeus because of their deception to Hercules. Aristotle wrote that the face of an ape is like that of man in many respects: it has similar nostrils, ears and teeth.[43]

Later, Isidore of Seville (c.560–636), an early Christian writer, wrote in his *Etymologiae* of the similarity between humanity and ape, and how it was possible that the animal could be treated as human with a motion and a mind, whether he was flat-nosed or not. He was a character to observe. In her study of the medicinal and scientific properties of plants and animals, *Physica*, Hildegard of Bingen (1098–1179), the writer, visionary, mystic and nun, said that apes were neither man nor beast. The difficulty may have been that classifying involved things being in-between: part human, part one thing, part a beast. And while terminology was created to distinguish one thing from the other, it may also have been a way to hide the fact that people then subconsciously knew what was really going on. When likeness was emphasised as a means of identification, it was framed according to the Creator's decree that 'Man should have dominion over the Beasts.' And so, a way to exert difference had to be found. Furthermore, the ape was often deployed to take on lowly human attributes such as the non-Christian, the sinner, the prankster, the figure who was up to no good. And the wayfarer.

Then, the thirteenth-century writer Bartholomew the

Englishman wrote in *De Proprietatibus Rerum*:

> The ape is simia in Greek and has that name owing to a flattened nose and so we call apes simias for that they are flattened in nose and foul and lined in the face. Or we call them simias and give them that name for likeness of reason, for in many ways, he counterfeit the deeds of men.

The construction of 'men' like apes is vividly expressed here. Apes were also deemed to be sinful, to make them lowly in God's creation. The ensuing creators of these mythic aspersions knew that, by words, the truth could hold. Distancing a creature metamorphoses them into how you want to see them. In *Apes and Ape-Lore in the Middle Ages and the Renaissance* (1952), H. W. Janson wrote that, 'in general terms, the ape / human / bestial is at the same time human / man / bestial.' Classifying animals with man and pitching one species against the other was the natural route to constructing the ape as an unworthy human.

So a kind of tense flirtation was played out that would witness the cunning antics of apes, and other animals such as foxes, with the increasing antagonism to itinerants as villains. Even chapmen, with legitimate commercial peddling roles, came to be seen as no more than vagabonds by the sixteenth century. They were often associated with wayfaring types who just could not be trusted. From the Middle Ages, chapmen were viewed as light of foot, and the equation of such people with certain animals was to orchestrate animosity towards them. While for the artist such representations could be jocular visual distractions.

Figure 11: *Bestiary,* Oxford, Bodleian Library, MS Bodley 764, fol. 16v, 13th century, 298 x 195 mm.

So, to see the wayfarer through the representation of the ape would not have been such a strange thing to do. In the *Bestiary,* such as in an example we see here (Oxford, Bodleian Library, fol. 16v, 13th century), there is a strong moral lesson about maternal protection. This is an account of a mother ape who walks, with her favourite on her front, the other clinging to her back. But since she is beset by hunters with arrows, she must run away. But in her tiredness she drops the loved child while the one borne on her back survives. Their little legs are shown all enveloped and coiled and tangled in her genital area. This heart-rending scene is a moment to impart the vulnerabilities of travelling and the harsh realities of survival, with the underlying cautioning against human neglect and suffering. Such a message was the nature of the Bestiary's instructional ploy.

This text also broke down barriers between humanity and animals, as the animal narratives were really describing human behaviour and offered lessons on how to behave through the allegory of the animal. And like other medieval texts, the Bestiary recognised our similarity to apes. To be an ape was to be slothful, dirty, gluttonous and drunk – all the things a human might be.

A Medieval Cartoon

Another medieval image where human faces look a little bestial is at the bottom of a folio from the thirteenth / fourteenth century manuscript of *The Golden Legend*, a compilation of stories about the saints, in the British Library (Add. MS 11882, fol. 220r, from the Life of St Cecilia, Plate 10). On this folio is a pen drawing of figures walking in a line: an adult, with a baby on their back, and three figures in front, two behind. They have pointed, jagged facial features, some have fool-like pointed hats on and some carry things: the adult a bowl and staff, although the main (man, father?) figure holds a menacing axe, resembling a cooking cleaver. Inscriptions or speech bubbles, written in English, accompany the figures. Each is made to look slightly different; the first figure from the left looks nude. He may even be very hot, as the bubble says, 'They die because of heat.' The right leg is slightly bent to show that he is walking. Behind him, two boys, facing each other, are saying, 'Sire we die for cold.' An image for all weathers and seasons showing that dispossessed wayfarers must always keep moving. To emphasise this, they have gangly bare legs and pointed or arched body movements. The eldest man behind them has stubble, and appears unkempt, like a rag and bone man. He looks ahead, as if to wonder what there is yonder, all at once carrying a bowl, as well as a long staff, while the baby on his back has another sort of vessel tied to their back. Behind father and baby, there is a smaller figure, staff aslant on shoulder with two vessels of some kind and a basket, who says, 'Sire I bear over-heavy' and behind him, a slightly smaller figure, also with staff, leaning on it to walk and a harp, well, a small harp, for a small child. You can hardly miss this doodle, as it is close to the page's edge and you might imagine that a scribe, bored with the laborious task of copying out script, rushed off some figures, where the ruled space for the text had ended.

There is no reason for them to be here, other than that the scribe, whose name was Alanus, looks as though he wanted a distraction, so painted in some figures – maybe some he had seen from the scriptorium window. Like the image of the mother ape and her young, the figures here are seen in profile. Wayfaring parents are protecting their young. They must fear abandonment, but they must be resilient in their rootlessness. Hang on they say, hang on. The audience could see the two creatures, an all in one – offering for our delectation human and ape as lowly characters, easy to class together. Like the mother ape Bestiary picture, the father has children to lose both in front and behind. Linear walking makes it hard to protect all, especially if you cannot carry and see them all at once.

Likeness is All Too Real
Ape and marginal humans are in the shadows but are also shadowing each other. In an 1158 Paris Embassy report by William FitzStephen, sent to Henry II's Chancellor, Thomas Becket, requesting the hand of the French king's daughter for Henry's son, the author speaks of a 'large procession, as well as packs and bags, over two hundred horses, a wagon and on the back of each sumpter-horse, a tailed monkey or "the ape that mocked the human face"'. Meanwhile, in Chaucer's 'The House of Fame' (1379–80), minstrels play outside the place and harpers are there imitating them, 'and countrefete hem as an ape, Or as craft countrefetth kynde.' So, we are poking fun at what we are propagating, that is laughing as we look at ourselves and the ape, replicating gaits, features, and the ability to be mocked. Ape parodying, wayfarers also parodying. Lest we forget, Darwin makes a connection between early man walking about the land as an intermediary figure, with the ape our common ancestor, who also walks upright. But long before Darwin, it seems the connection was written into the medieval consciousness as well.

Knowing deep down how close we were to monkeys and apes (even without any inkling of genetics or DNA to prove it) then, the wonder of it was visible and shaped in religious imagery. In the Wallace Collection in London, at the bottom of a late medieval miniature of the Virgin and Child, is a monkey clad in boots, a short tunic (revealing some of his hairy right back thigh) and a hood. He has his back to the viewer and is depicted standing in a woody vale. He looks back at us, his stick attached to a pack. I like to call him the monkey packman. He has no obvious reference to the Virgin. He is a world apart from the Virgin and Child, but as we now know, he shares up to ninety-three per cent of his DNA with them. Oh, and us.

The visual portrayal of animals causing disruption could be likened to people seen carelessly wandering – a reckless contrast in God's carefully ordered realm. Apes could also 'ape' or mock beggars, duping and tricking them as they went about their 'aping' business. Apes became an imaginative metaphor to show human behaviour. And in his *Natural History*, Pliny the Elder characterises apes as cunning animals, as they put on shoes, and so I think of the wretched state of Vladimir and Estragon, the two principal characters in Samuel Beckett's *Waiting for Godot* (1948–49). Are they reduced to merely imitating apes, as they fumble with boots in their endless waiting? I have read that the word Godot might be slang for boot in French – something like *godillot*. In Act One Estragon says that humans are pretty stupid – in fact just as the apes are. This is a play of limbo. Vladimir and Estragon hope against hope for something to happen beyond their repetitive chat, which in one sense is baffling, as they are acting in a play that relies mainly on dialogue.

It was a strong medieval impulse to express that apes were without reason and, therefore, unworthy. So they were merely beasts. And often evil at that. It was not very difficult for the moral and imaginative compass of the medieval mind to believe that what was seen in the forest was a beastly creature, or even a dirty demon or pulsating devil. Such creatures appeared as decoration – in stone corbels, gutters and misericords in parish churches, to remind people within the fold that there were social outcasts out there and the potential for their own ostracism. In doing this, people were instructed that if they did not act according to the Church, then the Church would act to remove them from God's order.

There was a sense, too, that imitation led you to become the very thing you imitated. And it is not so strange, this connection to animals. In that less sanitary time, animals were present in squares in towns, they were in courtly menageries, they were in people's homes and woven into their stories and imaginations. As Covid plagued and raged, fears arose that our proximity to animals, exacerbated by deforestation, was increasing once again. So, with the susceptibility of picking up the disease, the border of distinction, actual and metaphorical between humans and animals was unwantedly lowered again.

Yet while the makers of art that imitate or mimic use their powerful imagination, the result is often read as a weak defence against how imprisoned we are by our limitations, even if we want to be seen as superior to another species. Take St Christopher, in the Christian tradition, becoming a dog head, made to be less animal-like and more monstrous. Diogenes, the cynic, the ancient hermit, said one should turn one's back on the rat race and obtain autarchy, or self-government, apathy and freedom for happiness. Animals provide such a model. Diogenes also went about clad in a dirty cloak – for all seasons and used it as a blanket to sleep under. He masturbated in public and hurled abuse at passers-by and became known as the heavenly dog, while giving water to the animals to drink. He strove to find ultimate freedom of being.

Walking to the Wire

The strain running through some poetic expressions of walking is that it sets you free from your spiritual or mental imprisonment. Setting yourself free had untoward consequences though. Walking used to characterise a lunatic is observed in the eighteenth-century, Sonnet LXX (1797), from Sussex poet Charlotte Smith's volume, *Elegiac Sonnets* – 'On Being Cautioned Against Walking on an Headland Overlooking the Sea, Because it was Frequented by a Lunatic'. The poem is marked by an affinity with nature, but the sea emerges as a precarious place to walk: 'Is there a solitary wretch who hies / To the tall cliff, with starting pace or slow'. And 'measuring, views with wild and hollow eyes…' and later, 'In moody sadness, on the giddy brink'. The cliff is on the edge, so is the lunatic and their wandering. There are many types of 'brinks' when we walk.

When we move, we are bordered by fences and barbed wire threading through the rural paths. In summer, they are more concealed, but unless we get caught by wire when we crawl underneath or balance on top, and even without the spikes piercing our legs and arms, we can't ignore these infringements on our being. And more land enclosed has brought about an industry in making barriers and separations, prescient for today as well.

In the opening image for their 2016 exhibition – *The Road Less Travelled: Wayfaring and Alchemy, Amateurism and Wanderlust*, Kristen Kreider and James O'Leary photographed a fragment of scrubland on the ground beside the post for a section of wire, which, on the outside, has bits of string tied, hanging off and trailing away. The string softens the power of the fence. But perhaps that is just an illusion. The work makes the fence a site of architectural and political significance, while at the same time focusing on something insignificant. The exhibition's motive was that wayfaring pathways can be made anew by exploring new 'collaborations, processes and experiences'. The imprisoning borders can then break free. They emphasised the word nomadic. So, true connection lies in the exploration of new pathways, which continue to be followed but extended too. For the curators, the path is not A to B, but a journey that continues.

So, art moves on to create journeys, away from restrictions, but also moves apace with agility. In seeking a link with art long gone and art that must renew itself, artists play around with the face, mien, movement and behaviour of humans or animals. Making an expression caught into something long-lasting. Setting is also something to experiment with. In the grey, flecked white and tan cold-to-the-touch stone of Chichester Cathedral's north transept, a large installation called *Shadows of the Wanderer* (2016) by Ana Maria Pacheco brought dystopia inside just for a little while. She explored that closeness to the animals that we cannot get away from. In polychromed lime wood, sanded and stained, carved and painted, she made an assembly of figures, some with only trousers on, standing as if to guard a man carrying a figure on his back. The figures were clothed in birds' feathers and wings, collapsing humanness. The feathered attire came up close to their chins, a black, flecked with brown camouflage that may seem to be a protecting cloak. Their arms and hands were hidden, as were their legs; but their bare feet were visible. Maybe the artist was recalling the medieval statues struck, knocked and, at times, destroyed during the various iconoclastic waves of the early modern reformist period. The faces looked haunted, lost, disengaged. As if stripped of skin, full of anguish. The women had make-up; black disclike eyes made using onyx – some with mouths open as if crying out. Prisoners of their solidity and the space made up of arches and dark passages. In their stony setting, they looked as if they had been forced under a tyrannical lock, not that of the Kingdom of Heaven. And everything about the expressions, their stances, reeked fear, even under the vaults of God's watch, which made you almost feel like a sculpture with them. You were part of their silent, still performance as you walked around them, stood before them, and wondered whether they would go. The figure arrangement reminded me of medieval mystery plays, or a sculpted tableau of the Deposition of Christ, in which the constituent figures could be arranged and rearranged. As a spectator, you could eventually leave Pacheco's figures there, until the display would have been packed up by the artist and taken away. Each figure was once a series of braided, formed chippings, and before that a log. And before that, part of a tree that may also still be standing.

The unheralded fate of trees and wanderers, here now, gone in a flash. The statues, executed from wood to human form, look as though they could be too. Exiled figures to haunt us, like a repetitive dream – and in a space traditionally seen to comfort the needy. This artwork was a provocative stance against that, for if the figures had been placed on the corner of a street, our responses might not have been the same. No ground or space or lofty arch will necessarily protect.

Pacheco was born in Brazil in 1943, but she now lives in England and was the first woman to be Principal of the Norwich School of Art. I suspect she would find nothing curious about humans carrying baby apes on their backs. By the twentieth century, writers had found many ways to write of the untethered, using the meandering flexibility of language. The Dadaist / Surrealist Romanian-born poet Tristan Tzara (1896–1963), threw aside the conventions of word formation to create the seeming inexpressible of alienation and the wayfaring mentality of humanity. In *Approximate Man and Other Writings* (from the French – *L'homme approximatif*, 1931), he explored humanity's quest through torment, in some baffling poetic forms. He was writing at the time when more absurd language and the less understandable in art and word had been achieved. The Dadaist convention was to throw all sense of normality asunder and destroy and build up again, using an entirely different set of systems and structures. The poem uses a wide variety of images, many of which are taken from nature to avow solitary alienation, where nothing is as it seems. He assaults and violates words to create limbo language: 'solitude sole richness hurling you from one wall to the next / in the hut of bones and skin given you for a body', and then, 'freedom solemn torrent may you remove my flesh my barrier'.

Waiting for Godot again. Repeat. Shuffle. Repeat. Repeat, repeat. Estragon and Vladimir walk a bit. Stop. Walk a bit. Do it all over again. This is the sum of the play – Act Two, in part parallels Act One. Are the two men a double? But with variations on a theme. Beckett returning to the anguish of being. One of the most powerful plays of the twentieth century. Hard to say why. Just as *Waiting* is about repeat, I refer again to the play. Deliberate. Motif. Button on repeat. Brief. Raw. Visceral. Walking, waiting, hoping and surviving. Like wayfarers, Vladimir and Estragon walk and wait, hoping for something to get better. But the strength of the play is that we never quite know what they are hoping or waiting for.

Vladimir and Estragon seem to be on some sort of journey, yet they don't get far. They talk as they wait, stand as they look, point to their rags as they banter, limp as they go, sit as they feel pain (lots of that), eat carrots when they can; all the while trying to walk, and speaking in repetitive language. Plodding, then sitting, then standing, then sitting, then going on. Sometimes they get on, sometimes they don't. This is the sum of their play. Their surroundings are bare; we do not really know where they are (the stage setting in the script is a country road, a mound and a tree); and at the end, they talk about going, but we do not know where, other than off the stage. They have a teasing appraisal of who they are. In response to their interlocutor,

Pozzo, the tyrant with his chained slave, Lucky, Vladimir refutes the assumption they are beggars. Tinged with the prick of hardship, but to arouse the audience's curiosity, the figures are somewhere, there, for a while to make a passing drama, only to pass on when the play has ended.

The way Vladimir and Estragon talk is of the bareness and sparsity of things; their speech consists often of just one or two words, short and pithy – the abrupt dialogue of the ordinary. They talk of the ditch, a foot that is swelling, of the 'clap'. And they wonder about what they can do, whether all they look upon is the sum of life and they address the impulse to survive through walking and crawling. Here is the language of the outside, for the outside: foot-pain, ailments and adversity. They talk of basic human activities, as well as the life cycle of despair. And there are simple stage directions to boot, such as when Estragon has to appear, but with his head down. Throughout the play, the two main protagonists wonder if somebody will come, somebody, maybe Godot, maybe even God. There are a few Christian references: God(ot) may be seen as some sort of word pun to do with humanity and the cross, and they ask whether God is seeing them. Estragon conjures up a dream of the Dead Sea, its blue colour and going there for a honeymoon. Is blue for him Heaven? At one point, Vladimir even refers to Estragon going barefoot as if in shock, to which Estragon says that Christ did. As in the medieval Christian instructions, the poor were seen as good, ready to be free of sin and on the path to blessed redemption. There are references too, to the fear of strangers and others, but little is explained.

We love to guess, unpick, try to decode and interpret, but Beckett would have preferred we did not. Well, that is what he said. Do we believe him?

Towards the beginning of the play, Estragon and Vladimir talk about going their separate ways. The road emerges as a powerful theme, generating a sense of movement and progress. Yet the characters return to the same point, they never really move. Estragon says, however, that it would really be a shame if they did, and after a pause adds that they can think about the 'way' and 'wayfarers'. Who he regards as 'good'. We do not know though what he means by wayfarers. The sparsity of their situation is mirrored by the brevity with which they speak and the vagueness of what they talk about. And so, they occupy space, and a bewilderingly empty place. Where do they come from and where do they go?

The characters are strikingly drawn too, with something simple like a hat; bowler hats are worn in some *Waiting* performances. Like a Magritte picture of the man with the hat, more than once. He is depicted as if on repeat. Redolent of subconscious, mother, childhood, trauma. Then again, it might be none of these things. He might just be the man in the hat. All about him is simple. What we might say is that you are able to memorise the image better this way.

In this trophic-centred time, when every week brings newly branded and elaborate packaged wonders, vitamins, potions, liquids or vinegars, we devour these things with a strong gaze towards our healthy futures. Rather than just the simplicity of being. Gazing at wayfaring outcasts, whether for Beckett or the medieval illuminators, is to draw our attention to things we might find easier to ignore. Although these figures survive in Psalters and other manuscripts, the medieval wayfarer was always a marginal figure. Likewise, in *Waiting*, the sparse setting and surrounding is enlivened by these troubled travelling figures, but to those watching them, they are fleeting. For they go, so we can forget, unlike our bodies – which remain with us all the time, however we attend to them, however much we want to wrestle free from what they represent.

Yet alienation, while a common concern in the twentieth century, is far from being a modern phenomenon.

Walking Exile

The Desert Fathers knew exile all too well. Their exiled setting was sand and desert and heat. They courted voluntary exile, and imprisonment of exile, even when towns and cities were not established. In *On the Perfection of Monks,* Damian (11th century) said that Silvester 'wandered about in vagabond fashion to other places' but urged people to stay away from him.[44] Consider, too, the story of Theon, an anchorite near Oxyrhynchus who, 'Used to go out from his cell at night and keep company with wild animals, giving them to drink from the water which he had. Certainly, one could see the tracks of antelopes and wild asses and gazelle and other animals near his hermitage. These creatures delighted him always.'[45]

But the ragged medieval wayfarer, desperate for food, may not have known about the model of the Desert Fathers, or been persuaded by it as something to adopt. He had not repudiated any worldly goods. He was stripped anyway; he was a prisoner of his plight. The ape was freer.

While the idea of exile could be described in slightly wistful ways after the Romantic period, the idea of it as misfortune is still manifest in much of the literature. In Hardy's *Jude the Obscure* (1895), exile for Jude is emphasised by a warm inn where Jude meets Arabella. The scene makes him think of the 'tap-room on a Sunday evening when the setting sun is slanting in, and no liquor is going, and the unfortunate wayfarer finds himself with no other haven of rest.' The sense of going somewhere either to escape or face confrontation becomes something concrete. We see this too in Hardy's little play *The Three Wayfarers* (adapted from his story, 'The Three Strangers' 1883), where a gathering of people is unexpectedly drawn together in the same room. It also provides a snapshot of welcoming a stranger and, for that stranger, the vulnerability in going somewhere, but how that could modify or protect your plight. Timothy Sommers is in trouble and on the run as a condemned sheep stealer. He is taken into a home as a stranger – 'The rain is so heavy, friends, that I ask leave to come in and rest awhile', and is welcomed by the family of a shepherd who is celebrating the Christening of his baby with his wife and a few other revellers and players. Timothy finds a little sanctuary in the chimney corner while those around him speak of recent news of the hangman and stolen sheep. Soon after, the hangman comes in on his way, drinking and talking in such a way that Timothy feels a connection to the man. But the rest do not know his occupation. Timothy is nervous and asks the Lord to save him, as the Christening ignites his fear. Then a man called Joseph Sommers comes to the house, and he is suddenly turned into the condemned sheep stealer, assumed by his reaction as he sees his brother, who is Joseph. For some time, the people in the house talk about the sheep stealer and his impending execution. The Constable just happens to be in the house as well. For a while the audience will believe that Timothy is going to get away with his crime, as the play pivots on the lack of knowledge and the simplicity of conversation through which mistaken identity and subterfuge are framed. The party then starts singing, and the hangman reveals his tools, which causes a woman to faint at the revelation that he will hang the man in their midst, but they don't know it is he. Timothy then leaves, pointing to him as the criminal condemned. Of course, that is not the outcome, as that would be too predictable.

The writer George Borrow, with stick and bundle, was a wanderer for most of his life. Exile was something to consciously experience. For him, being on the move was best and he travelled to Morocco, Spain, Russia and Portugal, revealing a curious ambulant. Voyaging also meant being a voyeur – making a spectacle of those he saw on his travels, much of which was written up in *Lavengro*. In spending time with the Romany gypsies in Wandsworth in the 1860s as walker and traveller in Britain, he derived inspiration from meeting people he met as he walked. *Lavengro* is the story of his wandering, and meeting those who were not of his ken. Romany girls, tinkers and fellow travellers, even people who tried to poison him. He is keen for the reader to see him as a wanderer who has come out of his comfort zone; so, what is fantastical and what is real is pivotal. He makes no mention of maps, but leans on a milestone, with nine miles inscribed on it. The moon is also a guide, while streams provide comfort. He describes trees and stones, buildings, people and varying sorts of markers as he went. He 'meditates' as he goes, thinking about who he encounters. Sometimes, he rests for a few days, busying himself making fire, or with his 'kettles' just as a tinker might, mending and attending them. His writing is ridden with class judgements, which to an audience today would be unpalatable. A coachman, with hooked nose, red face and a 'black castor' on his head, sees him and invites him on; Borrow resists at first, as he was bound to walk. But the encounter immediately creates division, as he wants to sit on the 'box' next to the coachman, which the coachman refuses, as it is a place only for 'gentlemen.' The coachman then demands sixteen shillings, making an in road into what he calls his slender finances. What with 'flying horses' and changes of coachmen, he is thrown asunder.

Knocking on doors is done happily, seeing cottages selling beer, talking to strangers happens without question, as does the sense of being indebted to no one. On one occasion, he knocks on the door of a gentleman and asks the servant if the master is at home. The servant answers affirmatively while looking down at his shoes. But he quickly apologises to Lavengro, who grumbles about servants looking down rather than at the face. *Lavengro* is the story of a man with encounters, who is quick to judge, but that does not mean lack of kindness, for, before starting his walk, he remembers the apple woman of London Bridge and sends her a piece of gold, which is refused and returned.

Though the work may be autobiographical, Borrow practises the use of different voices. In conversations he is 'Myself', and the man writing is called George, who gives up a life in London to be a travelling tinker. Near the beginning, he remembers a childhood experience when a Jew knocked at the door who, he recalls, was probably a travelling salesman. Borrow was sitting outside in the sun, 'drawing strange lines on the dust with my fingers, an ape and a dog were my companions', while the Jew asked him questions, to which there was no response. Borrow recalls that the Jew then explained that children often threw stones at him and followed him. Borrow is a storyteller, you cannot always distinguish truth from fiction.

Here is a man with child-like wonder. There is a portrait of him by Henry Wyndham Phillips (dated to 1843) at the National Portrait Gallery. He is open-shirted, with his right hand gently clutching a black coat and with a subtle stroke of red on the waistcoat. His left hand and arm are concealed within the coat. He does not return our gaze as he looks out, conceiving of his next far journey perhaps, for Borrow was a man who walked and travelled a lot. He looks fresh and young, despite the grey hair, a sign, perhaps, that foreign trips for dispatches keep you youthful. Around the time that this portrait was painted, the first 'experimental telegraph wire' was created between Washington and Baltimore to send messages, intriguing when we consider that Borrow was a man who borrowed or lifted snippets and messages of conversation that he heard as he travelled, to become the words on his densely written pages.

He had a wayfaring creed, as he wrote in 1851: 'There's night and day, brother, both sweet things; sun, moon and stars, all sweet things; there's likewise a wind on the heath. Life is very sweet, brother; who would wish to die?' He bestows the joys of travel in reported conversations. He went about the country visiting castles, manor houses, monasteries, villages, towns and was 'welcome everywhere.' As a walker, the ground and its infrastructure were his anchors.

Feet, Path, Lanes
Did he consider the rabbits' and apes' paws touching the ground in all weathers, as he did the wayfarer's feet? That part of our anatomy, so essential to movement for survival. Feet ruled motivation rather than the head or the soul. It was steps that would lead them to what they needed most: food, shelter, water and welcome. The feet will get them what they need. Tim Ingold holds in *Culture on the Ground: The World Perceived Through the Feet* (2004), that boots and shoes imprison, even though it must be said they are useful walking tools. That view could not have been the thinking of the barefooted medieval wayfarers, who were, at times, in agony.

As I walk, I dream of past places deep in my memory. There are the paths around Cannizaro Park in Wimbledon that I so loved as a child, which were full of ornamental beds and ponds, groves and sunken gardens which gave me a sense of security. The trip to the country to pick bluebells in the woods, the mud catching in the grooves of my Wellington boots, what held meaning for me in my desire to see what was around the corner, or beyond the bend in the lane. The Italian countryside – the path to the house where the glow-worms whirred while lighting the way with their in-built flashlights on balmy summer evenings. The track down to the woods. Boars. Roaming our garden at night. A Kentish village, with the one path that took me to some sort of open landscape; though flat and unsurprising, it still convinced me I had a country scene on my doorstep. There are the paths around the lanes where I live now, from which you can see the line of hills as if drawn from charcoal, which used to be burnt in all the woods all around. I grew up in a garden of two levels. They were bordered by beds of roses. I ignored the plants and the planting, but the partition of roses constructing separations appealed to me. And from the tree at the bottom of the garden, I could then jump into my neighbour's huge garden, which was so big he never knew I was there. The path down the side of the house led to a large tree in the garden corner, where I was convinced the owl was too. As I tried to sleep, its hoot haunted me as I thought about it in the hollow of the tree outside, even though I knew it could not possibly eat me. Now, it is a source of deep comfort, for having not heard an owl for years I am now living in a place where I hear one. Although he does come and go. And I wish he would stay. And I don't know if it is the same one. And I know I will never see him.

I did not like all animals as a child. And I did not like mice or rats. Though I loved Rat (Ratty to his friends you understand). Yet I loved Mole (Moley to his friends you understand) even more – the tenderer, more feeling animal in Kenneth Grahame's *The Wind in the Willows* (1908). While 'wayfarer' held no particular meaning to me when I read the book as a child, I would now love to ask Kenneth Grahame why he used it here. It might be because he employed it as a mode of escape – as Rat, known as the wayfarer seafaring rat, says, 'take the adventure'. There is even a chapter entitled 'Wayfarers All'. Here, Ratty talks to another seafaring rat, who excites him with stories of the sea. And barefoot or bare-pawed they go.

And like others before him, Grahame disliked modern mechanisation and the mess that it brought – dirt and black, coal and grit. He was aware years and years ago how the discovery of industrialisation would widen the gulf between humanity and the animal kingdom. When they are looking for Badger in the Wild Wood, whom Mole has been wanting to meet, and as they see the snow fall, he writes: 'Holes, hollows, pools, pitfalls, and other black menaces to the wayfarer were vanishing fast, and a gleaming carpet of faery was springing up everywhere, that looked too delicate to be trodden upon by rough feet.'

When the book was first read to me as a child, it never occurred to me that I was reading about animals who, in nature's realm, in real life, wear no clothes. In the picture-book world, so realistic were their conversations, the picnic spreads, the boating talk, the preparations for going on the water – I think I thought that I was reading about people. After all, in many of the book's versions, the animals are illustrated wearing clothes. Grahame portrayed animals becoming like humans, with all their pettiness and trifling querulousness and worries. When I look back,

I see how Grahame used animals to show how trapped humans can be by their own blind behaviour. We act, then think, spoiling natural wonders as we go. Animals are our spoils, yet they are not ruining the land with their paws and claws; surely, they could teach us a thing or two. I like to think they could adapt in a changing landscape better than us humans.

Back to the in-betweenness of the ape and all the many ways in which to behold them. How will they survive without humans to mock? The ape looks perfectly at home on the painted page or on the colourful and decorative plant supports. An ape with arms outstretched, legs slightly bent on a curled-over tendril looks towards a figure in a short cape and pointed hat, with staff and begging bowl and swaddled baby on back, who also looks rather like an ape. Apes walk on borders with interlaced filigree patterns, they swing on tendrils. Apes move with foliage as well as humanity. They can also 'ape' a pedlar. Apes are agile creatures anyway, and thus they are natural givers to the page of movement and motion. The painted parchment apes *are* the apes. Imagine the manuscript's owner looking at these delicately painted creatures – surely they had a laugh?

As for learning myself how to imitate an ape, I don't think apishness is for me, for to 'ape' an ape would also be to go around naked. Dare I be tethered by such a state? Better, I think, to wrap myself in some fur or feathers. Or a lace or velvet drape. There are limits you know, I wish to continue walking.

Seven

Wayfaring Works 7:
Burying the Dead

There's the life for a man like me,
There's the life for ever.
Robert Louis Stevenson, 'The Vagabond' (1895)

Whether they caused suspicion or not, the medieval
wayfarer was viewed as an exile in the world they
were passing through. The jagged world of the wayfarer.
One step in front of the other in everyday existence.
Ragged clothes and the search for food, water, shelter and
kindness. The way is tethered by worry.

Wayfaring appeals to my vagrant mentality. Walking
reins in anxieties. But it also brings disquieting instability.
Then again, walking also allows an avoidance of goals and
end-games, and instead keeps a wondering, waiting, and
wandering fixed in the mind. And which inevitably leads
to frustration, which even the magpie can't compete with.
And so the meandering circle of walk or wait goes round
and round, on and on. Is all of this because it is easier

than to be stationary, chained to a desk and computer with nothing but never completed to-do lists? A sunny day means a carefree walk in the country, with a route that can then be ticked off and completed. But the call of work prevents that. So, imagine the relief when the day is rainy, grey, and cloudy. There is no brave decision to be made about staying in. And then there are the days when I want to smash my brittle astrological Cancer shell, and smash it onto the sands, or push it violently away to be whisked into the waves of the sea. Not so long after, my shell returns, seeks comfortable bed and armchair, and cups of tea to keep me at home. So, to be a wayfarer suits one side of me, but not the other. I have always been in conflict with walking out and staying at home. I am the agitated one in the firmament of the birds, who have predictable yearly migrations, destinations and returns. But I never quite reach mine. Probably because I don't know what it is to be, except for the one that is encroachingly certain. That is, the daily routine humming around me. The peregrine, regal and large in the British sky, comes from the Latin for wanderer – *peregrinus*. But he too would be a foreigner in this land, as there are no rocks (their favoured habitat) on a narrow English lane.

In rhapsodising times of staring at the landscape, giving words to musing observations, no destination was needed. But in medieval times, a firm and tangible endpoint was all that mattered. Each fugitive step was taken to get closer to help. Whereas the poetic words float fugitively, created from different days and different times within.

The wayfarer as a universal, the beacon of the unspoken

body, stands in amidst the rich threads of topography, folklore, legend, landscape, geography and history. The figure on the road or path arouses curiosity. Where are they going? Do they know what is round the corner? Where will they end up? Wayfaring has a romantic legacy, but a wayfarer, or its very suggestion, causes the fear of the other. The fear of those who walk behind you and who walk towards you. A fear that anybody moving can be suspicious, and is a figure to distance, remove, exile. The observer, too, plays a part here, transmitting unease to another traveller. It is all about time, distance, proximity and perception.

Wayfaring does not always work when you are in love or broken-hearted. Love-lost, through time, that break in love dismantles as easily as the spider's web on a hand and we say, 'I would rather be dead.' We mean it, then, as we cannot imagine a life without the person we have loved. Over the course of our existence, people have walked to their love, to find love, however 'tramp-like' they look, only to find their love is irretrievably locked out. William Browne's poem 'Britannia's Pastorals' (1614) is a lovingly wrought description of the sighs and joys of a shepherd on a riverbank. He thinks about Marina, the shepherdess leaving her flock, while singing to her, but with 'plaints' and the sadness of loss. So deep is his despair, he asks for forgetfulness, hoping that her image will leave his sorrowful memory and mind. And he hopes this will be for ever, as he 'Sings, sighs, and weeps at once'. To escape his woes, he goes to France and sings to the nymphs of Poitiers. In a dream, he sees Marina all in tears; he returns to sit, mourn, weep and dream by the River Tavy near Tavistock. One day, as he muses, he thinks he sees a man in the woods, or even a satyr, running. The rocks and beasts and the 'abhorred heads' of the serpents of his vision make him wonder if fortune had brought bad luck on the figure he sees before him:

> Wayfaring man, for aftertimes y-bore,
> Whoe'er thou be, that on the pleasant shore
> Of my dear Tavy hap'st to tread along...

Final Fare

And what of love and walking in time remaining? We all know that the road and the path disappear and, if the final destination is found, it is only to the place where none of us have yet been. That which were the burning caves of fear and despair in the Middle Ages, the judgement of either Hell or Purgatory. Heaven is more of an abstract though. It is pictured as blue and vast, whereas in medieval images of Hell, there are figures – demons, devils and dragons, and fiery pits, pitchforks and cauldrons. For those stumbling from inescapable hunger and thirst as they walked, the expectation of death and the afterlife might have been of great comfort, especially on ice-cold days in winter when dark descends all too early. Or any day. If sins were confessed, and all was well. With talk of the afterlife came the belief that while the body would be lost, the soul would go with you; you would not lose yourself entirely. Alongside the exhortation of how to behave in life for death, you were given the balm of eternal protection to anticipate. We are reminded of this in a poem – Anna Fitch's 'The Wayfarers' (1913), which includes the lines, 'Earth, I dare not cling to thee / Lest I should lose my precious soul.'

We have not quite forgotten how life after death was spoken about in times past. But for us, we try to cling onto life eternal in the here and now.

The Inevitable Way

My sense is that we could be learning better to prepare for the touchstone of death, as people were encouraged to long ago. I try not to be gloomy, but, as I write in 2024, I hear that humanity is living through terrible and unprecedented times. And the more this is said, the more it is believed. Moreover, I think we lose sight of not only our mortality and the inevitability of death. Acceptance of it is not trumpeted. Times are and always have been terrible; to live is to understand, if not accept. We avoid this, by being concerned with the present, or the banalities of the day. With the tap or the click, the press on the letter, the swipe, the meme, or the emoji, we instantly express our opinions about everything, but we do not look or anticipate our eternal destinies like people used to. Our sense of time and of time passing also gives us power. It has been shaped by the fact that we can now, for instance, see or hear programmes on iPlayer months after their initial broadcast. We pause, rewind, fast forward recordings on YouTube at will, then start, or pause, bending time to suit our whims and schedules. We can fix time: slow it down, or speed it up. We watch a live performance through the filter of our phones, the curious urge to record what we see. We can listen or watch the past, as much as we like. We can watch an Instagram reel in quick time or listen to a podcast on accelerated speed. And we habitually control images on social media by the tools of cropping, zooming, modifying colour, speed and focus. But we cannot manipulate our death or halt the time, hour, or minute of it, even though many try. Living with the illusion of putting time on hold, we do not prepare adequately for the end, as people had to in the medieval period, where life was seen as but a waiting room for the real, true and vital time after death. As I heard somebody say recently, 'Dying is not on in the West.'

On the contrary, we are told how to preserve life, en-couraged to walk and be active to keep our time and our life preserved. In other words, we can control our time by walking with it as well.

Even so, there are poems addressing our end, and our limitations.

Nineteenth-century capitulations on wayfaring tell of the open road, the long path and for the wayfarer, the seeking out of song and love. Barely concealed though, quite often is sorrow, with the anguish of the ever-encroaching end. We see this in Arthur Symons' 'Wanderer's Song' (1899), with the line, 'For the way's one and the end's one, and it's soon to the ends of the earth'. The apprehension of wayfaring led by time unalterable as evoked in Alice Meynell's poem, 'I am the Way' (1921). The third verse touches on the many aspects of wayfaring used in an artful sense – from how it can embrace restrictions, to how it encompasses moving and a moving forward, but without it being something tangible. At its heart is ill-aligned love, as the poem addresses the voice personified:

> I'll not reproach
> The way that goes, my feet that stir.
> Access, approach,
> Art Thou, time, way, and wayfarer.

Similarly, in 'Whither Must I Wander?' (from his *Songs of Travel and other Verses*, 1895), Robert Louis Stevenson addresses the eternal being on the road, where the only hope is the afterlife. Look down for the road that defined your being, and where the wind always blows, but then you will go where you want no longer:

> Home no more home to me, whither must I
>   wander?
> Hunger my driver, I go where I must.
> Cold blows the winter wind over hill and heather:
> Thick drives the rain and my roof is in the dust.
> Loved of wise men was the shade of my roof-tree,
> The true word of welcome was spoken in
>   the door
> Dear days of old with the faces in the firelight,
> Kind folks of old, you come again no more.

Wayfaring, then, in one sense, is time, moving forwards from suffering in life to facing death. To a place that we hope is motionless, kind, gracious, cloudless, blue-skied. Where there in an imagined Heaven is the offer of a perfect peach emblazoned with stars. The air free of melancholy, sorrow and striving, with chairs arranged in serried ranks, meetings, and levitations with those people we used to know and love.

We will never know.

Walking in this chapter is walking with the dead; we are with the last Work of Mercy, that is burying the dead. Is this the closest we get to a sense of the Divine? While on earth, admiring its natural wonders, while thinking about human frailty, the search through walking seeks something beyond us that is heavenly. Charlotte Smith, who lived and wrote at Storrington and Woolbeding in West Sussex, identifies that yearning in her Sonnet IV, 'To the Moon'*:*

> Queen of the silver bow! – by thy pale beam,
> Alone and pensive, I delight to stray,
> And watch thy shadow trembling in the stream,
> Or mark the floating clouds that cross thy way.
>
> The suff'rers of the earth perhaps may go,
> Releas'd by Death – to thy benignant sphere,
> And the sad children of Despair and Woe
> Forget, in thee, their cup of sorrow here.

Married at sixteen, and expected to care for her husband's twelve children, Smith left him within seven months and turned to writing sonnets. Sometimes, there were good reasons for crafting melancholy. Walking near Bignor Park today, where Smith was born, there are cars in Lord's Piece, kissing gates, bridleways, stiles, surfaced roads, a path by an arable field, footpath signs and named trails leading through to open fields, farm tracks and barns. All these things were beginning to be established as the existing pre-enclosure form and structure in the countryside changed. Ways of walking had to adapt too. Barriers are enough to break a heart to bring death forward – no longer was the right to roam bestowed on a trembling spirit.

And then, how we might long for time past and dread tomorrow. In Padraic Colum's poem 'The Wayfarer' (1881–1972), the encroaching heaviness of life is palpable. Here, path and movement are entwined, serving to illustrate the inexorable decline towards death, the road is a symbol of eventual surrender:

> Heavy the clouds upon the darkening road,
> And heavy too the wind upon the trees!
> The trees sway, making moan
> Continuous, like breaking seas.
> I walk this darkening road in solemn mood;
> Within deep hell came Dante to a wood –
> Like him I marvel at the crying trees!

We are also making moan. We are quick to observe difference in another and we might think we are unfamiliar to another. But does the wayfarer stand for our recognisable affiliation whoever we are?

Digital Exile

Time falters, time stops, we cannot mortally remain. If we put the medieval wayfaring image into a Zoom recording or animate it, we could watch the figures walk across the page, we could pause them to look more deeply. With a click or a mouse movement, we could leave these figures suspended in digital form. And we could delay letting them go. Then again, the wayfarer was controlled by the medieval visual experience too – as they were made to be decorative as well as functional. The page, then, only had to be turned. If a book was especially prized, the act of turning the pages became deliberate, reverent. Meanwhile, the gold leaf might get scuffed, or dirt from fingers or fingernails could mark the parchment. But, as humans, we cannot control our own way journey through life – our own wayfaring.

And so, in that sense, wayfaring may be about your eventual mortal exile. It touches on the inexpressible, to turn to faith for hope and the miraculous when all else in life has faded. In the hymn 'A Poor Wayfaring Man of Grief' (1826), the Sheffield poet James Montgomery (1771–1854) wrote haunting lines that resonate about earthly existence and something beyond:

> A poor wayfaring Man of grief
> Hath often crossed me on my way,
> Who sued so humbly for relief
> That I could never answer nay.
> I had not pow'r to ask his name,
> Whereto he went, or whence he came;

Yet there was something in his eye
That won my love; I knew not why.

And so, in the fifth verse, the man is given drink by the
poetic voice, with a reference to Christ on the Cross:

Stript, wounded, beaten nigh to death,
I found him by the highway side.

Indeed, the figure seeking help turns out to be Christ.
The hymn was also at the heart of an unpleasant episode
in the history of the American church. It was requested to
be sung by the so-called Prophet Joseph Smith, founder of
the Mormon movement, who was running for presidency,
before he was killed alongside his brother Hyrum in
Carthage, Illinois on June 27, 1844. His death followed
a series of events sparked by his order to destroy a local
newspaper, *The Nauvoo Expositor* (1844), which had criti-
cised Smith's practices, including claims that he supported
polygamy and maintained multiple wives. Supported by the
local council, the paper's destruction was a provocative act
that incited a mob. The brothers were arrested for declaring
martial law and blocking the free press. The reactions that
followed sound rather like Trump's incitement of crowds
in January 2021. And in the powerful voice that the media
employed to scandalise, another newspaper – *The Warsaw
Signal* – called on people to act with headlines such as
'Citizens ARISE, ONE and ALL!!! – Can you stand by and
suffer such INFERNAL DEVILS!' And while the brothers
awaited trial, the prison where they were being held was

stormed by about two hundred men. Before his capture, Smith escaped to Iowa, but he later returned to the fray, citing a dream in which he walked on water. No amount of criticism or media frenzy was going to stop him. Where is the difference between death and life, and between fact and fiction, when the flesh is weak, but the body fights on, when there is trouble with bodily principle and when it is believed the spiritual call is stronger?

'Wayfarer' continues to have resonance, often in religious or quasi-religious settings and in places designed to give people hope. I have never been, but there is the Wayfarers' Chapel in Palos Verdes, California (1949) – a building designed by Lloyd Wright, the son of Frank Lloyd Wright. It looks lush, inviting and green. Like a transparent balloon of childish expectation, it is airy, made so by copious sheets of glass. Above and around it, trees provide shelter, as well as enfolding those who might get married here. Indeed, the structure is so delicate and light in design, there is a sense the walls are made of foliage or that its structural timbers are in fact living branches. The building is also known as a tree chapel. The architect said he took inspiration from seeing the redwood trees of California bending over above him. In essence, Wright saw his architectural vision as one that provided no barrier between body and tree, between the natural world and human.

The chapel was the visionary idea of Elizabeth Sewall Schellenberg, a member of the Swedenborgian church, who wanted to build somewhere for the reception of 'wayfarers', a place where they could look out over the Pacific. The chapel looks like a venerated ancient sage, standing there with its branches bending and reaching out. It could almost be paralleling the bent gait of the exhausted wayfarer. This reminds me of the Canadian painter Emily Carr (1871–1945), who made painting trees her life-long work. Speaking of their charm, she said that they were better than humans, as they never pause, never question. 'They don't make a mess of things,' she said. The Wayfarers' Chapel imprisons the branches, embracing you to imprison your own mess and torment for a little while, and then be restored. Here you may stop, but then you will way-fare once more, hoping to leave the prison of your dreams.

And, just as trees gathered to help forget, animals are invoked to show the promise of the inexorable way. In the *Third Book of Aesop*, in 'Of the Merchant and the Ass', we are told that:

Many persons, even after death, are troubled and vexed. A merchant hurried along a road with an ass to get to a fair, beating the animal frequently with a whip so that he would carry his load more quickly, and thinking to gain thereby. The ass, seeing himself loaded and whipped while walking far and beyond his strength, reached the point of wishing for death, thinking that even after death he would be safer. And so, broken and tired out, he died.

Life to Fear
Where death was something to fear in the Middle Ages, but salvaged by the hope and promise of the after-life, now it is life. We cast doubt on our lives, we fret about our

health, our status, our identity, our purses, our minds. We do not prepare for death. Leaving it for another day, like the drawer of old newspaper cuttings that needs clearing out. Here is my box of life, which is the box of fear that I have easily curated, by just thinking about the trivial things I allow into my life and imagination, which I fear as well:

At night, one of the curtains has not been properly drawn (by me). I come downstairs in the morning and notice. I think that somebody has been in and altered the position of the curtains.

I leave a glass of water half-filled on the table. I think that somebody has been in to drink it.

The glass of water half-filled – how did it get there I ask? Since I didn't put it there.

I see my shadow in the fridge door, as light is coming in from the garden door near the kitchen. I sit in the kitchen and there are sounds coming from the fridge. I think there is somebody in there. It isn't the more plausible reason – that is cracking ice.

On walks, rustling in the low-lying growth, there is somebody lurking on all fours. It wouldn't be a bird or a squirrel I say to myself.

When a bird flies away as I walk, I jump. As if to say, that is not what a bird does.

A disc of mud on the road looks like a squashed mouse whose body has been laid out to be a shape symmetrical on all sides.

A tiny, blackened leaf and stem look like a tiny foetus of a bird with its tail growing.

At the side of the road, a white van has its engine running with somebody sitting inside. I want to start running. I imagine how I might use the stick I am carrying, in case the man in the van runs after me.

The car parked – somebody is waiting for me.

The monster ligaments heaving and stretching, contorting, dissolving into some part compressed emerging from a field border or gate. I am alarmed. Will it see me?

A junction of two roads. I take one, a man overtakes me, muttering, moaning. I am scared, I turn around and go back to the junction to take the other road.

I live in fear. Daunted.

As a child, when I went upstairs to bed at night, I had to look out of the long window at the top of the stairs on the landing to check that nobody was looking in. I was sure that there would be somebody there. They could easily suspend themselves in the dark. Like a bat, or seraph. Every night, I was sure somebody was staring at me. I did not know then that I was sensitive to thresholds and zones of safety, even though I knew what I found fearful. One of my most abiding memories is to do with tracks and boundaries. A car turning round on the grass by our house got stuck. The car had breached the drive and driven into our garden, and then got lodged in the wet grass, having skidded, throwing up the grass and the mud, and making a mess. I crouched inside, unable to look out. I tried to play with toy cars on a fort with my friend. But the struggle of the car distracted me and disturbed me for years afterwards.

I dreamt about my childhood neighbour with the big garden last night. Mr Benlian was Armenian and in the garden, with Eden-like temptations, the tomatoes in the greenhouse quite delicious. Nicola and I climbed onto an oak tree at the bottom of my garden, from where we could jump over a bit of broken fence to play in the garden of the free, where Mr Benlian the beneficent turned a blind eye to two young girls. The house was so far away at the top of the garden that he might not have even heard us. At Christmas, he would give his annual gift to the family – a big tin of Quality Street. And every year, he took us into the same room with the big windows looking out onto the garden and with the same squeaks in the same squeaky parquet polished floor. But, in the dream, he was different. He only had three teeth. He was walking out of a cupboard with three children. He was breaking free from it. There was wind whispering between the hinges and doors. It was enough to pull him back again. He then disappeared and took the path that led to eternity. As John Clare wrote on 23rd September 1824, describing his worry at leaving his children behind when he dies, the 'dark porch of eternity whence none returns to tell the tale of their reception'. All gone, for good.

I try not to be a hostage to fear when I walk. I try and banish thoughts that if I walk, I will die. But a medieval wayfarer would have thought that all the time as they confronted the hazards of their body and soul. If I see a man with a dog coming towards me, I feel relief. If he is walking on his own, I wonder what he is doing. He walks out, just as I do. I look back to check he is not following.

I could have learnt something from Maud Heath who knew walking and wayfaring:

> Thou who dost pause on this aerial height
> Where Maud Heath's Pathway winds in shade and light
> Christian wayfarer in a world of strife
> Be still and consider the Path of Life.

This 1838 inscription is found on a tall statue of Maud, the pedlar who walked to Chippenham, Wiltshire, every day to sell her eggs. The three-metre-high statue is on top of a hill at Wick, not far from where she spent most of her life walking from Bremhill. She is shown wearing a shawl and bonnet, with a basket beside her. The causeway is named after her, as she had raised enough money to leave funds to build this path, about five miles long.

Or I could be more like Will Parsons, the self-styled, but quintessential, valiant and sprightly modern wayfarer, who leaves home east to walk a long way west, not necessarily with a fixed number of miles to cover each day. Wayfaring he spells with a capital W, Wayfarer he spells with a capital W. He chats to his companion as he goes; his wayfaring is lively, raw, real – what he calls a 'fundamental human tramp on foot.' His wayfaring is reading maps, but getting lost too; laughing, talking, looking, letting go and recalling something lost. He sleeps outside, sometimes on ground where he shouldn't, and, if he gets found, he gently backs off; he tries sleeping in the church porch, or within a church lychgate, just as people found sanctuary there in the Middle Ages. He knows his herbs, miracle cures, the lie of the land, how rocks and crags work, the dips and dells, the moist and the dry, and indeed the names of trees and plants. For survival, he relies on the compassion of strangers – in the good old-fashioned way, by singing folk-songs to them. He might leave a coin at a trough where he has taken water, or trespassed. He engages with strangers who ask him what he is doing. He walks long distances, braving wind and wet, sodden clothes, and soaked sleeping bags. He confronts the land in all its habitats and moods in the way people used to. Sometimes, he longs to give up, but on he goes. And sometimes he wonders what he is doing, but on he goes; sometimes he worries about food and money, but still he goes on, busking, receiving the odd coin, a smile, or even the odd guffaw here or there. And there is even a short time spent with Dom the donkey, sleeping by a flint wall at Lewes Priory. He leaves his chestnut staff against a beech tree, imagining himself doing the same thing as many pilgrims long gone. Above all, Parsons walks amidst ancient stones, earthworks and ruins. He believes it is vital for us to remember how to keep close to the land, walking and singing with its contours, just as our ancestors did and always have done. Likewise, remembering the rituals that connected us. But his wayfaring is touch and sound, walking in growth or grime and in all temperatures.

Parsons can teach us that roads we walk, then, are not fearful. They are framed by hedges, trees or buildings, or a combination of both. You can walk ahead, turn around and go the other way, or cross. You might follow a golden glow, or the red roundel of light, like a flat felt beret in the sky. Or you might feel your way through mist and fog. But the paths are clearly marked. The path is the same. The signpost stands unchanged. It has a frame; with words tightly circumscribed by the border. All is tight and ordered. It is all around us and hard to unfurl. We see structure, safely placed, everywhere we go, even on a pedestrian street. But we do not really notice. The bits in between do not exist, as we are forced to follow lines – lines that dictate our direction, our gaze and sense of navigation. We rarely challenge these lines, unless we are refugees, prisoners or escapees. Along the border wall comprising the flimsy structure between the USA and Mexico, there is a place below for the hopeful, but also desperate Mexicans who can crawl underneath and escape to the other side. For a moment, they are over. In the safely beyond zone. But the area is so heavily policed on the other side, that the freedom they glimpse is only fleeting. Is the future an illusion, as they lie within a brief touch of it? It is the torment of the threshold, a moment suspended between despair and possibility. The Mexicans trying to escape their country are marginal beings in the seconds it takes to get under. They move one step into a new space – only to become transient again.

Enter through the light, your way is not dark. Enter through the light to find gold and colour. Your way explodes to brightness. Not so in the black and white film, *Wayfaring Stranger* by Andrea Luka Zimmerman, released in 2024. Enter the grey, too, and the wind and the driving rain, see the sizzling sausages cooked at a camp-fire, hear traffic noise, feel the hollowness of life. Devoid of dialogue, apart from a short piece of text spoken by Eileen Myles towards the end, the film charts the itinerant straits of seven female and non-binary figures who walk through strange and, at times, forbidding landscapes, echoing Shakespeare's speech, 'All the world's a stage' (Jaques in *As You Like It*, Act 2, Scene 7). There is no sense of a chronology, or narrative. They appear to co-exist but walk alone and apart as well. We do not know if they have left home, or whether they are returning home, or, whether they even have one. That ambiguity – where direction and destination are unclear – propels both the film and its audience. For just over an hour, viewers dwell in a blurry, temporary world. The figures walking, sometimes running, embody the tension inherent in wayfaring, that is, between solitude and mental desertion and the exhilaration of freedom. An old woman takes one of the wayfarers in, where she swiftly falls asleep, while another devours food left on a picnic table. Another walks through a 'Keep Out' sign, one dances uninhibitedly at a fair. The figures are remote, their gazes inscrutable. The camera lingers on close-ups of a plant, a cow, a sheep, and two dogs, reminders of the natural world. Haunting sounds accompany the figures' movements: some elemental like trees blowing, or rushes whistling; others indistinguishable, pointing to humanity's imprint on the land, while the soundtrack-song is the voice of Fern Maddie singing, 'I am a Poor Wayfaring Stranger'.

After the screening, a man in the audience said that 'wayfaring' is a neutral word; it has not been spoilt by capitalism or time, and that it was found in medieval peasant culture. At the end of all my solitary walking to think about wayfaring, I was chuffed. I looked his way to silently affirm his comments. I was tempted to speak to him. To say, yes, yes, yes. But would that have broken the spell of my own solitary wayfaring?

Seven people. The Seven Days of Creation. Seven Sins and Virtues and to save us – the Seven Works of Mercy.

Painted medieval wayfarers were rooted to the defined sections of a page, in their own space, but still part of a structure that defined them in their temporal world. As Barbara Babcock-Abrahams wrote, 'Marginal figures tend to be associated with market places, crossroads, and other open spaces which are "betwixt and between" clearly defined social statuses and spaces.'[46] In the Middle Ages, the wayfarer was at the edge of society's Divine Order. Struggling, poor wayfarers knew exclusivity, but not inclusivity. I wonder if they would have buried the dead along with others. There is probably nobody who has not at some point felt uncouth or unclear in the world enveloping them.

One word and its cognates give us a rich historical tapestry which describes a different set of marginal states. From cot to grave, from hate to love, and back again, we are all transients. At a time when we are seeing deforestation and the crude destruction and violation of the landscape we plunder, wayfarers also remind us of how the earth and soil, plants and trees have always been sources of comfort and nourishment, where walking was once conducted with a profound understanding of how they operated. As we face a frightening future in our relationship with the land, our peril laid bare by what we have done, wayfaring is also about loss at a time when earth's fragmentation has never felt so acute.

All a Border
In pandemic times, humanity was, to some extent, unified in trying to be borderless, in the global will to beat our universal enemy. The wearying adversary that dominated our lives for so long that it ultimately led though to the fierce tightening of borders to stamp out the virus. We wondered if they would ever come down again. We only became borderless beforehand by pretending, or through media channels or social media or politicians talking of humanity's universality. Knowing all along that being borderless is only for the privileged. Travel of any kind was severely restricted, agitated by a disease that knew no borders. And as we grapple with the borderless existence of climate change, we face another test of compassion and collective will, one that demands unprecedented unity. Here, another open-ended, indefinite question.

Wandering along a path when you feel barren inside gives you a replacement. The walk resolves the purposeless, the memories distort and disrupt.

Although when you face it, the inescapability of death is poignantly felt on the road, associated as it is with toil and struggle. Christina Rossetti's 'Up-Hill' (1861), like a melodious lament, explores the curiosity of journeying and the uncertainty of what lies ahead. It is tempting, though, to see it as her metaphor for the road having one eternal end:

> Does the road wind up-hill all the way?
> Yes, to the very end.
> Will the day's journey take the whole long day?
> From morn to night, my friend.
>
> But is there for the night a resting-place?
> A roof for when the slow dark hours begin.
> May not the darkness hide it from my face?
> You cannot miss that inn.
>
> Shall I meet other wayfarers at night?
> Those who have gone before.
> Then must I knock, or call when just in sight?
> They will not keep you standing at that door.
>
> Shall I find comfort, travel-sore and weak?
> Of labour you shall find the sum.
> Will there be beds for me and all who seek?
> Yea, beds for all who come.

Writers extolled the joys and virtues of walking and the freedom that it brought: footsteps, the forward direction, motion, two legs, exploring, curiosity, striding for heart and lungs, all these things bringing joy. And that sense of beyond the turn of the lane, over the mountain, behind the horizon. But that sense of something hidden and inviting could also be treacherous and final. Some wayfarers understood distance and perimeters and infinity, but only, in many cases, as markers of suffering. They walked along paths that can kill. There was no time to watch the shore that divides humanity from eternity. Their 'going' was not always the walking of roaming lovers or clusters of walkers gathering pace to look at something.

In (Sumerian) Mesopotamia, a hymn was sung to remember those travelling on government assignments, like Shulgi, who had run two hundred miles in a day. The hymn was known as the praise poem of 'Shulgi' (c.2020– 2000 BCE), in which he also summarises the things he did as king, and it is worth quoting in full, as it shows how humans are united all over and through time by the simple act of walking for hope:

> I enlarged the footpaths, straightened the highways
>   of the land,
> I made secure travel, built there 'big houses',
> Planted gardens alongside of them, established
>   resting-places,
> Settled there friendly folk,
> (So that) who comes from below, who comes from
>   above,
> Might refresh themselves in its cool,
> The wayfarer who travels the highway at night,

Might find refuge there like in a well-built city.

And while death and danger lie close to the surface when thinking about wayfaring, it never really relinquishes the hold it has as something that sounds negative. As Algernon Charles Swinburne wrote in 'Laus Veneri' (1866):

> And lo, one springe and you are fast in hell,
> Fast as the gin's grip of a wayfarer…

A shame.

In the murky light of the early morning, the way is wooded and wrapped in a gentle dark. The birds are squawking like scratchy oil-starved wheels, the owls are eerily loud and close. I cannot see the way of a straight line. But then a road turns to the left, and the trees vanish from view. At last, the early morning light does its rounds again. And the incandescence of the light in the room, the curtain chink bringing tentative light, loses its charm as a more brazen glow strengthens. The way is straight once more, and I am going into clarity. I walk home to finish writing the book. It is seven in the morning. I had been walking in a wood, staff in hand and coat drawn tight. At the top of the hill, there is a yellow aureole of light. It was late in spring to hear a fieldfare, a bird usually gone by now. It was making quite a noisy sound, but not as noisy as when there are others there too. The 'check check' was getting dimmer as some had already flown to hotter climes. The fieldfare is a bird of the north, and I imagined following it to Scandinavia. They come in October, and next year they will return to cooler summers. In the little woodland, the last remaining beech leaves on bushes are soon to fall. They hang on valiantly against winter's quickening grip, as their fading yellow leaves are lighting up, like haloes. I stop all the meandering, trying to scoop up the wayfarer from the earth, the guessing and more. As we all walk to the grave, and dance on silent, cold-stone gravestones, I think of the recurring inheritance of our walking. The wayfarers are there somewhere – hidden in the paths they walked. With their steps, they surely furrowed a track, however pedestrian. In our imaginations, perhaps they are the last ones standing. I see them now, going their way, still on the page's edge, fixed, permanent, but no longer jettisoned by perceptions of them. Luckily, they are lit by gold and the brush of hope in eternity.

Image & Text Permissions

Image Permissions

The Macclesfield Psalter, © Cambridge, The Fitzwilliam Museum, MS 1-2005.

The Seven Works of Mercy, Norfolk, St Andrew, Wickhampton, 14th century, courtesy of the church of St Andrew, Wickhampton.

Figure of a man, Yorkshire, Pocklington, All Saints, north arcade, 12th century, courtesy of Corpus of Romanesque Sculpture in Britain and Ireland.

Psalter-Hours, Baltimore, Walters Ms. W.82, fol. 193v, c.1315–25, 111 x 162 mm, Creative Commons Licence.

The Taymouth Hours, London, British Library, MS Yates Thompson 13, fol. 95v, c.1325–30, 170 x 115 mm, courtesy of the British Library Collection.

The Rutland Psalter, London, British Library, Add. MS 62925, fol. 47r, c.1250–60, 285 x 205 mm, courtesy of the British Library Collection.

The Ideal City, Fra Carnevale, Baltimore, Walters Art Gallery, c.1480–84, 77.4 x 220 cm, Creative Commons Licence.

The Seven Works of Mercy, West Sussex, Trotton, St George's Church, 14th century, courtesy of St George's Church, Trotton.

The Gorleston Psalter, London, British Library, Add. MS. 49622, fol. 48v, c.1310–24, 374 x 235 mm, courtesy of the British Library Collection.

The Ghent Book of Hours, Cambridge, Trinity College, MS B.11.22, fol. 23v, 14th century, image courtesy of The Master and Fellows of Trinity College, Cambridge.

Viburnum lantana, the wayfaring tree, Coloured engraving after J. Sowerby, 1796, London, Wellcome Collection, Creative Commons Attribution.

Our Mother, Grayson Perry, 2009, 84.5 x 65 x 65 cm, edition of 1, plus 1 artist's proof, cast iron, oil paint, string and cloth, courtesy of the Victoria Miro Gallery.

The Wayfarer, Hieronymus Bosch, Rotterdam, Museum Boijmans Van Beuningen, 1516, 71 × 70.6 cm, courtesy of the Collection Museum Boijmans Van Beuningen, Rotterdam.

The Ghent Psalter, Oxford, Bodleian Library, MS Douce 5, folio 74r, c.1320–30, 86 x 63 mm, courtesy of the Bodleian Library.

Bestiary, Oxford, Bodleian Library, MS Bodley 764, fol. 16v, 13th century, 298 x 195 mm, courtesy of the Bodleian Library.

La Legenda Aurea, London, British Library, MS Stowe 49, fol. 220r, last quarter of 13th or early 14th century, 270 x 180 mm, courtesy of the British Library.

Text Permissions

Thanks are due to the following publishers and people for kind permission to reproduce copyright material.

Gerald Maa for 'The Blighted Star Fruit' (2007).

The Black Widow Press for Tristan Tzara, *Approximate Man and Other Writings*, translated by Mary Ann Caws, from the Black Widow Press edition, 2005.

'Thalassography' *The Jaguar: New & Selected Poems* (Bloodaxe Books, 2024), reproduced with permission of Bloodaxe Books.

Alan Jackson for 'The Grim Wayfarer'.

Acknowledgements

To all the institutions and libraries who kindly helped me track down material and references for wayfaring words: the staff at the Keep: the East Sussex Record Office, the Warburg Institute, Senate House Library (University of London), Institute of Historical Research, the Norfolk Record Office, the British Library, University College Library and the Lewes Library. Amanda Townsend for kindly opening the church at Trotton and for giving me so much of her time. To the parish of Wickhampton for supplying me with images for the book. To Rita Wood, who introduced me to the Pocklington wayfarer. To my early readers: Edmund Flett, Richard Janssen and Mary Charrington. To Benedict Flett for razor-sharp copy-editing and proof-reading and to Peter Gaskell for help with formatting text and images. To the publishing students at the University of Exeter who used a manuscript draft as a publishing project / proposal. To Richard Willis, publishing director at the University of Exeter's publishing degree programme, who saw the potential in the manuscript and was very helpful with advice and encouragement along the way. To Tor Falcon whose painting of Reymerston in the Brecks is on the front cover. To Debbie Ardley, Camilla Nelson and Paris Back for giving me launch-pads for the book. And last, but not least, to Alice Carter for her beautiful book cover design and to Sam Carter who believed in the book and saw it through to publication day.

REFERENCES FOR QUOTED MATERIAL

1   'Mr Whistler's Ten O'Clock', *The Correspondence of James Mc-Neill Whistler* [https://www.whistler.arts.gla.ac.uk/miscellany/tenoclock/]

2   West Sussex Burial Index, Par 141/2/1

3   West Sussex Burial Index, Par 124/2/1

4   East Sussex Record Office, SHE2/7/29

5   Dom David Knowles, *The Religious Orders in England,* vol. 1 (Cambridge, 1962), p. 130

6   Walter Skeat, ed. *Complete Works of Chaucer* (Oxford, 1972), Book 2, metre V, line 127

7   Agobard of Lyons, 'On the Deception of Certain Signs', [https://sourcebooks.fordham.edu/source/Agobard-OntheDeceptionofCertain Signs. Asp], translated by W. J. Lewis, from the Latin text, pp. 237–243 in *Agobardus Lugdunensis*, Opera Omnia, ed., L. Van Acker (Turnholt, 1981)

8   Henry Lucas, 'The Great European Famine of 1315, 1316 and 1317', *Speculum* 5 (1930), pp. 343–377, p. 359

9   *The Simonie: A Parallel-Text Edition*, ed. from MSS Advocates 19. 2. 1, Bodley 48, and Peterhouse College 104, eds. Dan Embree and Elizabeth Urquhart (Heidelberg, 1991)

10   From *On the properties of things:* John Trevisa's translation of *Bartholomaeus Anglicus De proprietatibus rerum* ed., M. C. Seymour (Oxford, 1975)

11   Quoted in 'Hegel, Duchamp, Warhol, Beckett', in Lois Oppenheim, *The Painted Word, Samuel Beckett's Dialogue with Art* (Michigan, 2000), p. 59, footnote p. 107

12   Tim Ingold, *Being Alive* (London, 2011), pp. 12–13

13   Given under our Privy Seal at Westminster, July 8, 42 Edward III, minstrels return home from Brabant, 1368

14   J. M. Escreet, *The Life of Edna Lyall* (London, 1904), p. 8

15   *Gospel of Pseudo-Matthew*, Chapter 20, translated from the *Ante-Nicene Fathers*, p. 377

16   *Summa Confessorum*, ed. F. Broomfield (Paris, 1968), 7.2. 19.2, pp. 402–03

17   Thomas Wright, *A History of Domestic Manners and Sentiments* (London, 1862), pp. vii–viii

18   Thomas Wright, p. 74

19   Audrey Lucas, *E. V. Lucas: A Portrait* (London, 1939), p. 85

20   Quoted from George Hothersall, 'Vagrants in 18th-century West Sussex, *West Sussex History*, no. 95 (pp. 19–24), October 1995

21   Hothersall, pp. 19–24

22   Susan Owens, *Spirit of Place: Artists, Writers & The British Landscape* (London, 2020), p. 284

23   An Act for Inclosing Lands in the parishes of Maxey… and Helpstone, in the County of Northampton, 49 Geo. III. Sess. 1809

24   He was commenting on the position of the poor and travelling poor, as quoted in *The Poor in the Middle Ages*, Michel Mollat (London, 1986), p. 243

25   *Medieval Learning and Literature, essays presented to R.W. Hunt*, eds. J. J. G. Alexander (Oxford, 1976), pp. 398–422

26   *Ipswich Journal*, Saturday February 27th, 1813

27   Francis Blomefield and Charles Parkin, *An Essay Towards a Topographical History of the County of Norfolk…* Vol. VI, 1807, p. 230. See the Patent Roll, 10th of Edward II, p. 2, no 32

28   *Warenniana – Ancient Letters and Notices Relating to the Earls de Warenne. Partly from original MSS*, by W. H. Blaauw, *Sussex Archaeological Collections*, Vol. 6, 107–128

29   *Calendar of the Patent Rolls, Edward III, AD 1330–1334* (London, Her Majesty's Stationary Office, 1893), 3 (ii), pp. 129–30

30   Humbert of Romans, *Opera de vita regulari*, ed. J. J. Berthier (Rome, 1888), II, pp. 193–95

31   Tales of the Monks from the *Gesta Romanorum*, ed., Manual Komroff (London, 1936)

32   *A History of the Richard Watts Charity*, E. J. F. Hinkley (Rochester, 1979), p. 10

33   'Household Accounts from Medieval England', in *Records of Social and Economic History*, ed. Christopher Woolgar, new series, CVII, 1992, 200–27 and XVIII (Oxford, 1993), pp. 577–79

34   *The Pilgrimage of the Life of Man* by Guillaume de Deguileville ed. F. J. Furnivall (London, 1904)

35   David Dymond, *The Norfolk Landscape* (London, 1984), p. 74

36   Quoted in *Sussex Archaeological Collections,* Relating to the History and Antiquities of the Counties of East and West Sussex, Volume 123 (The Sussex Archaeological Society, Lewes, 1985), p. 154

37   Bonington Moubray, *A Practical Treatise on breeding... all kinds of domestic poultry... And rabbits* (1842), pp. 186–87

38   William Langland, *Piers Plowman*, The Donaldson Translation Middle English Text Sources and Backgrounds Criticism, edited by Elizabeth Robertson and Stephen H. A. Shepherd (New York, 2006), p.163

39   *The Poetical Works of James Chambers,* 1820 [https://archive.org/details/poeticalworksofj00chamrich]

40   Swaffham Ecclesiastical Parish, Swaffham, Norfolk, Norfolk Record Office, PD 52/150/2, from the Poor Law records

41   East Sussex Record Office, QDB/2/2/1327

42   Bodleian, MS. Douce 308, *Bestiarie d'Amour,* early 14th century, fol. 89v

43   Aristotle, *Historia Animalium,* II, 8–9, 502 a–6, from the works of Aristotle (Oxford, 1910)

44   *Sayings of the Desert Fathers,* the Alphabetical Collection (Michigan, 1975)

45   *Lives of the Desert Fathers,* trans. Norman Russell (Kalamazoo, 1981)

46   'A Tolerated Margin of Mess' The Trickster and his Tales Reconsidered', *Journal of the Folklore Institute*, Vol. 11, No. 3 (March, 1975), pp. 147–86

Selected Bibliography

PRIMARY SOURCES

Aelred of Rievaulx, *La Vie de Recluse*, ed. C. Dumont, Sources Chretiennes, 76 (Paris, 1961)

Agobard of Lyons, *On the Deception of Certain Signs,* [https://origin.web.fordham.edu/halsall/source/Agobard-OntheDeceptionofCertainSigns.asp], trans. W. J. Lewis

Annales Monasterii de Bermundeseia Annales Monastici, vol. III, Rolls Series (London, 1866)

W. H. Blaauw, *Warenniana – Ancient Letters and Notices Relating to the Earls de Warenne, partly from original MSS* (Sussex Archaeological Collections, Vol. 6, 107–128)

Joseph Bosworth, *An Anglo-Saxon Dictionary* ed., Thomas Northcote Toller (Oxford, M DCCC XCVII)

F. Broomfield, ed., *Summa Confessorum* (Paris, 1968)

Calendar of the Patent Rolls, Edward III, 1330–1334 CE (London, Her Majesty's Stationary Office, 1893), 3 (ii), 129–30

Samuel Fox, ed., *King Alfred's Anglo-Saxon Version of Boethius, De Consolatione Philosophiae* (London, Bohn's Antiquarian Library, 1864)

G. Fransen, ed., *Summa Elegantius, in Iure Divino, seu Coloniensis,* (Vatican, 1969)

Robert Gregg, trans., Athanasius, 'Epistula ad Marcelinum de interpretation Psalmorum' 11, *The Life of Antony and the*

Letter to Marcellinus, The Classics of Western Spirituality (New York, 1980)

Humbert of Romans, *Opera de vita Regulari,* II, ed. J. J. Berthier (Rome, 1888)

Manuel Komroff, ed., *Tales of the Monks from the Gesta Romanorum* (London, 1936)

Roy F. Leslie, ed., *The Wanderer* (Exeter, 1985)

Frederic Madden and Walter William Skeat, eds., *The Lay of Havelok the Dane* (E Gutenberg edition) [https://www.gutenberg.org/files/32049/32049-h/32049-h.htm]

A. L. Mayhew, ed., *Promptorium Parvulorum,* First English-Latin dictionary, from MS. in the Chapter Library, Winchester (London, 1908)

Palladius, *The Lausiac History*, trans., R. T. Meyer (London, 1965)

M. C. Seymour, ed., *On the Properties of Things: John Trevisa's translation of Bartholomaeus Anglicus De proprietatibus rerum* (Oxford, 1975)

Thomas George Tucker, ed., *Concise Etymological Dictionary of Latin* (Halle, Saale, M. Niemeyer, 1931)

East Sussex Record Office, SHE2 / 7 / 29, PTS / 2 / 1 / 1, QDB / 2 / 2 / 1327 West Sussex Burial Index, Par 141 / 2 / 1

West Sussex Burial Index, Par 124 / 2 / 1

Database of Poor Law records for West Sussex

Other Literature

J. J. G. Alexander, ed., *Medieval Learning and Literature*, essays presented to R. W. Hunt (Oxford, 1976)

Samuel Beckett, *Mercier and Camier*, ed., Seán Kennedy (London, 2010)

Francis Blomefield and Charles Parkin, *An Essay Towards a Topographical History of the County of Norfolk*, Vol. VI (Norfolk, 1807)

Michael Camille, *Image on the Edge: The Margins of Medieval Art* (London, 1992)

Michael Camille, *Mirror in Parchment: The Luttrell Psalter and the Making of Medieval England* (London, 1998)

W. G. Clarke, *In Breckland Wilds* (London, MCMXXV)

David Dymond, *The Norfolk Landscape* (London, 1984)

J. M. Escreet, *The Life of Edna Lyall (Ada Ellen Bayly)* (London, 1904)

Thomas Hardy, *The Three Wayfarers, A Play in One Act* (Dorchester, 1935)

George Hothersall, 'Vagrants in 18th-century West Sussex', *West Sussex History*, no. 95 (pp. 19–24) October 1995

Tim Ingold, *Being Alive* (London, 2011)

J. J. Jusserand, *English Wayfaring Life in the Middle Ages*, translated from the French by Lucy Toulmin (New York and London, 1889)

Dom David Knowles, *The Religious Orders in England*, vol. 1 (Cambridge, 1962)

Audrey Lucas, *E. V. Lucas: A Portrait* (London, 1939)

Henry Lucas, 'The Great European Famine of 1315, 1316 and 1317', *Speculum* 5 (1930)

Lois Oppenheim, in 'Hegel, Duchamp, Warhol, Beckett', *The Painted Word, Samuel Beckett's Dialogue with Art* (University of Michigan Press, 2000)

M. R. James, *Norfolk Archaeology* (Norwich, 1917)

Susan Owens, *Spirit of Place: Artists, Writers & The British Landscape* (London, 2020)

Dante Gabriel Rossetti, *Poems and Translations including Dante's Vita Nuova and the early Italian Poets* (London and Toronto, 1912 first published, then 1930)

Tom Williamson, *Rabbits, Warrens & Archaeology* (Stroud, 2007)

Thomas Wright, *A History of Domestic Manners and Sentiments* (London, 1862), originally published in the *Art Journal*